Juliet Ash is a lecturer in Fashion Design History and Theory at Ravensbourne College of Design and Communication. She was co-editor of *ZG* magazine, and has contributed articles on aspects of fashion design to a number of books. She was co-editor of *Components of Dress*.

Elizabeth Wilson is the author of a number of books, including *Adnorned in Dreams: Fashion and Modernity* (1985), *Hallucinations* (1988), and *The Sphinx in the City* (1991); and with Lou Taylor she co-authored the book of the BBC 2 fashion history series *Through the Looking Glass*. She was a founder member of the editorial collective of *Feminist Review*, and is currently a member of the *New Left Review* editorial board. She has written for numerous magazines and newspapers, and has broadcast on British, Dutch, Danish and Australian television. She is Professor of Social Studies at the Polytechnic of North London.

D0147471

CHIC

A Fashion Reader

THRILLS

Edited by Juliet Ash and Elizabeth Wilson

UNIVERSITY OF CALIFORNIA PRESS

Berkeley • Los Angeles

University of California Press
Berkeley and Los Angeles, California

First California Paperback Printing 1993

Published by arrangement with Pandora Press

10   9   8   7   6   5   4   3   2   1

Library of Congress Cataloging-in-Publication Data

Chic thrills : a fashion reader / edited by Juliet Ash and Elizabeth
   Wilson.
      p.   cm.
   Originally published: London : Pandora Press, 1992.
   Includes bibliographical references and index.
   ISBN 0-520-08339-3
   1. Costume.   2. Fashion.   3. Clothing and dress—Psychological
aspects.   4. Costume—Symbolic aspects.   5. Clothing trade—Economic
aspects.   I. Ash, Juliet, 1949–   .   II. Wilson, Elizabeth, 1936–   .
GT520.C48   1993
391—dc20   92-36413
                                                               CIP

The paper used in this publication meets the minimum requirements
of American National Standard for Information Sciences—Permanence
of Paper for Printed Library Materials, ANSI Z39.48–1984. ⊗

For Bill and Pat (JA)

For Angela and Eleanor (EW)

Contents

Haute Couture versus Popular Style

Utopias and Alternative Dress

Chic Thrills

Introduction

We live in times of crisis – environmental crisis, crisis of capitalism, crisis of socialism, global crisis. And if, at one level, it would be easy to dismiss talk of a 'crisis' in fashion and the garment industry as trivial by comparison, we would argue that clothing and its vicissitudes reflect rather accurately the wider crises of world dimensions.

There is also the 'sexual crisis' of the 1990s. Fashion, like the theatre and ballet, but more than other fields of art and design, has suffered the tragic deaths of the talented young, mostly from HIV-related illness. So the threat to fashion comes from more than one direction.

These threats are of the present. A different kind of threat – to the artistic and ideological status of fashion – is of long standing; fashion has always faced the difficulty of not being taken seriously. There have always been plenty of critics and moralists – ranging from fifteenth-century divines to twentieth-century radicals – who have raged against it, although it has always had its supporters too, those who have argued passionately for its centrality to human concerns. The debate between the two camps seems irresolvable, and reflects the ambiguity which lies at the heart of fashion and indeed all forms of dress.

Fashion has dualities in its formation, a reputation for snobbery and sin. It separates individuals one from the other in appearance, and yet draws them together with common identities. It expresses inner selves, yet aids disguise. It is obsessive about outward appearances, yet speaks the unconscious and our deepest desires.

The skills required for the making of fashion are not necessarily specialised; it is made in abundance by all people who put together fabrics and colours, and bought and sold in abundance by those whose values are determined by money. Fashion is universal, and yet in its best-known and most discussed form – haute couture – is available only to a minority. The process of its making is a part of everyday imagery – the 'weaving of lies', the 'knitting together of ideas' – yet traditionally the fashion business has implied elitism. Historically it has rarely been afforded the serious contemplation reserved for the arts of literature, painting, sculpture, music and theatre, nor has its analysis competed successfully with the debates conducted around the popular cultural forms of the last half century: television and popular music. In recent years, however, the critical obsessions with design in architecture, advertising and product design have gradually extended to include fashion.

Costume historians have long produced empirical work of great sensitivity, and the strength of this work must have created a foundation upon which more adventurous theories of fashion could be built in the 1980s, when a creative convergence of cultural studies and art history with 'style journalism' encouraged a new, and theoretically much more sophisticated interest in the meaning of dress. Feminist writing has played a key role here. At the time this seemed like a great leap forward; at last fashion was carving out a place for itself in the cultural mainstream. Yet in retrospect it may seem that the growing intellectual respectability of fashion in some sense presaged the crisis of the fashion industry at the end of the eighties, was even in a sense a part of it: fashion, previously central to daily life and taken for granted, even if it was despised as frivolous, began to be taken seriously only when the commercial basis of its mainstream importance came under threat.

The search for the meaning, or meanings, of fashion has a long history, but the development of fashion theory in the twentieth century has been paradoxical. The intuitive brilliance of Quentin Bell[1] and Cecil Beaton[2] aside, fashion historians attempted to explain dress by means of theories which constituted an attack on the value and legitimacy of the whole fashion project so dear to their own hearts – for it seems likely that those who have studied and written about dress are prompted at least in part by interest in the subject, and by enjoyment of clothes, yet the main message of the theories of fashion upon which they relied was negative.

In other words the use of theory, in an attempt to demonstrate the importance of dress, seemed to lead only to its further denigration. This delegitimation took three forms in particular. In the first place, fashion could be condemned on a number of economic grounds. Here, the work of Thorstein Veblen[3] was influential. Writing at the end of the nineteenth century, he objected to the 'conspicuous consumption' of fashion – and of nineteenth-century bourgeois culture in general. In his condemnation of fashionable dress he was influenced by the dress reform movements of the period. He argued that fashionable dress was an important feature of female subordination, in particular the subordination of the bourgeois wife, whom, following Marx and Engels, he saw as a chattel, as in many ways she was. Fashionable dress, in his view, functioned to proclaim the status and wealth of the husband. Over and above that, the workers, mostly women, who made the fashionable clothes, were obscenely exploited, as Engels[4] and many others had protested long before.

The second line of attack on fashionable dress has emerged from the standpoint of psychology. J. C. Flugel[5] explained fashion – and ultimately all clothing – as a neurotic symptom. More recently, Alison Lurie[6] has also drawn on psychological explanations for the way individuals dress; dress for her is a form of communication, but often expresses messages of which the wearer is *unconscious*. Attempts to transmit a conscious message by means of dress are thus held up to ridicule; the punk *thinks* s/he is emitting a message of political rebellion, but is actually expressing the infantile feelings of an angry baby (the classic psychoanalytical put-down of all revolutionaries). Lee Wright's article in this volume, by contrast, represents a new and more sophisticated approach to the interpretation of the meaning of clothes.

Thirdly, Veblen and many others assumed that snobbery and status consciousness motivated the fashionable. As each new style was devised, it was taken up first by those at the top of the social pyramid. When the style was rapidly copied by those further down the social scale (the 'trickle down' effect), those at the top discarded it in disdain, quickly producing a new fashion, which was again as quickly copied in an endless cycle of envy and 'keeping up with the Joneses'. Recent work, however, has demonstrated that there can just as easily be a 'trickle *up* effect.[7] Angela Partington explores the working-class approach to fashion, which can sometimes be universalised.

Within the fashion world there has also emerged a stylistic challenge to conventional fashion photography. Rosetta Brooks discusses the divergence in the late 1970s and early 1980s between commercial and naturalistic representations of women in fashion photography, and Teal Triggs investigates the iconography of masculinity as it was redefined in this medium ten years later.

Chic Thrills takes its position on the cusp of two decades. It draws on the exciting new work done in the 1970s and 1980s, and particularly on the seminal analyses of Dick Hebdige[8] and Anne Hollander.[9] Yet it looks forward to the 1990s. It attempts to present, from the varying positions of its contributors, a political history of fashion ideas in order to challenge the recycling sterility of the 1980s era of consumption, and looks forward to a Second Millenium, where, if the 'deep, passionate forces of fashion' are to continue, 'the most pressing need for the new generation of designers is to think ideas'.[10]

For, although the 'designer culture' of the 1980s may have assisted the production of a more sophisticated *analysis* of fashion, it did not necessarily produce more original fashion. Neil Spencer suggests this was so as far as menswear, for example, was concerned.

The refinements in analysis and representation alluded to above came at a time when, as we can now see, vast changes have occurred within the industry. By the late 1980s the euphoric 'designer' scenario was under threat from the economic downturn: growing unemployment, high property values, high mortgage rates, under-investment and a generally recessionary climate. The whole fashion hype was always somewhat hysterical in Britain – a country whose textile industry has gone into serious decline, and whose clothing industry is sustained by continuing dependence on sweatshops and the most exploitative forms of homeworking.[11] Of course, as Ellen Leopold points out in her article about the American garment industry in the early twentieth century, genuine modernisation of the garment industry has never occurred. And yet within these technological restrictions women have often organised themselves as workers and envisaged new forms of life and consumption. Sheila Rowbotham explores this in her work on women textile workers during the 1848 revolution in France.

Paris, Italy and even Japan have also had their problems. Paris haute couture in fact has changed out of all recognition during the 1980s. Paris continues to be a commercial fashion centre, but the role of the actual clothes has changed. The designers make few clothes today for private customers. The French government increasingly supports the idea of Paris as not only a European but as a world centre for the business and marketing of fashion, and Katherine Hamnett and Romeo Gigli are only two of the non-French designers who have decided to show their collections in Paris in recent years. Yet early in 1991 Philippe Webster[12] described how the Paris haute couture houses have been forced to turn to high finance for survival, 'transforming a structure of mainly family-owned firms'. A £2-billion luxury firm, LVMH, now owns Christian Dior, Givenchy, Parfums Christian Lacroix, Lanvin, the cosmetic firm L'Oréal and Balmain. LVMH has decreed that Balmain is to stop designing haute couture altogether, in order to help it break even. The recession in the United States and the crisis in the Gulf have devastated Paris haute couture, but couture's financial difficulties had begun some time before. For some years now, haute couture design has been making losses and has become primarily a gigantic advertisement for the sale of profitable scents, cosmetics and accessories.

Perhaps haute couture was never quite what it professed to be. Valerie Steele reassesses the work of Chanel from a fresh perspective, which places her more solidly among the other *women* designers of her period, while Lou Taylor's investigation of the murky period of the Nazi occupation of Paris raises crucial questions about the relationship between fashion and politics.

Despite the continuing dominance of Paris as a world fashion centre, fashion, both as industry and as style, is increasingly globalised, as indeed is youth culture – and clothes play a key role in youth culture, as Judy Rumbold and Carol Tulloch demonstrate. Unlike the 1950s, 1960s and 1970s, when subcultural styles tended to be in opposition to mainstream fashion, in the 1980s youth fashions increasingly influenced the mainstream. However, British

Vogue recently bemoaned what it sees as a generation turning its back on high-turnover fashion in favour of functional sweats and parkas – a new version of what Angela Carter called 'recession chic' in the 1970s.

Ethnicity also plays an increasingly important part in the youth style scene. The question is whether new uniforms erase or glorify ethnic style and difference. Naseem Khan explores the ambiguities of an ethnic fashion coming to grips with both its own history and with Western design and commerce.

A 'fashion crisis' in some ways similar to today's crisis occurred in the late nineteenth century, when 'anti-fashion' in the form of rational and/or aesthetic dress emerged as a protest against the artificiality and waste of fashionable attire. (There was also a movement against the widespread use of birds' feathers and the consequent mass slaughter of birds.) Articles by Aileen Ribeiro, Kate Luck and Linda Coleing variously explore some of the alternative aspirations of utopian dress, whether expressed in utopian literature, in the Arts and Crafts movement, or in utopian political groups. Kate Luck's research into the history of trousered dress challenges the stereotypical view that this was the invention of a few American feminists in the mid-nineteenth century, and links it rather to earlier socialist and millennial movements.

Today, ecology and green movements are at the centre of anti-fashion, of which the most important manifestation is the campaign against the use of animal fur. The anti-fur movement is particularly strong in Britain and the Netherlands, and has been interpreted, again in British *Vogue*, as part of a general decline in interest in fashion. At the same time, the slump in the fur trade, and the closing down of fur retailers and fur coat departments in stores such as Harrods and Selfridges may be due in part to developments within the trade, and cannot be attributed entirely to the efforts of campaigners.

The Green campaigner and the 'fashion victim' represent opposing sides in the great contemporary divide between authenticity and consumerism, kitsch and taste, nature and the unnatural, excess and austerity – or what William Rees Mogg recently described approvingly as the 'new puritanism'.[13]

Postmodernism seems on the whole to fit more easily with a kitsch, unnatural, urban and consumerist sensibility than with the 'new puritanism'. It has been commandeered in support of widely varying views: sometimes it is hailed as a radical impulse, as the disintegration of oppressive modes of thought and/or oppressive systems; then this disintegration appears to permit oppressed 'Others', hitherto silenced, to emerge. Yet often it has appeared to celebrate culture's lowest common denominator, revelling in popular 'bad taste' and the 'schlock' of the urban wilderness. Elizabeth Wilson suggests that what it does for fashion is to reveal the playful, arbitrary and chosen aspects of personal identity, to which dress makes an important contribution. Postmodernism acts as a name for the Zeitgeist in which fashion, rather than naturalising the arbitrary, as Roland Barthes insisted, *denaturalises* supposedly natural gender and other identities, and thus it has a radical potential in calling attention to alternative possibilities.[14] Katrina Rolley demonstrates how one particularly marginalised group (lesbians) were able in an earlier period of upheaval and reform to use deviant dress to express their sexuality and thus to define themselves, both individually and as a different kind of sexual couple.

The early 1990s have both economic and cultural parallels with the end of the nineteenth century. Then, too, there was a recession after over-expansion of the retail trade. Can we then argue that the *fin de siècle* cultural developments of the 1890s bear any similarity to the 'decadence' of 1990s' postmodernism? Hilary O'Kelly considers some of these implications in Anglo-Irish dress in the late 1890s and early twentieth century.

Fin de siècle art of the late nineteenth century expressed the extremes of decadence and prophesied that it would also characterise the twentieth century. It was pessimistic and yet glorified its negativity; it was cynical and ironic as it reacted against the emergence of finance capital as a dominant force in world economies – a dominance that was to reign over the tragedies and (few) glories of the twentieth century.[15] As J. K. Huysmans in *A Rebours* commented:

> After the aristocracy of birth, it was now the turn of the aristocracy of wealth the caliphate of the counting house . . . the tyranny of commerce with its narrow-minded, venial ideas, its selfish, rascally instincts . . . The result . . . had been the suppression of all intelligence, the negation of all honesty, the destruction of all art; in fact artists, and writers in their degradation had fallen on their knees and were covering with ardent kisses the stinking feet of the high placed jobbers and low-bred satraps on whose charity they depended for a living . . . This was the vast brothel of America transported to the continent of Europe; this was the limitless, unfathomable, immeasurable scurviness of the financier and the self-made man, beaming down like a shameful sun on the idolatrous city, which grovelled on its belly chanting vile songs of praise before the impious Tabernacle of the Bank.[16]

Finance capital still dominates in the 1990s, yet its contradictions, witnessed by Huysmans at their birth, contain the seeds of its own destruction. Subversive impulses, moreover, are still evident in the world of design, and Juliet Ash explores some of them in her piece on Vivienne Westwood. The inspiration for fashion designers in the next decade may well be located in the moulded clothing of rubber gloves worn by plumbers and the felt boot linings of eskimos – then the bike messengers of the world's cities might become the gods and goddesses of the street-as-catwalk. The fabrics of Guatemala constructed fittingly by the West with seams, may be replaced by the simplification of city forms. Martin Margiela (Jean Paul Gaultier's former assistant) produced such a collection in Paris for spring 1990. He transferred the location from the Tuileries gardens, the home of the rich, to a ghetto of the inner city, where local African children accompanied models on a catwalk surrounded by crumbling walls. Ethnic style and deconstructivist fashion met in a 'third world' *arrondissement*, accompanied by rap music. It was the fashion elite that was displaced. Similarly, Romeo Gigli's spring 1990 collection, when shown in New York for the first time, was greeted with disdain by the rich, uptown, fashion 'victims', but with delight by the downtown art world.

Corporate style, having attempted to standardise culture by postmodernist means, may yet be brought down by those who work in the image industry, if they can harness their inventiveness to the urgency of creating a radical yet realistic alternative for the twenty-first century.

Notes and References

1 Quentin Bell, *On Human Finery*, London, 1968.

2 Cecil Beaton, *The Glass of Fashion*, London, 1954.

3 Thorstein Veblen, *The Theory of the Leisure Class*, London, 1957. (Originally published in 1899.)

4 See Friedrich Engels, *The Condition of the Working Class in England*, Moscow, 1970. (Originally published in 1844.) See also E. P. Thompson and Eileen Yeo (eds), *The Unknown Mayhew*, Harmondsworth, 1973.

5 J. C. Flugel, *The Psychology of Clothes*, London, 1930.

6 Alison Lurie, *The Language of Clothes*, London, 1981.

7 Ingrid Brenninkmeyer, 'The Diffusion of Fashion', in Gordon Wills and David Midgley (eds), *Fashion Marketing*, London, 1973.

8 Dick Hebdige, *Subculture: The Meaning of Style*, London, 1979.

9 Anne Hollander, *Seeing Through Clothes*, New York, 1971.

10 Bill Cunningham, in *Details*, New York, 1990.

11 Annie Phizacklea, *Unpacking the Fashion Industry: Gender, Racism and Class in Production*, London, 1990.

12 Philippe Webster, 'A Scent of Battle Rises', the *Guardian*, 4 January 1991.

13 William Rees Mogg, 'For the Pure shall inherit the earth', the *Independent*, 31 December 1990.

14 Roland Barthes, *The Fashion System*, London, 1987. (Originally published in 1957.)

15 See Mikulas Teich and Roy Porter (eds), *Fin de Siècle and its Legacy*, Cambridge, 1990, for a discussion of the *fin de siècle* phenomenon.

16 J. K. Huysmans, *Against Nature*, trans. Robert Baldick, Harmondsworth, 1966. (Originally published in 1881.)

Imagery and Language

ELIZABETH WILSON

Fashion and the Postmodern Body

POSTMODERNISM

These days, culture critics have become accustomed to take shelter under the great umbrella of postmodernism which has conveniently opened during the past decade to shelter us from the torrents of cold water so often poured upon those who attempt to take popular culture (and I include fashion in that category) seriously. The term 'postmodernism' appears to perform a function similar to that of the term 'decadence' applied to the 1890s: although the times and the terms are different, perhaps there is something about the end of a century that impels us to find a dominant theme, a mood, as we slide towards an end that is also a beginning. In the 1990s this impulse is intensified because we are approaching not only the end of a century, but the end of a millennium. As it turns out, we are doing so in global circumstances that seem more and more strange and fearful: we are living in a world turned upside down, with the disintegration of the Eastern European bloc and indeed of the Soviet Union as a single entity, with threats of ecological disaster, and the spectre of instability and wars on a global scale. However much we disbelieve prophecy or pride ourselves on not being superstitious, the well-known predictions of Nostradamus and the long-established threat of nuclear Armageddon add a fateful tinge to an increasingly gloomy mood.

Postmodernism gestures towards all this in a word. The terms 'postmodernism' and 'postmodern' have seeped into semi-popular language as shorthand for a vague, general 'Zeitgeist' (spirit of the times). They have become code words for a tremendous sense of change and upheaval, in Western societies at any rate, as much at the cultural level as at political or economic levels. The great quantity of writing and debate on the subject of postmodernism has been one of the ways in which we have tried to come to terms with, or at least to express, this sense of an at times quite overwhelming change.

Above all, postmodernism expresses a mood of ambivalence:

Postmodernism has this odd double standard where you're convinced that capitalism has triumphed: there's the market on one hand and everybody's better off and everybody plays their different music, but on the other hand we're also equally convinced that there's incredible misery in these societies, they're getting worse rather than better . . . And we know that both things are true and also that they are incompatible. [1]

The postmodern social landscape has a kind of ghastly kitsch excitement about it. Its 'hallucinatory euphoria', and the glittering, depthless polish of the postmodern urban scene reflect a world denuded of feeling. [2] Arthur and Marilouise Kroker note the 'suffocation of natural objects' (the extinction of nature), a 'general economy of excess', and fashion as one particular 'spectacular sign of a parasitical culture which, always anyway excessive, disaccumulative, and sacrificial, is drawn inexorably towards the ecstasy of catastrophe' [3] – their 'excessive', over-the-top-language offering one kind of postmodern response to what they analyse.

The idea of postmodernism fascinates, while appearing to celebrate the most kitsch and degraded aspects of our culture. It is a distorted, or thwarted, utopian impulse, which twists the problem – of alienation at the polluting ugly underside of consumer culture – into a kind of solution. Postmodernism expresses at one level a horror at the destructive excess of Western consumerist society, yet, in aestheticising this horror, we somehow convert it into a pleasurable object of consumption. Some critics have therefore felt that postmodernism has given the most vulgar aspects of commercial culture an undeserved respectability. It is also attacked as trivialising, or even as a fascistic justification of unjustifiable cruelty and excess.

There *are* powerful objections to the use of postmodernism as a term. Some, for example, question its usefulness as a portmanteau category:

It is often difficult to see how the concept transfers from one medium to another . . . The postmodern is . . . perceived by different writers as essentially aligned with quite varied, and sometimes opposed, political positions. Postmodern architecture has generally been seen as in some senses reactionary; postmodern dance, on the other hand, is associated with developments which are progressive (aesthetically and politically). [4]

It is precisely as a portmanteau concept, however, that I wish to defend the term. To me it indicates the aestheticisation of dystopia – the knife-edge quality of so much contemporary culture as well as our contradictory responses to that which is made pleasurable. It is useful to have a world that names our confusion, and our aspirations towards changes we cannot really imagine. Attempts within disciplines such as architecture and philosophy to define 'postmodernism' more rigorously, although useful in one way, essentially miss the wider point. And the point is the ambivalence.

FASHION, FEMINISM AND POSTMODERNISM

Postmodernism supposedly challenges the distinction between unique art and mass culture and between 'art' and 'craft'. As a result, cultural critics have felt freed to explore the meanings of popular culture, and to analyse and often to defend artefacts such as soap opera and romantic novels.

The feminist challenge to a gendered aesthetic value system has been a powerful component of this re-evaluation. We can now see much more clearly how some aesthetic forms have come to be stereotyped as 'feminine' and how they are then almost automatically judged as less important, less worthy, less 'great' than more 'masculine' kinds of art. For example, throughout the nineteenth century anything 'detailed' or 'ornamental' was judged feminine and inferior; and this distinction was carried on into twentieth-century modernism.[5] Aesthetic products have traditionally been equally diminished in value if their audience or consumers were or were thought to be women; this was true, for example, of romantic fiction and soap opera.

So the postmodern breaking down of aesthetic divisions has opened a space for the reappraisal of what was traditionally seen as the feminine, and postmodern culture criticism has provided a forum which has been used by feminist writers to explore subjects once considered unworthy of serious attention, while insisting on the validity and seriousness of a feminine/feminist point of view.

There are important implications here for the discussion of fashion, for it has been a cliché of even some of the best fashion literature that dress is an entirely feminine domain. James Laver and J. C. Flugel set out this view very powerfully, arguing that the 'great masculine renunciation' of the early nineteenth century had placed men outside fashion.[6] Now, feminists have begun to explore the meanings of fashionable and other kinds of dress. This exploration has gone against the grain of a traditional feminist suspicion of fashionable dress: many feminists reject fashion because of the way in which it reinforces the sexual objectification of women; for its associations with conspicuous consumption and the positioning of women as economic chattels, as property, and because it is held to be uncomfortable and to render women helpless (high heels and pinched-in waists, for example, can impede movement). It is alleged that it has an association with privilege and wealth and hence unacceptable class and race connotations.

The development of an explicitly feminist interest in fashion in the 1980s might therefore seem surprising, and *has* met with criticism from those who have misperceived it as a simple and uncritical celebration.[7] In fact it is an attempt to explore and to analyse one of the most immediate and important everyday cultural manifestations, one which we neglect at our peril.

Clothing in Western society is paradoxical. When we dress in the prevailing fashion, we are both trying to conform, yet simultaneously to individualise ourselves. Clothes socialise our bodies, transforming them from King Lear's 'poor forked thing' into the cultural being. Our dress constitutes our 'appearance'; the 'vestimentiary envelope' produces us as social beings. In Kaja Silverman's words: 'clothing and other kinds of ornamentation make the human body culturally visible . . . clothing draws the body so that it can be culturally seen, and articulates it in a meaningful form . . . Clothing is a necessary condition of subjectivity . . . in articulating the body it simultaneously articulates the psyche.'[8] Dress is the cultural metaphor for the body, it is the material with which we 'write' or 'draw' a representation of the body into our cultural context. Indirectly, at least, then, the postmodernism debate has helped rescue the study of dress from its lowly status, and has created – or at least *named* – a climate in which any cultural or aesthetic object may be taken seriously.

Secondly, postmodernism appears in a much more immediate and restricted way to explain some of the features of fashionable styles that dominated the 1970s and 1980s. Fredric Jameson identified pastiche and eclecticism as essentials of postmodern style in a wide range of artefacts and aesthetic productions, and these were certainly features of haute couture and its high street imitations from the late sixties onwards. (In 1989 the French designer Martine Sitbon was introducing pastiche, or 'retrochic', versions of 1970s fashions which were themselves a pastiche of the 1940s!) Although I question whether pastiche *is* confined to the recent period in dress,[9] it certainly did become a cliché of fashion journalism in the 1970s that there was no longer one 'line', no longer fashion, but fashions, a kind of compulsory pluralism of styles.

FRAGMENTATION, FASHION AND POSTMODERNISM

It would be possible to argue that this pluralism was and is a faint echo of the postmodern 'end of grand narrative' – the idea, advanced by postmodernist philosophers, historians and sociologists, that we can no longer subscribe to the eighteenth-century Enlightenment belief in continuous progress, evolution and the dominance of scientific rationality. It is also argued that we can no longer believe in the history of the world as being the single 'grand narrative' of the history of Western civilisation. For one thing, our culture of global mass media feeds us so much information that a massive cultural eclecticism is the only possible response. It is simply no longer possible to imagine that the history of the West is the history of the world; and if we can no longer perceive history as a linear progress from barbarism to civilisation, then it follows that there are many histories, many 'stories'. None has primacy over any other. We must also reject – the postmodernists say – those other 'grand narratives' of theory: the work of thinkers such as Marx and Freud, who claimed to have developed overarching theories that could explain *everything*. In postmodern thought this is judged as not only Eurocentric, but also as inevitably coercive. This kind of theory exemplifies the tendency of knowledge to be a means of domination; the more knowledge is 'totalised', the more it will create a prison house of information and theory from which there is no escape.

The bombardment with representations and information to which we are all subjected is seen in postmodern writings as leading to 'fragmentation'. This has become another popular catchword of postmodernism. Sometimes it appears to refer to the bombardment of the individual by culture and information from multiple sources. This is then seen as an experience that is impossible to convert into a meaningful whole. This is the fragmentation of knowledge (as when the 'grand narratives' of history and philosophy are at an end, as mentioned above). At other times, it is the fragmentation of identity that is discussed; this, too, has more than one meaning. For some writers fragmentation in this sense seems to mean that identity is always to some extent a fiction; drawing on psychoanalysis, they have argued that the concept of identity is an ideology of false wholeness, a repression of unconscious impulses. Others, by contrast, have described a collective psychological way of relating to the postmodern world – with a 'schizophrenic' blankness, a loss of feeling, a 'hallucinatory euphoria' which refuses to be disturbed by an objectively disturbing reality – and then fragmentation refers to a split between thought and feeling.

A further inconsistency in the debate is that on the one hand there is discussion of the fragmentation of individual identities, yet elsewhere we are told that suppressed or minority groups and various 'Others' now have an opportunity to come forward, and that postmodernism gives these a chance to express themselves, to assert, find or retrieve an 'identity'. Blacks and other ethnic minorities, women, and lesbians and gay men all have a place here.[10] In this way postmodernism is given an anti-racist and anti-sexist dimension. Yet is not the very idea of a *coherent* 'black', 'African', 'female' or 'gay' identity incompatible with the notion of individual fragmentation? Can there be such identities in a fragmented world?

On the other hand, why should anyone suppose that the 'white Western male identity' – a particularly powerful one, one would have thought – is fragmenting, and yet these identities of the 'Others' capable of sustaining themselves? Recent research, however, suggests that white American males are indeed 'suffering from growing feelings of anxiety, isolation and defensiveness'. They experience a 'lack of identity and belonging in the face of assertive

ELIZABETH WILSON

minorities who emphasise their difference'. The growing assertiveness of women compounds this anxiety. It is not that white American men are actually losing their power, but they are no longer the numerically dominant group, and by the year 2000 will comprise only 30 per cent of the workforce, according to the American Bureau of Labour statistics. In their case, 'loss of identity' seems to mean that they feel threatened when other groups lay claim to any larger share of the cake.[11]

Postmodern 'fragmentation' may therefore express the loss of identity of the white male critic writing about postmodernity. At the same time in a fragmenting world others feel that they can in some way 'choose' the identity they were born with, or redefine and rework it. Yet ultimately we do not choose our bodies, so postmodern playfulness can never entirely win the day.

Despite the different and inconsistent ways in which 'fragmentation' and 'identity' are used in discussions of postmodernism, as concepts they are of interest in relation to dress. Dress could play a part, for example, either to glue the false identity together on the surface, or to lend a theatrical and play-acting aspect to the hallucinatory experience of the contemporary world; we become actors, inventing our costumes for each successive appearance,

Postmodern fashion? Dress designed by Joyce Thé, Amsterdam, photographs by Inez Van Lamsweerde for Modus, edited by Pauline Terreehorst, published by De Bailie, Amsterdam (courtesy of the photographer)

disguising the recalcitrant body we can never entirely transform. Perhaps style becomes a substitute for identity, perhaps its fluidity (in theory it can be changed at will) offers an alternative to the stagnant fixity of 'old-fashioned' ideas of personality and core identity, perhaps on the contrary it is used to fix identity more firmly. Either way, we may still understand dress as one tool in the creation of identities. For example, in New York in 1990 Afro-Americans were looking to Africa in search of their roots and an alternative means of cultural expression. This gave rise to styles of clothing as well as to many other varieties of aesthetic experimentation. In fact, at least since the 1960s, black women and men *have* used style to express collective identities, in opposition to the dominant culture, and long before that 'outsider' groups of all kinds used style to create a 'counter-culture'. These styles have normally expressed social dissidence. They also, interestingly, often involve a critique of and an alternative to current norms of beauty. Punk, for example, was a ferocious onslaught on 'normal' beauty. 1960s Afro styles expressed a directly political statement in the slogan 'black is beautiful'.

Any investigation of counter-cultural dress forces us to recognise that individuals and groups use dress in subtle ways to create meaning, to locate themselves in society in a variety of ways. Women and men do not just imitate those above them in the social ranking order; on the contrary they may use dress to reinforce class barriers and other forms of difference (for example black hairstyles for both sexes which cannot successfully be imitated by whites).

FASHION, FOUCAULT AND THE BODY

Both in oppositional or counter-cultures and in the mainstream of society, dress and body together are used to create a given desired effect. Paradoxically, it is just that body we have not chosen that we try hardest to alter, in part through the medium of adornment. Yet relatively little has been written about the relationship of fashion to the body. Although adornment is used in many cultures with the aim of altering the body, in the West discussions of body shape continue to be dominated by moralistic concerns regarding health and women's oppression. It is a popular view, for example, that fashion designed for the youthful, even prepubertal, body and the use of very young fashion models from the 1960s onwards, starting with Twiggy, has in some sense 'caused' anorexia nervosa.

In questioning such types of explanation I have no wish to minimise or trivialise conditions such as anorexia, but I do question such an oversimplified understanding of cause and effect. Many women follow fashion, perhaps diet from time to time, but are not anorexic. Nor has anorexia decreased during the 1980s, a decade when fashions were not uniformly prepubertal as they were in the mid 1960s.

A more fruitful line of inquiry is that suggested by Michel Foucault. He has been accused of discussing the body as a passive object, of treating it as the ultimate 'given', as a kind of bedrock or raw material for the play of the social, but at least he puts the body back into the social sciences, understanding that it is a social construction as well as a biological entity. As anyone who has tried to diet knows, it is actually rather difficult radically to alter the shape of one's body. Yet dress and adornment in virtually all cultures have been used to do precisely this: from tattooing and neck rings to the dyeing and curling of hair and the use of high heels, both women and men have worked hard to produce a 'different' body.

In *Discipline and Punish* Foucault charted the growth of surveillance and the ways in which forms of power are deployed throughout society by means of specific practices. He was interested in the development of forms of drill, physical education and generally in 'reform' – all of which acted to produce the 'disciplined body', the body 'apt' to perform more efficiently and carry out a wider range of tasks and activities; or perhaps just to enact a 'representation' of efficiency and order. By implication the enormous growth of uniforms in the nineteenth century would also contribute to this 'regime' of discipline. Also, fashions undoubtedly were used in bourgeois society, both then and later, as a form of regulation, control and social policing. The study of mourning dress illustrates this especially clearly. Every detail of material used and ornamentation or its absence had a specific meaning.[12]

It is perhaps something of a cliché to state that the whalebone, canvas and steel corset of the nineteenth century (discipline enforced from without) has given way to the corset of muscle produced by exercise and diet of the twentieth century (discipline internalised and produced from within). From this point of view the nineteenth-century tight-laced corset – almost always denounced as a direct form of coercion and restriction, and as key to the creation of the Victorian woman as 'exquisite slave' – was less morally and psychologically coercive than the contemporary obsession with diet and exercise. (Also, some women found the corset reassuring and in its own way comfortable, a supportive shell or armour placed between the individual and the world.)

Just as we oversimplify if we see Victorian women's fashions as *only* operating to restrict women, so we are equally mistaken if we see the rise of twentieth-century fashion as representing *only* increased freedom and liberation. In the modern British prison system, women inmates now wear their own clothes instead of a uniform. This change, made in the 1960s, was interpreted as liberal and progressive, yet it has another side to it. As early as 1836 a Frenchman, Dr Parent-Duchâtelet, who published a pioneering investigation of prostitution, was arguing that the registration of prostitutes was necessary as part of their 'individualisation'. Every prostitute must have her own dossier, because the better the authorities knew the individual woman in question the more successful their surveillance of her would be.[13] Parent-Duchâtelet's argument seems almost to anticipate Foucault, while prison reformers gave very similar reasons for the doing away with uniforms in British women's prisons – if female prisoners dressed as they pleased they would 'reveal' their personalities more fully than had been possible in a uniform intended to degrade and to reduce the personality of the prisoner. (The male prison governors of women's prisons have also seen fashion and cosmetics as promoting a more acceptably heterosexual culture in women's prisons.)

Thus, the way a woman prisoner dresses and makes herself up is redefined. It is no longer a kind of luxury of which she must be deprived as a punishment, still less is it a form of vanity and self-regard to be eradicated. Rather is it an important duty to the self, establishing self-respect and an ordered way of life, and assisting conformity to an approved sexual identity. There are fashions in virtue, too; behaviour the Victorians defined as vain and selfish, contemporary welfare culture perceives as well-socialised conformity. To fail to 'take a pride' in your appearance is to be an 'inadequate' individual.

Here again we find an echo of Foucault, this time of his last works, Volumes Two and Three of *The History of Sexuality: The Uses of Pleasure* and *The Care of the Self*. In these works he studied ancient Greek and Roman etiquette, dietary and other 'practical' writings from the pre-Christian period, and he finds in them 'the development of an art of existence dominated by self-preoccupation'.[14] He concentrates on rules relating to diet and sexual activity. These last writings of Foucault illuminate not only the period which he was investigating, but also our contemporary world. Foucault drew a parallel between then and now: both were periods, he argued, in which traditional forms of morality and belief were crumbling, or in transition, and were therefore periods in which individuals had in a real sense to create their own ethics. The correct 'care of the self' involves an appropriate attitude towards the relationship of one's body to the world: this is an embodied ethics.

In these last works Foucault was less concerned with power, but in *Discipline and Punish* and in other writings from the 1970s he discussed power as pervasive. All social interaction involved power relations. All kinds of disciplinary activities represented a deployment of power. However, this power, or these powers, necessarily generated resistances. Knowledge was control, yet inevitably gave birth to rebellion. When the nineteenth-century sexologists defined homosexuality and other 'perversions', their use of knowledge was regulatory and controlling, an exercise of power, yet homosexuals twisted their definitions into a subversive, resistant identity: the gay identity – an identity signalled with clothing, jewellery, hairstyles and body movements.

Sex is one kind of power. The relationship of sexuality to dress and fashion was perhaps overstated by some of the earlier costume historians and theorists, such as James Laver and J. C. Flugel. Laver, for example, wrote of the 'shifting erogenous zone'; fashion, he argued, emphasised now one, now another part of the female body in order to prevent men from becoming sexually bored. This, he claimed, accounted for the eroticisation of the back in the 1930s, and in part for the rise and fall of hemlines. One glaring problem with Laver's argument is that it explains fashion purely in terms of men looking at women and completely ignores women's active construction of themselves as sexual beings. Another costume historian, Cecil Willet Cunnington, even saw fashionable dress as *creating* the erotic body from rather unpromising materials. He wrote that female fashion triumphed over Nature. By comparison with her dress, a woman's body was 'deplorably limited, hampered by its bad shape and dull colour; a monstrous pink lollipop flavoured with S.A. [sex appeal]!'[15]

The recent feminist cultural interest in women's dress has incorporated something of an implied reaction against the idea that women's dress is only about sexual allure – a view, after all, which rested on conventional ideas of women as concerned only to attract men. Instead there has been more emphasis on all other social meanings of dress. Yet clearly sex and dress are closely related. In 1987, when HIV infection was becoming a heterosexual concern, some journalists were puzzled by the increasing sexiness of women's – and men's – dress, with tight, short skirts and dresses inspired by the Paris designer, Azzedine Alaia, and much use of leather and even rubber. One tentative explanation was that this surface of sexual display functioned as a kind of 'touch me not' armour, with voyeurism replacing actual sexual contact. Three years later, and motifs from fetishism, bondage, erotic lingerie and skin-tight sportswear dominated a showing of the work of young, avant-garde Dutch designers at the Balie Café in Amsterdam, part of the launch of *Modus* by Pauline Terreehorst.[16] The book, like the show, went to the edge; it celebrated the romantic association of fashion with forbidden areas of sexual experience, and its illustrations in particular did not evade the fetishistic elements and often ambiguous sexual politics of dress. Some groups of lesbians and gay men have long adopted a similarly controversial strategy, while it is a characteristic of soft-porn imagery that it is more about the partly undressed than the absolutely nude female body. Clothing, in fact, has the unique characteristic of being able to express ideas about sex and the body while simultaneously it actually adorns the body. Its 'ecstatic fantasy'[17] articulates sex on the body of the wearer.

These insights move us away from the simple, moralistic rejection of fashion which has characterised so many left-wing radical movements. They surpass the view put forward, for example, by Stuart and Elizabeth Ewen, who mourned the way in which American immigrants followed fashion, interpreting this as a loss of traditional culture, and as a 'displacement' of 'real' rebellion on to something trivial.[18] Today we are forced to take a more complex view: clothes act as an extension of self and body; in a very immediate way they represent

'Lesburados' –
lesbian subversion of
accepted dress codes,
photograph by Della
Grace (courtesy of
the photographer)

culture; they will necessarily represent the dominant values of the culture (blue for a boy, pink for a girl, for example – almost the first thing that happens to a newborn baby is that it is colour-coded and thus gendered); yet this dominance will itself open the way to a counter-discourse, to reinterpretation and resistance. And these style wars *are* 'real'. The conquered Scots and Irish were forbidden to wear the kilt by their English conquerors, because the kilt was seen as a potent symbol of Celtic identity, as virtually a call to rebellion. Zoot suits caused riots on the West Coast of America in the 1940s. The field of dress·codes is a site of struggle for control of the power to define situations and ourselves; to create meaning. We can still acknowledge that dress is a powerful weapon of control and dominance, while widening our view to encompass an understanding of its *simultaneously* subversive qualities.

Contemporary interest in fashion is consistent with what has been described as the postmodern shift from an emphasis on knowledge to one on being, 'from knowledge to experience, from theory to practice, from mind to body'.[19] For fashion is more than a language. True, it communicates. It is also tactile, visual, it is about touching, surfaces, colours, shapes. It embodies culture. A more radical aim than the suppression or eradication of fashion would therefore be its extension, its proliferation, a multiplication that would ideally include its emancipation from stereotypes of gender, race or age. The 'Rational dress' of the late nineteenth century was in its own way as coercive as fashionable dress, morally at least, while as Meaghan Morris has said, describing the culture of 1970s radicalism, including feminism:

> We hear a lot these days about superficial style-obsessed postmoderns: but the smart young things about town have very little indeed to teach the Left about the politics of authoritarian control through style. We're the ones, after all, who installed a ruthless surveillance system monitoring every aspect of style – clothing, diet, sexual behaviour, domestic conduct, 'role-playing', underwear, reading matter, 'accessibility' versus 'obscurantism' in writing and art, real estate, interior decoration, humour – a surveillance system so absolute that in the name of the personal–political, everyday life became a site of pure semiosis. And this monitoring process functioned constantly to determine what styles, which gestures, could count as good ('valid', 'sound') politics, and which ones could not.[20]

Value systems are inevitably embodied in our dress. Perhaps what was wrong with the eighties was not a style obsession, but that styles, of dress at least, expressed all too well the enterprise-culture ethos of the times. In a kind of reverse resistance, the riot-engendered style of the poor (Punk) was converted into the style of dominance and of a success whose boots were indeed made for walking, and were indeed going to walk all over you. Which is not to say that the process can't be reversed.

IN CONCLUSION

Fashion, like postmodernism itself, remains ambivalent. When I visited the exhibition of Pierre Cardin fashion at the Victoria and Albert Museum in January 1991, I re-entered the eerie world of *disembodied* dress. In one way the display was very old-fashioned, in that it was accompanied by a commentary which must have been put out by the Cardin publicity department – full of hyperbole, banal, and reeking with the idea of Designer as Genius. By contrast the aura created was futuristic, with a weirdly humming space machine pulsating with subdued light in the centre of the room. Strangest of all were the dead white, sightless mannequins staring fixedly ahead, turned as if to stone in the middle of a decisive movement. It was like being in an Arabian Nights' story, or a fairy tale in which some malign being has petrified a whole population. The clothes themselves were brilliantly coloured, clear, incisive of cut, fancifully futurist, yet simple. But without the living body, they could not be said fully to exist. Without movement, they became both oddly abstract and faintly uncanny. Nothing could have more immediately demonstrated the importance of the body in fashion, and this goes to support the assertion that the study of fashion has an important role to play in bringing forward a consideration of the body in cultural studies.

At the same time, the uncanniness of the museum display, with clothes suspended in a kind of rigor mortis, offered a seductive example of 'hallucinatory euphoria', a glimpse into a dystopia of depthless colours and inhuman brightness, a veritable imitation of life.

Notes and References

1 Fredric Jameson, 'In Conversation with Stuart Hall', *Marxism Today*, August, 1990.

2 Fredric Jameson, 'Postmodernism: or the Cultural Logic of Late Capitalism', *New Left Review*, no. 146, July/August 1984.

3 Arthur Kroker and Marilouise Kroker (eds), *Body Invaders: Sexuality and the Postmodern Condition*, London, 1988, p. 45.

4 Janet Wolff, 'Postmodern Theory and Feminist Art Practice', in Boyne and Rattansi (eds), *Postmodernism and Society*, London, 1990, pp. 192–193.

5 Adolf Loos, 'Ornament and Crime', in Ulrich Conrads (ed.), *Programmes and Manifestos on Twentieth-Century Architecture*, London, 1964. (Originally published in 1908.) See also Adolf Loos, 'Ladies Fashion', in Adolf Loos (ed.), *Spoken into the Void: Collected Essays 1897–1900*, trans. Jane Newman and John H. Smith, Cambridge, Mass., 1982. (Originally published in 1900.)

6 See James Laver, *A Concise History of*

Costume, London, 1969a; James Laver, *Modesty in Dress: An Inquiry into the Fundamentals of Fashion,* London, 1969; and J. C. Flugel, *The Psychology of Clothes,* London, 1930.

7 See Sara Lovibond, 'Feminism and Postmodernism', in Boyne and Rattansi, 1990, op. cit.

8 Kaja Silverman, 'Fragments of a Fashionable Discourse', in Tania Modleski (ed.), *Studies in Entertainment: Critical Approaches to Mass Culture,* Bloomington, 1986, p. 145.

9 See Elizabeth Wilson, 'These New Components of the Spectacle: Fashion and Postmodernism', in Boyne and Rattansi, 1990, op. cit.

10 See Andreas Huyssen, 'Mapping the Postmodern', in Andreas Huyssen, *After the Great Divide: Modernism, Mass Culture, Postmodernism,* London, 1988.

11 Simon Tisdall, 'Anxious White Males Green in America's Tossed Salad', the *Guardian,* 2 January 1991, quoting the work of Anna Duran of Columbia University.

12 See Lou Taylor, *Mourning Dress: A Costume and Social History,* London, 1983.

13 A. J. B. Parent-Duchâtelet, *De La Prostitution Dans La Ville de Paris,* Paris, 1836.

14 Michel Foucault, *The History of Sexuality, Volume Three: The Care of the Self,* Harmondsworth, 1984, p. 238.

15 Cecil Willet Cunnington, *Why Women Wear Clothes,* London, 1941, p. 52.

16 Pauline Terreehorst, *Modus,* Amsterdam, 1990.

17 Cecil Willet Cunnington, op. cit.

18 Stuart Ewen and Elizabeth Ewen, *Channels of Desire: Mass Images of the Shaping of the American Consciousness,* New York, 1983.

19 See Roy Boyne, 'The Art of the Body in the Discourse of Postmodernity', in *Theory Culture and Society: Special Issue on Postmodernism,* vol. 5, nos 2/3, June 1988, p. 527.

20 Meaghan Morris, 'Politics Now (Anxieties of a Petty-bourgeois Intellectual)', in Meaghan Morris, *The Pirate's Fiancée: Feminism Reading Postmodernism,* London, 1988, p. 178.

ROSETTA BROOKES

Fashion Photography

The Double-Page Spread:
Helmut Newton, Guy Bourdin & Deborah Turbeville[1]

Fashion photography has traditionally been regarded as the lightweight end of photographic practice. Its close relationship to an industry dependent on fast turnover makes the fashion photograph the transitory image par excellence. For historians and critics concerned with isolating 'great' photographic images and according them enduring significance, the commercial sphere of photography – the domain of the everyday image – represents the debasement of a conventional history of photography. Fashion advertising, in particular, is seen as negating the purity of the photographic image. We see the typical instead of the unique moment or event.

Given this prevalent critical and historical attitude, photographers are inclined to regard the 'captured' moment, as opposed to the contrived, stylised fashion shoot, as the most powerful point in the photographic process, the point at which the 'real' world reproduces itself. It is considered more creative than the mass-production processes which are seen as stamping the image with the uniformity and monotony of a commodity. This has prevented a serious investigation of those features of photography which have been produced by the combination of these processes. Although photography has its origins in the reproduction of nature by the machine, fashion and advertising photography must be studied, as Walter Benjamin recognised in the 1940s, as a process of the mechanical reproduction of the *contrived* image.

Throughout the 1980s and as the 1990s progress, fashion photography reflects more and more the segmentation of the fashion market-place – between mass production at one end and couture at the top. The blurred photographic image which rejects both the garment and the human body relies on the viewer's familiarity only with the designer's logo. This type of imagery is apparent in the promotional material of Yohji Yamomoto, Issey Miyake and Comme des Garçons and represents the upper end of the market, the 'creativity' of innovative couture design, which has potential for inclusion in a retrospective of 1980s and 1990s fashion photography in an art gallery. Whereas the proliferation of fashion advertising imagery, particularly in mail order catalogues, represents the mass-production end of the market-place and is most visible in the United States and Britain. American fashion photography has been little affected by more 'impressionistic' couture promotional material and has tended towards a 'lifestyle' imagery at both ends of the market. Here the viewer is required to identify with the purchasing of the garments rather than with the 'mood' or imagined potential of a Yamomoto collection. In mass-produced fashion advertising the image is not simply something we see; it is also something we 'wear'. The mass circulation of photographic images emphasises our awareness of self-image, and establishes a relationship between the particular and the typical.

Historians of photography have yet to do justice to this 'other' side of photography, possibly because it is too familiar. How does one look at photographic history and do justice to the processes which make the imagery typical and transitory, without selecting certain great images for their uniqueness? Changes in the nature of advertising and fashion photography necessitate an analysis, as well as a reappraisal of the caricatures of commercial photography. In the late 1970s and early 1980s there were dramatic changes in street photography; one of these aspects was the advent of the intimacy of the double-page spread.

HELMUT NEWTON: MANIPULATING STEREOTYPES

Many see the 1970s representation of women in advertisements and especially in fashion photographs as a sort of masculine counter-offensive against the feminist consciousness of sexual stereotyping. That some of the significant individual contributions to this change happened to come from women in no way contradicts the claim that we saw then the development of the most perniciously sexist imagery yet encountered in the very core of sexual stereotyping, fashion photography.

Fashion photography in the 1970s in one sense produced nothing particularly new, no recognisable ideal like Jean Shrimpton or Twiggy in the 1960s. No particular look or appearance dominated the decade. Models seemed to come straight off an assembly line, representing a well-established physical norm. Most conspicuous was the repression of the model's distinctive individuality. She was wholly identified with her type, and seen not as an individual but as a model.

Stereotyping appeared to occur through suppression of the awareness of stereotype and by identification with the unique. The dynamics of fashion are embodied in the dualism of the world itself: fashion is what is general and typical, and yet it is also restricted and individual. Another peculiarity of the fashion photograph is that it is positioned on a threshold between two worlds: the consumer public and a mythic elite created in the utopia of the photograph as well as in the reality of a social group maintained by the fashion industry. One distinctive feature of fashion photography in the 1970s was that it converted utopias into dystopias.

The Helmut Newton model is one of a type, presented with the cold distance of a fleshy automaton, an extension of the technology which manipulates her and converts her into an object. Her veneer, which is at one with the gloss of the image, is to be flicked past and consumed in a moment. When the models strike up stereotyped poses, it is their deadness and frozen quality that strikes the viewer most strongly. The suggestion that they are frozen from a narrative continuum emphasises their strangeness and their discontinuous, fragmented nature, like film stills isolated from the cinematic flow.

Some have interpreted the strange, unusual settings in the work of Guy Bourdin and Helmut Newton (accidents and suicides) as the intrusion of a 'real world' into fashion photography. I think the reverse is true: it is because scenes of rape and death are commonplace in film and television that they can be treated with such distance in fashion photography. The aura of a particular kind of image, not the aura of the streets, is utilised. The artificiality of the image is emphasised. It is the deathly aura of mediation which encases everything in gloss. Newton's harsh colours, particularly his use of red and blue, make an association with poor quality reproduction, and thus invoke the limitations of the medium.

The emphasis upon the alien and artificial qualities of the picture makes a straightforward accusation of sexism problematic. All fashion photography, as the dominant currency of female images, could be seen as inherently sexist, manipulating exchanges between self and self-image. Yet this exchange is conventionally suppressed in the image of the moment, as it binds us to a model of femininity beyond existing norms, converting them into stereotypes. To recognise an image as a constraint, as a violation or repression of femininity, is to glimpse the demise of a stereotype going out of circulation. Each ascendant, newer image promises to escape those constraints. Accordingly, fashion photography seeks to suppress any sense of the strangeness of sexual typification, the conversion of femininity into a static type or commodity. The sense of stereotype must be reserved for hindsight in the succession of female images.

Newton manipulates existing stereotypes; their alienness is accentuated, and yet they are almost archetypes in their sexual dramas. The passive reclining woman offers no threat; she is completely malleable, a dummy made of flesh. The object of gratuitous sexual violence and violation, she offers no resistance, but because of this she becomes unreal, like de Sade's libertines. As the threat of personality diminishes, her image-like quality transports her beyond the eroticism of the living to the fetishism of the inanimate object. She fits into dominant stereotypes so completely that she ceases to connote any reality apart from the images which constitute her.

For example, by mixing dummies with live models in the French *Vogue* of June 1977 Newton makes impossible an unambiguous erotic response (from either sex). Instead, the picture sequence directs voyeuristic attention to the conversion point between object and flesh, and to their deathly reciprocity in the photographic act. While the photographs are erotic, the eroticism is a part of the process of mediation itself.

Many of Newton's more successful photographs hold a distanced engagement with the manipulative devices of fashion photography and with the process of mediation. Those alien features present in suppressed form in fashion photography and current images of women are exposed and made explicit. The image is presented as alien, as a threat rather than an invitation. Stereotypes are presented as falsity.

GUY BOURDIN: 'A TRAP FOR THE GAZE'

In the post-war period the growth of mass production and reproduction was greeted in some circles as a threat to individuality and to the uniqueness of human activity. The horrific spectre of the totality of industrial culture was the familiar expression of a fear of what seemed inevitable as a result of consumer culture: the false universalisation and homogenisation of human experience. Theodor Adorno saw the stamp of the machine everywhere, reducing everything to a 'sameness', reflecting and reinforcing a sense of alienation in all aspects of private life and experience. As mass entertainment and advertising became more dominant, they increasingly levelled experience down to the 'lowest common denominator'. The threat of the culture industry was the production and reproduction of sameness in all spheres of cultural life. Adorno saw the media as part of a great machine serving to encompass, assimilate and absorb all opposition and all individual variation by acceding to the sameness of machine production.

Current cultural trends could be interpreted as posing quite the opposite threat: the loss of common cultural experience. The decentralisation of fringe cultures and the increase of minority opinions cannot be accounted for in the view which foresees the media industry triumphing in a uniformity of cultural experience. For Marcuse, writing in the same period as Adorno, avant-garde art as oppositional culture was depleted by absorption and assimilation into mainstream 'affirmative culture'. While this may seem prophetic in view of the current state of art, indifference to oppositional art is the result not of a depletion or assimilation of its meanings, but of its isolation. It appears as one cultural ghetto among many, with its own diminishing media stake. It is not that the values of a minority culture are distorted and absorbed into the mainstream, but that, on the contrary, they pose no threat at all.

The principle of negation itself, which avant-garde culture once represented, is now built into all spheres of cultural activity. Even disco music, a human expression – dance – aligned with the rhythm of the machine, is negated in groups like Kraftwerk, for whom the machine pulse which 'animates' disco dance is the object of morbid contemplation. It is not merely a 'progressive' extension of popular culture. What is incorporated is negation, which guarantees a sort of all-round authenticity. We can enjoy it either for itself, or alternatively for its parody of itself. Irony mediates our experience, our alienation. It is, however, no escape from it.

Tolerance of mechanised cultural products has risen to a higher level: an acceptance of the limitations of the medium in an engagement with the process of mediation. As Adorno and Horkheimer said: 'The triumph of advertising in the culture industry is that consumers feel compelled to buy and use its products though they see through them.'[2]

They could not, however, have predicted the peculiar route to this triumph. From the vantage point of the 1940s and 1950s when they were writing, it was difficult to imagine that a fashion photographer would ever have occasion to complain that his work was being censored by the machinery that Adorno predicted would incorporate cultural producers like Helmut Newton. Yet Newton's complaints about English *Vogue* are echoed by fashion photographers who have begun to talk about being 'given free rein' by magazines. When Guy Bourdin claims to be an artist, he is laying claim to a specific type of formal problem encountered with a particular kind of image in circulation. It is not so much that 'the double page is his canvas', but that the double page is *not* canvas that is the basis of the claim.

Canvas stands in antithesis to his material, to the texture of mechanical reproduction. In Bourdin's work, the double page is not the vehicle for communicating the image, but is a structure characteristic of a particular kind of encounter. He organises his images around the form of mechanical reproduction, around the divide of the double page and the turn of the page. In a fashion photograph in French *Vogue* of May 1978 the female voyeur/ spectator figure is divided by the centrefold as she watches the almost symmetrical division of her reclining self-images. To turn the page is not only to open and close the spectacle of the fashion spread, but is also to cut up the figure with which we are spatially identified – to open and close her legs. The model is completely engulfed in the vertical divide as though by a mistake in binding, leaving the two legs isolated on facing pages.

At other times the double page becomes its own mirror. In a March 1976 French *Vogue* spread, a colour reproduction faces a black and white reproduction of almost the identical scene, as though frozen from successive moments. The process of reproduction itself is being reproduced. With these more dramatic formal devices, spatial relationships are set up within the picture which rebound upon the strangeness of our ordinary encounter with the double page, with the photograph and with the advertisement itself. In a photograph in French *Vogue*, May 1978, we are re-directed from the object (the product) to the spatial ambiguities of its setting, which jar with the expectations built into encounters with photographs and advertisements. Bourdin enhances the spatial strangeness of the conventional spread, to accentuate the alien quality of what is unfolded in that horizontal continuum and around the vertical division in the process of unfolding. This spread best exemplifies the division and alternation of shallow and deep spaces, which is used to juxtapose façade and depth, the frontality of the image with the three-dimensionality of the setting. Bourdin plays upon a hesitation in the spatial and temporal expectations of the double page, emphasising the alien manner in which both product and advertisement are positioned. Brechtian distancing techniques and the formalist 'exposure of the device' have become mainstream.

Bourdin's shoe advertisements provide a case in point. Without the manufacturer's name as caption, some would be unrecognisable either as advertisements or as having shoes as their subject. In a passing encounter with the image that the fashion magazine produces, it is profitable to exert the negative principle as a subversion of the neutrality of 'flicking through'. An arrest of vision is required at all costs – even at the expense of accentuating the alien quality of clothing itself. Our sense of puzzlement seeks double confirmation which is provided by the product name.

A 'trap for the gaze'[3] may be the solution to the immediate pressures of the market, but the implications of an increasing dependence upon an enlarging and increasingly autonomous advertising industry are less easy to estimate. The autonomy and independence from the product achieved by the product-image seems to promise a fulfilment of the totalitarian ideal of propaganda for its own sake. In 'The Work of Art in the Age of Mechanical Reproduction', Walter Benjamin saw fascism as the 'political consummation of [art for art's sake]', in an elevation of propaganda to a new level of aesthetic self-justification.[4] The emancipation of the image from its caption, and of the product-image from the product, means that the advertising image has become the pure imperative, not divisible into form and content, the pure veneer, the absolute facade for and of itself.

DEBORAH TURBEVILLE

This new autonomy of the product-image has created another market sector. The collecting of ephemera, the practice of surrounding oneself with old and sometimes not so old advertisements, is now almost a cliché of middle-class lifestyles. A large business has established itself, selling not so much old as 'fixed' brand images. Mass production exploits the borderline between consuming and collecting, between connoisseurial attention to qualities, and the sheer neutrality of the product-image in the context of the cash exchange. Obsolete product-images have been revived as nostalgia for the mythical past of the product itself. There is an obsession with the conversion point between the currency and redundance of the image.

In the same way, fashion trends in the 1970s were predominantly nostalgic. Even more recent sci-fi and high-tech fashions came over as a nostalgia for older stereotypes of 'futurism', as a taming of images of technology which once were threatening. But recent forms of revivalism are not specific attachments to a specific bygone age; they are more romantic nostalgias for some 'essence' – peasant life or primitivism in the late 1960s, or some vague idea of Hollywood 1930s' glamour in the early 1970s. This nostalgic undercurrent has come to dominate and has almost caught up with itself: in 1989 the French haute-couture designer Martine Sitbon was showing pastiche 1970s' garments, the originals of which had themselves been pastiche recreations of 1940s' fashion.

Nostalgic attachment to the immediate past becomes an attachment to the process of turnover, a narcissistic identification with the alien qualities of one's own past. That point of self-awareness at the juncture of the up-to-the-minute and the out-of-date becomes an identification with the very process of mediation that fashion represents.

The photography of Helmut Newton and Guy Bourdin radiates a knowing self-awareness of fashion photography and its falsities. These photographers convey the sense of an impenetrable veneer, resistant to the very movement of stereotypes. In the work of one of the best women fashion photographers, Deborah Turbeville, a different sense of the alien nature of the image is represented as a sort of hesitation between self-images. In many ways her photographs are at variance with characteristics of the work of her male counterparts. For example, her models are not chosen for their identity with a stereotype, but usually for their divergence from the type or image which they appear to represent. At its best her work involves this hesitation between the image presented by the model and the image presented by the picture, although finally the meaning is always communicated by the latter. Conveying this uncomfortable relationship with the model's self-presented image pushes her towards portraiture, or her models towards acting. However, she is clearly not satisfied with communicating the strangeness of the female image through the illustrative neutrality of the photograph. In her book, *Wallflower*, her photographs are presented scratched, violated and montaged together.

In the foreword to this book she describes her photographs as:

. . . like the women you see in them. A little out of balance with their surroundings, waiting anxiously for the right person to find them, and thinking perhaps that they are out of their time. They move forward clutching their past about them, as if the ground of the present may fall away. [5]

Perhaps they accede a little too easily to the automatic overlay of nostalgia resulting from the association of limited colour range with the faded photograph, or with the technical qualities of early photography. Her work seems unresolved, as she herself says: 'My pictures walk a tight rope . . . I am not a fashion photographer, I am not a photo-journalist, I am not a portraitist'.[6]

Whatever the viewer's opinion of the 'success' of her pictures, it is interesting that a photographer preoccupied with the kinds of self-image mass circulation produces should find the fashion spread the most accommodating site for her exploration, however provisional she may feel this to be.

Whether the recent dominance of the 'alien' fashion image is an extreme expression of the autonomy of fashion photography, whether this implies a distancing from the form of coercion which the fashion spread represents, whether it constitutes the elevation of the advertisement to a higher power and greater autonomy, or whether it is the beginning of a break up of that structure of representation, these questions have implications far beyond fashion alone.

EDITORS' NOTE: We were unable to obtain permission to include the images mentioned in this article. They were the photographs by: Helmut Newton (in French *Vogue*, June 1977, and also in *Sleepless Nights*, London, Quartet Books, 1978, p. 139); Guy Bourdin (French *Vogue*, May 1978, and also *Vogue Book of Fashion Photography*, New York, Coudé Nast, 1979, pp. 218–9); Charles Jordan shoe advertisement (French *Vogue*, Spring/Summer 1975, and also in *History of Fashion Photography*, International Museum of Photography, Alpine Books, 1979, pp. 190–1); Deborah Turbeville (in *Wallflower Portfolio*, London, Quartet Books, 1979).

Notes and References

1 This article (now revised) first appeared in *Camerawork*. I should like to acknowledge the writings of John Stezaker, especially his idea on stereotyping. I refer to 'Archetype and Stereotype', a paper delivered to the Photography Convention organised by the Department of Psychology at Southampton University, and to *Fragments*, published by the Photographers' Gallery, London.

2 Max Horkheimer and Theodor Adorno, 'The Culture Industry: Enlightenment as Mass Deception', in *The Dialectic of Enlightenment*, trans.

John Cumming, London, 1973.

3 Jacques Lacan characterises all pictures as 'traps for the gaze', but the phrase is used in the context of a discussion of the use of distorted images to 'catch' the eye and maintain the engagement of the gaze.

4 Walter Benjamin, 'The Work of Art in the Age of Mechanical Reproduction', in *Illuminations*, trans. Harry Zohn, London, 1973, p. 244.

5 Deborah Turbeville, *Wallflower*, London, 1979, p. 1.

6 Ibid., p. 1.

TEAL TRIGGS

Framing Masculinity

Herb Ritts, Bruce Weber & the Body Perfect

Fashion magazines not only document but also construct new modes of gender identification and commodification. In particular, fashion photography continually challenges notions of gender politics and the conventions of traditional fashion photography. In the 1970s, portrayal of *women erotica* in the fashion images of Helmut Newton and Guy Bourdin responded to and confronted changing concepts of feminity.[1] Shifting patterns of consumption and the proliferation of gay and feminist social critiques paved the way for the emergence of the 'new man' in fashion photography of the 1980s. The decade brought a variety of definitions and representations of masculinity, simultaneously conceiving the male as father, lover and breadwinner. In this different context masculinity was used to express a social and physical power established through emphasis on portrayal of the body. The body is either draped with garments establishing recognised signs of social and sexual status, or is devoid of garments establishing a new-found strength by representations of the physique. The 'fashion signifier' is no longer the garment but the male nude. This second skin became merely another form of garment. Fashion photographers such as Bruce Weber and Herb Ritts construct and confront these images of masculinity in numerous images for fashion magazines.

THE SET-UP

Three distinct types of image emerged depicting the garment in the fashion photography of the last decade. Firstly, an observable trend towards abstracting garments on the human form fulfilled, ostensibly, the postmodernist's aesthetic of fragmentation. This type of image appeared in popular magazines such as *Details*, *The Face* and *i-D*, and later filtered through to the 'upmarket' press, where it emphasised cut, texture and the drape of fabric over the body. The selectivity of the cropped image focused on attitude and style of dress. Secondly, the garment discarded the human figure, finding itself progressively isolated on the fashion page. Single garments by designers such as Issey Miyake and Bill Blass were portrayed as exotic still-lifes. In the absence of the human form, the garment's cut, shape and texture could be examined more critically. Finally, the rise of the 'new man' was accompanied by a plurality of masculine identities which sought to maintain a balanced tension between emotional and sexual existence.[2] The appropriation and application of female physical and emotional qualities (e.g., softness, submissiveness, passivity, etc.) to the representation of males was achieved within a newly constructed arena which drew heavily upon imagery of the pre-cultural human state. Employing the new *bricolage* of male representation and the 1980s emphasis on fitness, the garment was cast off revealing not the traditional female form but the body perfect of the male nude. This process of shedding the garment is exemplified best in the Levi's launderette advertisement (1986). Nick Kamen removes his Levi jeans liberating himself sexually and subverting the conventions of the launderette as a feminine/domestic sphere. The nakedness of the male body is not an invitation to eroticism, for it has been anaesthetised by the apportion of female traits.

In examining the anatomy of gender, material categories may be created to endow the male or female domain with distinguishing signs.[3] Likewise in relation to the body, categories of differentiation might be established to explain the relationship of men and women in the fashion photograph: primitive/cultured; natural/spiritual; unclothed/clothed; vulnerable/controlled; subordinate/dominant. Prior to the 1980s, these divisions in the context of fashion photography were based on traditional gender views of product-image. The roles have now been reversed. Maleness has been reconstituted and is revealed as in its primitive state before commodification. The dismissal of conventional images of femaleness accompanied a major shift which re-addressed the balance of male and female sexual divisions. Traditional roles have been redefined so that when both sexes appear together on the fashion page the woman is no longer subordinate to the man, nor is she pictured in a subordinate position. These ideas are readily apparent in the fashion photographs of Weber and Ritts, who explore independently the pre-cultural state of the commodification of the male and the notion of the second skin.

THE SHOT

In Herb Ritts's photograph for Valentino Furs (*Vanity Fair*, September 1988) two male nudes exemplify the transference of sexual power and the concept of the natural. Two male nudes cower behind the fur-clad and stiletto-heeled female whose facial expression and posture suggest a command over the scene. The male nudes are found in positions of submission, their faces buried in the fur coat and their genitalia hidden by muscular thighs. The female remains firm, confident, in control and clothed. Her second (fur) skin though signifies a naturalism which the naked male body reinforces as a subordinate rhetorical clothing. The fashion photograph is complete when the visual transference is made.

The transition of the male from a primitive state to cultural commodification is exemplified in Bruce Weber's 'sport' photograph for Calvin Klein (below). Set in a vague theatre of marbled tiles and walls, the actors are dressed in white Calvin Klein jeans, the uniformity of attire denoting a uniformity of sexual position. One male figure is seated, composed, but pouting as his gaze reaches out towards the viewer. The other two males strike an s-curve sculptural pose, gazing away from the body of the woman. They stand passively behind the female who restrains them with her extended arms. This inhibition of movement with the image restricts the semi-clothed males to a natural/primitive and not yet commodified cultural state.[4] The division between male and female domain is made clear.

Photograph by Bruce Weber, Vanity Fair, *December 1988 (courtesy of the photographer)*

The construction of masculine identity is often consummated by the resort to classical martial culture and the activity of sport. Weber and Ritts legitimise the nude, bestowing authority to their treatment of the male body by appropriating the martial/athletic sculptural form. Herb Ritts's images for designer Giorgio Armani feature male torsos who assume physically exerting positions to advertise hosiery. Physical power is denoted by the muscular tones of the male body whether seen in a state of action or inaction. The body is viewed as both aesthetically and sexually pleasing although the latter is not readily accessible. Bruce Weber extols the perfection of the athlete's body in his 1984 LA Olympic series (in *Bruce Weber*, Twelvetree Press). The archer poised on a group of rocks in the forest draws the arrow across the string of the bow ready to take aim, like Apollo, as archer. The corporeal culture of the Greeks distinguished them from the barbarians. According to Clark, participants in the Olympic Games competed naked as early as the sixth century BC thus purging themselves of physical and spiritual inhibition.[5] The cult of wholeness and the physical beauty of the Greek body implied that the 'evils' of sensuality and pure aestheticism could not materialise. The intangible nature of the Greek sculptural form places 'desire' out of reach. The same tension is manifested in Weber's subjects but is heightened by the voyeuristic nature of the photographic image.

The clearest depiction of the desire to portray physical perfection and the transference of gender is found in Ritts's juxtaposition of male and female nudes as classical sculptural forms. This appeared in December 1990 in a fashion editorial layout for *Vogue*. 'Heavenly Bodies' mythologises both the male and female form. The narrative of the body perfect is the elevation of the human to the divine. The replication of classical modes positions the female on pedestals wrapped in lush white cloth. The persona and gender of the gods are transformed through props worn by the human forms. Apollo, portrayed as female, is adorned with the archer's gold bow and arrows.

The postmodernist parody of history and fragmentation of the body is summoned as male nudes appear juxtaposed with second-century marble figures of the Nike of Samothrace and the fifth-century relief of Artemis. Like an earlier Armani advertisement, one of Ritts's models appears without a face (others appear without arms) emulating the incomplete relics of Greek sculpture and ostensibly relinquishing personal identity. But the absence of a face does not preclude personage. The viewer's attention is drawn instead to the athlete's torso which evinces a new means of identity and a clear association with the Greek ideal. As if to emphasise these points, the accompanying text is taken from the writings of Keats, Shelley, Byron and Tennyson, recounting the traits of Greek gods and goddesses. The male and female nudes are thereby associated explicitly with Greek gods and icons, and the nude is bestowed with pagan religious authority and totemism.

THE BREAK-DOWN

Recent fashion photography employs and captures the male body as a complex signifier. Kenneth Clark, in his seminal study *The Nude*, distinguishes between the nude and the naked. Whereas the naked is to be without clothes, the nude is a form of art and as a conventionalised form possesses the authority of classical tradition. Clearly this is a force at work in many of these 'neo-'neo-classical images. Clark further contends though that photographers engage themselves in a search for the 'perfect' in the physical sphere.[6] In this realm, the nude acts as a landscape or portrait for the photographer and facilitates his/her choice of subject. But Clark argues too that photographers are not able to satisfy the canon of perfection without imitating other artists' views of the naked body (e.g., sculptors, painters, etc.). The camera does not deceive.

The gradual acceptance of the 'New Man' has negated the portrayal of male erotica in the images of Herb Ritts and Bruce Weber. These photographers, through their fashion imagery, are framing masculinity by responding to and confronting new perceptions of the Male Body Perfect.

EDITORS' NOTE: We were unable to obtain permission for some of the images mentioned in this article. They were the photographs by: Herb Ritts (photograph for Valentino Furs in *Vanity Fair*, September 1988; and the photograph in British *Vogue*, December 1990); Bruce Weber (*The Archer* in *Interview*, January 1984, and in *Bruce Weber*, Los Angeles, Twelvetrees Press, 1983).

Notes and References

1 Rosetta Brookes, 'Sighs and Whispers in Bloomingdales: A Review of a Bloomingdale Mail-Order Catalogue for their Lingerie Department', reprinted in Angela McRobbie (ed.), *Zoot Suits and Second-Hand Dresses: An Anthology of Fashion and Music*, London, 1989.

2 Jonathan Rutherford, 'Who's That Man', in Rowena Chapman and Jonathan Rutherford (eds), *Male Order: Unwrapping Masculinity*, London, 1988, p. 32.

3 For example, Dick Hebdige has suggested in relation to automobile design, that objects engender sexual differences which can be delineated along a constantly shifting chain: man/woman; work/pleasure; production/consumption; function/form. *Hiding in the Light*, London, 1988, p. 87.

4 Roland Barthes, *The Fashion System*, New York, 1984, p. 302.

5 Kenneth Clark, *The Nude: A Study of Ideal Art*, London, 1957, p. 20.

6 Ibid., p. 4. John Berger took a similar stance and elaborates the discourse in suggesting: 'A naked body has to be seen as an object in order to become a nude'. John Berger, *Ways of Seeing*, London, 1972, p. 54.

KATRINA ROLLEY

Love, Desire and the Pursuit of the Whole

Dress & the Lesbian Couple

UNION

Our heart is the same in our woman's breast,
My dearest! Our body is made the same.
A similar heavy destiny has weighted our soul,
We love each other and we are the perfect hymn.

I decipher your smile and the shadow on your face.
My softness is the same as your great softness,
Sometimes it even seems that we are of the same race . . .
I love in you my child, my friend and my sister.

Like you I love the lonely water, the breeze,
The far-away, the stillness and the handsome violet . . .
With the power of my love, I understand you:
I know exactly what pleases you.

See, I am more than yours, I am you.
You have no cares that aren't mine also . . .
And what could you love that I don't also?
And what could you think that I don't also?

Our love is part of infinity,
Absolute as death and beauty . . .
See, our hearts are joined and our hands are united
Firmly in space and in eternity.

Renée Vivien[1]

Miss Teddy Gerard (left) and Miss Doddy Durand, photograph by Bassano, 1914 (courtesy of the National Portrait Gallery, London)

'In the first place', explains Aristophanes in Plato's *Symposium*, 'there were three sexes – male, female and hermaphrodite – and 'each human being was a rounded whole, with double back and flanks forming a complete circle. . . . Their strength and vigour made them very formidable, and their pride was overweening; they attacked the gods,' and Zeus retaliated by bisecting them.

Man's original body having been thus cut in two, each half yearned for the half from which it had been severed [and] . . . it is from this distant epoch . . . that we may date the innate love which human beings feel for one another, the love which restores us to our ancient state by attempting to weld two beings into one and to heal the wounds which humanity suffered. . . . Those men who are halves of the being of the common sex, which was called . . . hermaphrodite, are lovers of women . . . Women who are halves of the female whole direct their affections towards women and pay little attention to men [and] . . . those who are halves of the male whole pursue males.[2]

Love, according to Plato, is 'simply the name for the desire and pursuit of the whole',[3] and this coupling could be achieved through the union of similar or different halves. However, for lesbians living in Europe during the first half of this century – in a society which recognised heterosexual difference as the only basis for the welding of two beings into one – the pursuit of the whole could be fraught with difficulty, particularly if the couple wanted the world to acknowledge their union.[4]

A multitude of institutions and traditions served (and serve) to validate the heterosexual couple. They were welded together by legal documents, religious ceremonies, cohabitation, the production of children, shared names and a shared grave and, until recently, such a union could be extremely difficult to dissolve. No such institutions, ceremonies or traditions existed to validate the lesbian couple; in fact lesbian desire – the desire of same for same – remained largely unacknowledged until the early twentieth century. Regardless of this official silence women did desire each other, form lasting partnerships and want public acknowledgement of their unions, but their options with regard to the latter were both limited and problematic.

If they tried to tell people 'the truth' about their relationship the couple were likely to inspire revulsion rather than recognition (especially at a time when emotional and sexual lives were rarely subjects for general discussion). If they were wealthy or independent they might live or work together, thus making clear an emotional union, but this union could easily be perceived as a marriage of convenience rather than desire – a consolation prize for the absence of a man. Either of these options also limited recognition of a couple to those who knew them personally. How, then, could two women indicate that their union was a free and deliberate choice, and how could they assert their status as a couple to every chance acquaintance and casual observer?

'Unless twin sisters are dressed in identical clothes and do their hair in the same way', Colette observed with regard to her perceived likeness to the actress Polaire, 'people seldom exclaim at their striking resemblance.' However, 'from the day when . . . [Colette] cut off [her] too long hair, a number of clever people discovered'[5] how similar the two women looked. When Colette and Polaire were 'fitted out with three precisely similar costumes'[6] their likeness caused even more comment, and if the onlooker knew that they were not twins, or even sisters, they were bound to accept that some other relationship existed between the two women.

For centuries familial ties had been made visible through dress, with parents and children, siblings, and in particular sisters, being dressed alike. Uniforms, be they imposed or voluntary, serve both to distinguish the wearers from the rest of society and to bind them together into a unified body. Thus the lesbian couple who dressed alike emphasised both their special closeness and their difference from the rest of society. They were a pair rather than two individuals and such visual unity gained in strength and meaning by being freely chosen: 'My child, my friend and my sister . . . I am more than yours, I am you.'

However, whilst dressing the same, as sisters or twins, might communicate emotional closeness, what of the physical relationship? In a society which allows desire only in difference, which perceives active desire as a masculine prerogative and which taboos incest, dressing as sisters would tend to suppress rather than express the suggestion of a physical relationship. Even if some form of physical relationship was allowed by the viewer, in the absence of active 'masculine' desire such a relationship might be dismissed as unimportant. As Renaud says to his wife, Claudine, in Colette's novel *Claudine Married*:

> You women can do anything. It's charming and it's of no consequence whatever . . . Between you pretty little animals it's a . . . how can I put it? . . . a consolation for us, a restful change . . . or, at least a kind of compensation. It's the logical search for a more perfect partner, for a beauty more like your own, which reflects your own sensitiveness and your own weakness . . . If I dared (but I shouldn't dare), I would say that certain women need women in order to preserve their taste for men.[8]

In the case of Colette and Polaire it took the masculine presence of M. Willy, Colette's husband and 'manager', to add a sexual edge to the couple, who might otherwise have been taken for 'real' twins or sisters by the unknowing observer. Willy turned them into a *ménage à trois*, sexualising both the women's relationship with him and their relationship with each other. As Colette puts it, 'On the days when our manager took us out to restaurants in our "twins" disguise [Polaire] was constrained . . . and her shrinking made people stare and smile more maliciously still.'[9]

Willy's use of Colette and Polaire was clearly exploitative and although his presence sexualised their relationship with each other, it also ultimately focused the attention back on him, as the site of the active, 'masculine' sexuality. But what if this active sexuality was separated from the body of the man and situated instead in the body of a woman? Active 'masculine' desire need not be located in the body of a man – something the sexologists implicitly recognised when they defined the 'congenital invert'[10] as a woman with a male mind and a female body. If one of the women within a lesbian couple took on 'masculine' desire it served the dual purpose of both sexualising the women's relationship with each other and also excluding any male intruder. The couple was already balanced and complete in itself, there was no room for another man.

The only way to make the mind visible is through its physical embodiment, and the masculine mind of the active, congenital invert was represented on the bodies of many of the lesbians who appeared in late nineteenth- and early twentieth-century literature; literature produced at a time when 'the immanent truth of appearances . . . was a constant theme in . . . medicine, phrenology, physiognomy, and eugenics'.[11] Thus whilst Renaud dismisses Claudine and Rezi's relationship as meaningless, Colette underlines Claudine's own experience of it as both sexually and emotionally valid by investing Claudine with a masculinised body: 'I was proud', Claudine says, 'of my muscular tallness, of my slender grace, more boyish and clear cut' than the 'white and gold' Rezi.[12]

Whilst this masculine lesbian body is a commonplace in literature, transformation and display of the body obviously held difficulties for the 'real life' lesbian couple who wished to make public the sexual nature of their union. For them, the body was displaced on to clothes, which are at once more malleable and more fixed than the body. Clothes both disguise and reveal the body, they are more easily changed than the body but they do not themselves change, as the body does. Clothes can transform the body, fix its meanings and make them visible.

For lesbians who chose to use it, dress could bind two women together, transforming them from individuals into a united couple. It could also, through the use of gendered dress, suggest heterosexual difference and the presence of active 'masculine' desire within the sameness of lesbianism. (Did this reverse the heterosexual sexualisation of women's dress and make masculine dress sexual within the gendered lesbian couple?) Thus both emotional and physical love could be expressed – through dress that was both similar and gendered – and the couple could be perceived as complete within itself.

This visible expression of emotional and physical unity bound the lesbian couple together not just in the eyes of the world, but also in their own eyes. Looking the part, like playing the part, helps to create, define and reinforce our identity. As Virginia Woolf writes:

Vain trifles as they seem, clothes have, they say, more important offices than merely to keep us warm. They change our view of the world and the world's view of us . . . Thus, there is much to support the view that it is clothes that wear us and not we them; we may make them take the mould of arm or breast, but they would mould our hearts, our brains, our tongues to their liking. [13]

Whilst wishing to avoid oversimplistic equations between power, sexuality, masculinity and masculine dress, clothes do play a vital part in both creating and displaying the gender ideals of any particular period. The adoption of masculine dress might well have stimulated, liberated or sanctioned desire between two women.

Vita Sackville-West gives dress a central role in her account of the beginning of her passionate relationship with Violet Trefusis.

An absurd circumstance gave rise to the whole thing; I had just got clothes like the women-on-the-land were wearing, and in the unaccustomed freedom of breeches and gaiters I went into wild spirits; I ran, I shouted, I jumped, I climbed, I vaulted over gates, I felt like a schoolboy let out on a holiday; and Violet followed me across fields and woods with a new meekness, saying very little, but never taking her eyes off me, and in the midst of my exuberance I knew that all the old under-current had come back stronger than ever, and that my old domination over her had never been diminished. I remember that wild irresponsible day. It was one of the most vibrant of my life. [14]

In response to Vita's awakening masculinity Violet drew on all her 'knowing' femininity in 'the supreme effort to conquer the love of the person she had always wanted'. [15] For dinner, later that same day, she wore:

a dress of red velvet, that was exactly the colour of a red rose, and that made her, with her white skin and tawny hair, the most seductive being. She pulled me down until I kissed her . . . Then she was wise enough to get up and go to bed; but I kissed her again in the dark after I had blown out our solitary lamp. She let herself go entirely limp and passive in my arms. (I shudder to think of the experience that lay behind her abandonment.) I can't think I slept all that night – not that much of the night was left. [16]

As the relationship developed both women appear to have experienced and expressed their union in terms of gendered roles. Vita talks of possessing a 'dual personality . . . in which the feminine and the masculine elements alternately preponderate', [17] and it was the masculine Vita whom Violet loved – Julian, Dmitri, Mitya – not the feminine Vita who belonged to her husband

and children: 'Mitya, you could do anything with me, or rather *Julian* could. I love Julian, overwhelmingly, devastatingly, possessively, exorbitantly, submissively, incoherently, insatiably, passionately, despairingly. Also coquettishly, flirtatiously, and frivolously.'[18]

Before the relationship began, however, these gendered roles were not so fixed. As adolescents dressing up, it was Violet who 'chased [Vita] with a dagger down the long passage of that very ancient Scotch castle',[19] and in a letter from Celon in 1910 Violet addressed Vita as 'my incomparable sister of the velvet eyes'.[20]

There are various possible explanations as to why Violet and Vita chose (consciously or unconsciously) to eradicate such ambiguities once their friendship developed into a passionate affair. Vita's masculinity helped to explain their relationship – the 'inevitable' attraction of opposites – and gave it a similar importance to Vita's marriage to Harold Nicolson. Vita's 'dual nature' also, simultaneously, safeguarded this marriage and kept the wife and mother and the masculine lesbian at a safe distance from each other. The ideals of both masculinity and femininity remained intact – cohabiting rather than co-mingling – in Vita's bisexual body.

Violet and Vita's perceptions of their relationship may have been influenced by the work of the sexologists but even if they had never heard of congenital inversion they had, like the men who theorised lesbianism, been brought up within a society which saw emotional and physical union as the prerogative and result of heterosexual difference. This heterosexual dichotomy was not simply imposed upon the lesbian couple from without but also came from within, shaping their experience of love, desire and the pursuit of the whole and influencing the way they expressed that experience. This is not to suggest, however, that difference within the lesbian couple was the same as difference within the heterosexual couple. As Joan Nestle argues with reference to the supposedly rigid 'heterosexual' roles of butch and femme in the United States in the 1950s: 'Butch-femme relationships, as I experienced them, were complex erotic statements, not phony heterosexual replicas. They were filled with a deeply lesbian language of stance, dress, gesture, loving, courage and autonomy.'[21]

Vita's relationship with Violet was not her first lesbian affair. Prior to this she had been involved with another childhood friend, Rosamund Grosvenor, and in this relationship the masculine/feminine dichotomy does not appear to have been pronounced, if present at all. Gendered roles within lesbian relationships were, like masculine and feminine roles within heterosexuality, fugitive rather than fixed. They changed with time, were shaped by the class, race, age, occupation, etc., of each partner, and shifted in relation to the dynamics between the two women.

In the late 1950s Joan Nestle 'walked the streets looking so butch that straight teenagers called [her] a bulldyke',[22] but in lesbian bars she was recognised as a femme. When Una Troubridge wore feminine dress it identified her as a lesbian in relation to her partner, Radclyffe Hall, but when she presented herself in isolation from her lover, for example in her portrait by Romaine Brooks, she adopted masculine dress so as to communicate her sexuality.[23] In relation to Renaud, Claudine is feminine, in relation to Rezi she is masculine, and her short hair, youth, and beauty elicit responses from both heterosexual women and masculine lesbians.

Violet and Vita took this gender masquerade one step further and actually passed as man and woman whilst in Paris. Through the adoption of masculine dress Vita became Julian, 'a rather untidy young man, a sort of undergraduate, of about nineteen'.[24] Julian's masculinity allowed the lovers to experience the privileges of heterosexuality and to make their relationship public: to see it acknowledged by the theatre audience amongst whom Violet lay back 'in an abandonment of happiness' and gave herself up to her lover's 'scandalously indiscreet caresses';[25] to see it reflected in the eyes of the taxi driver who 'smiled knowingly and sympathetically'[26] at Julian as he would never have done at Vita.

Julian and Violet – the 'poet' and his 'mistress' – could become 'a part of [Paris], essentially. As much a part of it as the hairy concierge and the camelots who wear canvas shoes and race down the boulevards nasally screaming, "La Petue! La Presse!"'[27] Vita and Violet – lesbian lovers – could expect amused tolerance at best – of the kind that the heroines of Radclyffe Hall's *Well of Loneliness* experienced:

A few people might stare at the tall, scarred woman in her well-tailored clothes and black slouch hat. They would stare first at her and then at her companion: 'Mais regardez moi ca! Elle est belle, la petite; comme c'est rigolo!' There would be a few smiles, but on the whole they would attract little notice – ils en ont vu bien d'autres – it was post-war Paris.[28]

Violet and Vita's relationship was sparked off by Vita's adoption of breeches and was at its most passionate when she masqueraded as Julian. Stephen (heroine of *The Well of Loneliness*) and Mary's 'earthly passion' was changed into 'a love made perfect, discarnate',[29] as the couple stood amongst Stephen's 'neat . . . suits, . . . orderly piles of shirts, crepe de Chine pyjamas' and 'hand-knitted silk'[30] stockings which the 'womanly' Mary longed to darn. Claudine and Rezi's love blossomed in the latter's 'perpetually overheated dressing-room' where 'Rezi dresses and undresses'[31] and Claudine watches her admiringly. Clothes, it seems, often played a central part in lesbian relationships in both life and literature.

As Elizabeth Wilson points out, 'Stephen's apparel almost *is* her sexuality, and her sexual attraction is mediated through her masculine garb.'[32] Once gender was freed from the body endless possibilities came into play. A lesbian couple's bodies might be the same sex, but what gender were they? Masculine? Feminine? Or a combination of the two? And if so in what proportions? As Joan Nestle puts it: 'When we broke gender lines in the 1950s, we fell off the biologically charted maps.'[33] How else was a woman recognisable as a lesbian except through her body, her clothes, and the dialogue between the two? 'I loved my lover [Nestle writes] for how she stood as well as for what she did. Dress was a part of it: the erotic signal of her hair at the nape of her neck, touching the shirt collar; how she held a cigarette; the symbolic pinky ring flashing as she waved her hand.'[34]

The lesbian's ability to change her gender through manipulation of her self-presentation, thus exposing the artificiality of society's masculine and feminine ideals, clearly had the power to disturb the onlooker. Compton Mackenzie, in his novel *Extraordinary Women*, attempts to reassure the reader by emphasising the body as the fundamental site of sex and gender. Rory Freemantle, a stereotypical 'congenital invert',

> did not allow evening to interfere with her masculine style. She came down to dinner at the Augusto in a good imitation of a dinner-jacket, though without the stiff-fronted shirt which she would have liked to affect every night, but which owing to the inconsiderate femininity of her bust caused her so much discomfort that she could only affect it on the grandest occasions.[35]

The femininity of Rory's body, Mackenzie asserts, triumphs over her masculine dress, just as her tears regularly dislodge the monocle from her eye.

Reality, however, was not so reassuring. Clothes articulated lesbian desire and simultaneously exposed 'gender as a masquerade'.[36] They expressed this desire, communicated it, gave it permission to exist and maybe even created it. Gendered dress for the heterosexual couple displayed and exaggerated the body, emphasising the difference. Gendered dress for the lesbian couple disguised and transformed the body, creating difference.

> Go to a party with a cute SM butch I fancy. She's taller than me. I feel quite femme. She turns up in a leather mini-skirt, fishnets and stilettos. I've never seen her looking so comfortable. I wear lounge suit and black tie. Halfway through the evening I yearn to change clothes with her, but her feet are bigger than mine. No good unless I've got the stilettos too. Tell her about it anyway. We flirt all night and then fuck like rabbits back at my place.

Barbara Smith[37]

Notes and References

1 Renée Vivien, *The Muse of the Violets: Poems by Renée Vivien*, Tallahassee, Florida, 1982, p. 73. (Originally published in 1923.)

2 Plato, *The Symposium*, Harmondsworth, 1951, pp. 59–62.

3 Ibid., p. 64.

4 The word lesbian is both historically specific and difficult to define. It appears here as shorthand for the different words with similar, although not identical, meanings which have been used over the centuries. It defines, in this context, a woman who forms her primary sexual and/or emotional relationships with other women.

5 Colette, *Earthly Paradise*, Harmondsworth, 1974, p. 143. (Originally published in 1957.)

6 Ibid., p. 144

7 Vivien, op. cit.

8 Colette, *Claudine Married*, Harmondsworth, 1972, p. 95. (Originally published in 1902.)

9 Colette, op cit., 1974, p. 144.

10 'Invert' was the term used by many of the sexologists, in particular Havelock Ellis whose works were most influential in Britain, to describe homosexuals of both sexes.

11 Lisa Tickner, *The Spectacle of Women: Imagery of the Suffrage Campaign 1907-14*, London, 1987, p. 169.

12 Colette, op cit., 1972, p. 137.

13 Virginia Woolf, *Orlando*, Harmondsworth, 1945, p. 108. (Originally published in 1928.) My thanks to Lisa Tickner for reminding me of this passage.

14 Nigel Nicolson, *Portrait of a Marriage*, London, 1974, p. 105.

15 Ibid., p. 106.

16 Ibid., p. 107.

17 Ibid., p. 108.

18 M. Leaska and J. Phillips, *Violet to Vita: The Letters of Violet Trefusis to Vita Sackville-West, 1910-21*, London, 1989, p. 103.

19 Nicolson, op. cit., p. 29. The BBC Television series *Portrait of a Marriage* (1990) also sought to banish such ambiguities when it reversed these roles and depicted the masculine Vita chasing and finally overwhelming the feminine Violet.

20 P. Jullian and J. Phillips, *Violet Trefusis: A Biography*, London, 1986, p. 152.

21 Joan Nestle, *A Restricted Country: Essays & Short Stories*, London, 1987, p. 102.

22 Ibid., p. 100.

23 Katrina Rolley, 'Cutting a Dash: The Dress of Radclyffe Hall and Una Troubridge', *Feminist Review*, no. 35, Summer 1990, p. 63.

24 Nicolson, op. cit., p. 111.

25 Leaska and Phillips, op. cit., p. 115.

26 Ibid., p. 116.

27 Ibid., p. 115.

28 Radclyffe Hall, *The Well of Loneliness*, London, 1982, p. 328. (Originally published in 1928.)

29 Ibid., p. 326.

30 Ibid., p. 324.

31 Colette, op. cit., 1972, p. 80.

32 Elizabeth Wilson, *Hallucinations: Life in the Post-Modern City*, London and New York, 1988, p. 48.

33 Nestle, op. cit., p. 108.

34 Ibid., p. 104.

35 Compton Mackenzie, *Extraordinary Women: Theme and Variations*, London, 1928, p. 55.

36 Wilson, op. cit., p. 53.

37 Barbara Smith, 'Shock, horror – Butch turns Femme', *Pink Paper*, no. 19, 31 March 1988.

NEIL SPENCER

Menswear in the 1980s

Revolt into Conformity

What did men wear before menswear? Fashion folk spent much of the eighties proclaiming, designing, photographing, and selling the 'revolution in menswear', so it's worth recalling the pre-revolutionary epoch of the Great British Male to remind ourselves of the extent of our transformation. What's so different?

Not much. The suit still rules absolutely as what a man must wear to be taken seriously in society – as we shall see, its command in an authoritarian and retrospective decade was more absolute than ever – while outside of bohemian circles a man is still not considered fully dressed without a tie. Though equipped with a far fuller wardrobe – thanks to the menswear boom and a general upsurge in affluence – the office drudge of the eighties wore much the same as his counterpart in the twenties or fifties. An unpleasant mac, a dowdy overcoat, a shaggy jumper and slacks for weekends, an insistence on dour colours from the sludge spectrum unique to the GBM, a sullen resistance to sock-changing – some things just don't change. Only the creeping arrival of Euroman, with his suspect peacockery and his handbags, threatens the dull purity of this strain.

Alongside this uniform of respectability, which in Britain descends in an unbroken chain from royalty to the suburbs, exists the uniform of jeans, blouson, T-shirt and trainers that clothes almost every other GBM. In contrast to the office drudge, the working (or unemployed) drone of today looks strikingly different from his antecedents in their demob suits, cloth caps and overalls. Hunched into a technicolour bomber jacket, hands in pockets and elbows flapping, indigo legs tapering spindily into rubber shoes, ass and belly hanging – much of working-class male Britain now resembles budgerigars in running shoes. The Hunt Ball may still dress in the style of its grandfathers, but on the football terraces of the Stanley Matthews era, the aliens have landed.

This is an altogether new silhouette in twentieth-century fashion; originating in fifties' teendom via James Dean, it is now seen on men in their sixties, and considering how unflattering it is to all but the athletically inclined, its popularity is astonishing. (Latterly, sportswear has helped disguise the sagging male gut, while implying that the degenerate inside the tracksuit is actually doing something about his physical problems – but that's another story.)

Though these two GBM looks may be regarded as contrary poles rather than as mutually exclusive looks, the area that falls outside their embrace – the zone of the 'menswear revolution' – is, in practice, small. The fashion pages of the newly established male fashion press strutting their bold colours and shapes; the now-subsiding rash of Next; Ralph Lauren tradition at Marks & Spencer; the Italian fashion machine; feminism and the new man: their collective impact on the GBM has been puny. Conformity and solidarity rule alongside mediocrity of design and material, and if the GBM's sartorial self-awareness has been raised an iota or three in the last decade, the 'menswear revolution' has also helped stifle the British tradition of eccentric dressing. These days even dotty squires come off the peg from Hackett's.

What made the 'menswear revolution' of the eighties so fascinating was not that new looks were created and better clothes more widely marketed (both were), or that fresh fortunes were made – though this remained a powerful motor, in keeping with both the times and rag trade tradition. Menswear was an idea whose time had come – 'everything has been done in womenswear' went the cry – and one which offered the media a handy microcosm for the contrary social currents set in motion by 'new right' governments at home and abroad. Any crack in the social consensus demands a new set of sartorial codes; the trauma of dismantling the welfare state, a notion embedded deep in the post-war British psyche, demanded a revolution. New codes were duly found to reflect the realigned status quo, which from the outset demanded that everyone 'knew their place', that the 'haves' be readily distinguishable from the 'have nots'.

Never before had the GBM enjoyed such a choice of clothes, a mirror world of the wider 'choice' being offered by the new government. Instant upward social mobility – the carrot ahead of Mrs Thatcher's stick – gave rise to the second biggest fashion movement of the decade – the yuppie. In his over-sized pinstripe suit, fake Jermyn Street striped shirt, authentic Jermyn Street brogues, hair swept back in brilliantined glory, the yuppie was Cecil Parkinson made manifest, a paradigm of 'enterprise culture'. Margaret Thatcher, of course, was the yuppie mum; when she railed against the 'nanny state' no one seemed to fit the description better than herself.

The new cult of the label ensured that social mobility could be bought off the shelf. It was as if the new regime could not tolerate the social gaffes of the seventies' *nouveau riche*; the suburban kitsch of purple swivel chairs and ankle-tickling carpets, footballers in kipper ties with a knot as big as your ankle, the tacky Mediterranean tan of medallion man. The label, which was suddenly flipped through fashion's looking-glass to the outside of the garment, was not only the apogee of conspicuous consumption, it bestowed the certainty of good taste for which previous *nouveaux* could only grope. Every jumped-up young estate agent or futures-dealer knew to aspire to Paul Smith and Giorgio Armani and had the readies to buy them. Acute as ever, the Japanese coined a word for the label 'junky' – *miha* – a condition venerated in the 'shopping and fucking' novel, a genre dedicated to making the latter as mundane as the former.

While the yuppie aped ruling-class tradition – the big shouldered, double-breasted business suit, the yachting blazer, polished black Oxfords from the quad – the country's male elite did not surrender up its threadbare wardrobe so easily. Though it occasionally toyed with yuppie and Euroman – Prince Charles in an Italian suit, a junior cabinet minister in gaudy tie – it mainly retrenched itself in dull tradition; barbours and wellies signify rural squiredom, old school ties and Tricker's hunting slippers a style that can't be bought from French design houses. The need to be seen as pre-yuppie money made the Sloane Ranger a fêted species for a few years, and called into being shops like Hackett's to supply young fogeys with the requisite gnobbly tweed jacket and itchy tattersall shirt.

The biggest male fashion movement of the eighties was inevitably not among the newly enfranchised but among the dispossessed millions who piled up the unemployment statistics. Unemployment as much as aesthetics ushered in the era of the anorak, trainer and jeans as the bog-standard garb of the working-class/unemployed service-sector GBM. Cheap, practical, hard-wearing, the look also identified with the macho heroism of le rocker, with the icons of Dean, Brando, Presley, and with eighties' counterparts like Springsteen and Cruise, and is now Regular Guy garb from Hong Kong to Hounslow to Houston, all of which watch the same Levi's ads.

While jeans and a C&A bomber were what grown-up poor people wore, there were more studied responses to the stick of new austerity that accompanied the yuppie carrot; exquisitely torn jeans adorned the 'Hard Times' cover of *The Face*, while the long macs and second-hand suits of the 'Oxfam brigade', with their doomy Joy Division rock and George Orwell haircuts, made a suitable fanfare for the advent of the dreaded 1984. In one sense Oxfam chic was a lament for the passing of the old working-class certainties, much like Bleasdale's *Boys from the Blackstuff*. From here on in, the only mufflers and hobnail boots to be seen were in the haywain and haircut films of the Heritage industry, alongside Rupert Everett in Eton crop, linen shirt and braces.

The effects of the new right's social engineering aside, there were other, and perhaps more significant forces at work, to which the 'menswear revolution' was in part a response. Central has been the concept of the 'new man'. Sounding like a term from Nazi ideology, the term implied no less fundamental a transformation of human nature; the creation of the post-feminist, non-sexist male. Like the thousand year Reich, one suspects the 'new man' is a doomed idea. His begetting, however, was unavoidable. The rise of feminism and the advances of the women's movement demanded some kind of response from men, however feeble. The 'male feminist' proved deeply creepy and unappealing to both genders, not least because of his unsexy 'woollyback' wardrobe.

Indeed, sartorial matters proved deeply troubling to most sectors of the left during the eighties, from the 'disgrace' of Michael Foot's donkey jacket at the Cenotaph to the accusations of yuppie sell-out that greeted the arrival of Neil Kinnock's groomed and fragrant Red Rose Rallies, and their overseer, the ever dapper Peter Mandelson. Citizen Ken Livingstone, in his fawns and flares, exemplified GBM drabnitude and politically died, while GLC lawyer and dandy Paul Boateng prospered in Gaultier. Tony Benn, in his DMs and button-downs, maintained an even keel. As for the donkey jacket, it started the eighties on the back of *Socialist Worker* street sellers, and ended as a double-page advertisement for Liberty's, replete with paisley shoulders.

The new man was always as much the creation of women as of men, a kind of projected animus that roamed the rails of menswear looking for fun, eventually becoming a well-dressed *yeti*, a mythical creature thought to exist, much speculated upon, occasionally sighted, but damnably evasive. A few years ago I conducted a straw poll of female aquaintances on the subject of the new man. 'I know they wear Paul Smith,' said one magazine editor, 'but I've never met one.' 'A friend of mine went out with one once,' went another typical answer, 'but it didn't work out.'

Though at first it seemed like a media fad – set 'em up with the picture of a tender, bare-chested hunk holding a baby, then shoot 'em down when reality fails to follow suit – the new man has proved more enduring than expected. Deeply in touch with his anima, and the suppressed female side of his nature, yet retaining the admirable male values of paternity, strength, and virility, he continues to haunt the sexual arena. At first he was derided as a wimp, the real-life victim of the symbolic castration of men by feminism. New man also became gay collaborator. Pop's 'gender bender' boom of the early eighties – Phil Oakey of the Human League in lipstick, Boy George in frocks – was followed by Jean Paul Gaultier's celebrated 'men in skirts', while stylist Ray Petri put his *Face* male pin-ups in DMs and boxer shorts. For a while 'new man' became father, a young buck saddled with a baby but taking on his responsibility, as in the numerous baby movies of late eighties' Hollywood (*Raising Arizona, Three Men and a Baby*, etc.), while film and rock stars increasingly took to posing with their offspring.

Most recently the new man has become realist rake, a style exemplified by Jonathan Ross (whose early success revolved as much around his exemplary wardrobe as his show). This is essentially 'new man' as lad, though the new rake is as likely to be in steady partnership or marriage as on the tiles; he takes his commitments seriously. He is not, however, neutered, and wears his sexuality proudly. He is steeped in the realpolitik, rather than the ideology, of sexual relations, and he is increasingly the focus of the men's magazines, where the traditions of collective male lust are refined and renewed in articles like 'Measure your manhood without using a ruler' (*GQ*), or 'Girls Girls Girls, one hundred women we'd die for' (*Arena*), or 'Women we'd like to take to lunch' (*Esquire*). It is one of the ironies of the male press that while outvying each other in red-blooded heterosexuality, and murmuring asides to their female readers, their substantial gay readership is addressed only through homoerotic fashion plates (which are often posed, styled and snapped by gay men).

The men's mags depend in part on men's newly found self-consciousness about their appearance and identity, but they have also given women new ideas about the shape of their menfolk, who have learned for the first time how it feels to be measured against the male equivalent of the dolly model. 'Why don't you look more like this?' ask the women, dangling a shot of some cleft-chinned animal beauty draped in a grand's worth of Hamnett. As the decade wore on the subject of female erotica and pornography became an increasingly popular media hunting ground, an evolution of the growing power of women to dress (or undress) men. This was no longer confined to a devoted wife's selection of a tie for an important occasion (scene from a thousand old films) but became a full-scale invasion of menswear by female designers like Westwood, Hamnett, Cappellino and Farhi, though all modified rather than revolutionised the central tenets of menswear, and were often dismayed by the conservatism of the male market.

Another major social current to which British menswear has responded is race, and the emancipation of a new generation of black Britons has been as central to fashion as it has to sport and entertainment. In fact black Britain could be said to be the synthesis of all three. One origin of the now ubiquitous sportswear is reggae chic in the late seventies; when Bob Marley started posing in his football gear and donned a red, gold and green tracksuit he set in motion more than he knew. By the early eighties tracksuit 'n' trainer was in vogue in ghettos from Watts to Moss-side, and has remained the staple fare of hip-hop ever since: Run DMC (who composed 'My Adidas' and were rewarded by sponsorship from the company); Public Enemy, LL Cool J – all have worked out in sportswear.

In general, though, seventies' UK black style was overturned; 'earthman' shoes, ex-army 'jungle greens', woolly hats and other signifiers of ethnicity and militancy were abandoned for the language of emancipation: crisp Italian suits, or the MA1 jackets, gold chains and hi-top trainers of Afro-Americana. Outclassing the 'grey boys' in the 'gears' stakes became a matter of pride; Frank Bruno's Saville Row suits, Lenny Henry's comic character 'Delbert' with his 'sponditious' trousers and 'crucial' jackets, the fact that the sharpest shop assistants on the King's Road were usually black; all were outcrops of the same mood.

The rediscovery of jazz (another aspect of the wider retro mood) brought other traditions of black dress to the fore. The Zoot Suit, the embodiment of bagginess, was re-cast by the likes of Blue Rondo a La Turk, led by Wag Club founder Chris Sullivan and dressed by Demob, who were an impressive example of sartorial form over musical content. Be-bop threads were back, along with young men with horns, dusky chanteuses, and clubs wreathed in blue cigarette smoke. The romanticism of jazz was evoked in lager adverts, pop videos, fashion shoots, film flops like *Absolute Beginners* and box-office hits like *Bird* and *Round Midnight*. Miles Davis, a leading edge rake since the forties, was on T-shirts in his 1961 mohair suit and in Gap adverts in his 1991 incarnation.

British jazz was riven apart by all this, caught up in a style wars squall beyond its comprehension. Young poseurs who knew more about Charlie Parker's wardrobe than his solos were one thing, but the new breed of talented black players who now came to symbolise British jazz – Courtney Pine, Steve Williamson – also dressed with poise, insisting that the average jazzbo's grubby T-shirt, unkempt beard and beer-soaked jeans showed 'lack of respect' for the music. Appropriately, Williamson's 1990 debut LP was launched at Armani's Brompton Road salon.

Black designers also appeared; several of them, like Charlie Allen, part of the tradition of Caribbean tailoring. This was also the case with Jazzy B of Soul II Soul, whose successful bid for World Domination was launched not by the group playing live (indeed, there were no musicians, just DJs, tapes and singers), but by fashion shows, dancers and clothes shops; the most intimate collusion of pop and rag trade since Westwood and the Sex Pistols.

Male fashion continues to be more influenced by music and movies than by fashion houses, which is why the Italians love to wardrobe *Miami Vice* or *The Untouchables*. Rolling up suit sleeves came in with Michael Jackson's 'Thriller' and continues to sort out the lads from the yuppies; rockers (other than teddy boys) rarely feel comfortable in suits. Both rocker and mod looks prospered through the early and middle eighties. The Reaganite return to the Cold War fifties (the last time the United States felt good about itself), ushered in an era of quiffs and shaved necks, of pumping iron and hulking physiques in 'power suits' with shoulders like cliff tops (Superman also returned). The trans-formation of Bruce Springsteen from wispy-bearded wimp to muscular Joe Six-pack in motorcycle boots and bandana, yawping 'Born in the USA', exemplifies the shirt. There are numerous rocker cults – billy, punk, metal, etc. – but the uniform remains essentially the same. Le rocker survives partly because it is tight, which despite a decade of flapping Yohjis, is still what most Westerners consider sexy.

The influence of British Mod was more subtle, and was tangled up with US retromania and the appropriation of the preppy look by continental Europe, but it was no less pervasive. Several eighties' fashion shakers had mod backgrounds. Paul Smith, *Face*-founder Nick Logan, stylist Ray Petri and numerous retailers had spent their youth as clothes-obsessed moddy boys in loafers and Fred Perrys. Paul Smith's creations were basically updates of mod, with a nod to the Edwardian world of the traditional gent's outfitters; Smith bought up stocks of old shop fittings to give his shops the requisite glow of burnished wood, and was also able to capitalise on the established rag trade of his native Nottingham.

The clothes which sixties mods yearned for were mostly hard to obtain US imports – shrink-to-fit Levi's, loafers, wing-tip brogues, Fred Perry tops, Ivy League suits, button-down shirts – which in the United States were the uniform of the collegiate middle class, the North American equivalent of Jermyn Street respectability. This was the 'tradition' which Ralph Lauren now sold the world, along with manly, check lumber shirts, hiking boots and other trappings of the Western Frontier, and a logo which suggested you belonged to the polo-playing classes. Though the package was as hokum as the ranch Lauren bought himself (importing mature trees to show how long the place had been around), it was popular, not least with his European imitators.

Suddenly every shirt, every pair of chinos (another preppy item to achieve mass popularity) had a label boasting their maker's pedigree. Blousons sported lettering in pidgin English claiming that the wearer belonged to the Saskatchewan Husky Trading Company or some other unlikely institution. Crested blazers and naval brass buttons replaced such homely 1920s obsessions of the seventies as Fair Isle jumpers, tweed baggies, collarless shirts and Hovis ads.

Today, the mod/preppy tradition is the *lingua franca* of menswear, the skeletal wardrobe of most men who consider themselves 'dressers', and what people mean when they drop that over-used epithet 'classics with a twist'. One of the greatest achievements of this twist – apart from making some beautiful, though often over-priced clothes – is extending the range of men's accessories with which to dress up one's 'classic'. Braces, cufflinks, belts, scarves, handkerchiefs, watches, socks, hats, fountain pens, wallets and more all became available in a variety unprecedented since the days of Jeeves and Wooster. The intricacies of the Edwardian 'gentleman's wardrobe' now became available on every high street, right down to the foreseen production and style.

Mod culture proper, which since its sixties' heyday had mutated through skinheads, soul boys, the Mod Revival (The Jam et al.) and Two-Tone (Specials et al.), re-emerged in the eighties as the Casual. The casual shared his predecessors' predilection for neatness and elitism, for soul music and dancing, for dress that could pass muster both sides of the wire; respectable in suburban shopping centres but loaded with detail and meaning for the initiate. His clothes sense, though, was oriented more to Italy and France than to North America. He brought guile and violence to the cult of the *miha*, 'taxing' other casuals by quite literally stealing the clothes off their backs, while it was folklore that the most violent football hooligans were the most expensively dressed (much to the initial bafflement of the police and public, who still expected their hoodlums to be shaven-skulled boot boys). Influential on the growth of the casual was the continuing success of English football teams, particularly Liverpool, in European competition. Hordes of English 'away' supporters fell ravenously upon the boutiques of Bologna, Milan, Naples and Rome, pillaging them for Armani, LaCoste and Fiorucci with which to out-trump the terraces of domestic rivals.

Three successive 'summers of love' from 1988 to 1990 wrecked the tribal distinctions of young Britain, which imploded under the impact of 'rave' culture and the widespread use of Ecstasy as clubland's, and later rock and roll's, drug of choice. The fashion consequences were immediate and widespread, as the hot-weather minimalism of surf shorts, fluorescent T-shirt, bandana and baseball boots undermined label-based elitism, the first of several knock-backs for the fashion industry. Spending disposable income on 'E' and warehouse parties (neither particularly cheap) simply proved more rewarding for many than splashing £80 for a Comme des Garçons shirt.

The new baggy, unisex look of loose jeans, long-sleeved T-shirt ('the fashion garment of the nineties', according to John Galliano) and Wallaby shoes proved massively popular, and ushered in a hippy influence last sighted at the start of the seventies. Pop likewise headed back to the sixties, rather than to the fifties, for inspiration; to jangling guitars, mop top beat groups with pouting lips (Stone Roses, Charlatans, etc.). The ghosts of Hendrix and Morrison prowled again; the former as soundtrack to a Wrangler ad, the latter in Oliver Stone's *The Doors* biopic. The sixties had become a *verboten* zone under Thatcher, decried by Norman Tebbit and chief constables as the root of our societal problems. Things had unravelled dangerously under their 'permissive' sway; everything from AIDS to the Crime Wave to left-wing subversives in education could be traced back to the same sixties root. Made taboo, the lure of the sixties proved too tempting to ignore, while under the onslaught of deepening eco-crisis, the rural and spiritual orientation of hippiedom looked less dippy than for a decade.

The menswear boutiques have shifted accordingly; the flowered shirt made an unexpectedly widespread return, leather has given way to suede, shaved necks to floppy fringes. More than ever, it seems, male Britain is divided into two breeds: those who wear suits to work and those who don't. The rag trade itself has been hard hit by the recession, and with the removal of Mrs Thatcher from office, the 'menswear revolution' is starting to look as much of a mirage as the 'economic miracle'. Already the Thatcher years look like a distant and time-bound era, and are presented as an inexplicable aberration even by Cabinet ministers who presided over them. The sartorial codes are shifting too; Mrs Thatcher's taste for fine clothes had been one of her trademarks (reaching its pinnacle during her last few weeks, when her outfits became more and more lavish); now we have the epoch of the 'men in grey suits', as her supplanters became known. And who more grey, more Great British Male, than John Major himself, in his dull serges and M & S white shirts. This is government by bank manager, the day of reckoning after the spending spree. The golden age of menswear may already be over.

LEE WRIGHT

utgrown Clothes for Grown-up People

Constructing a Theory of Fashion

This essay tests the validity of the method – qualitative research – as a way of constructing a theory of fashion.[1] A theory can only be constructed if an interpretation, translation or meaning is made. To apply or map theories on to the subject is to assume their application. My aim is to 'listen' to the focus of study and articulate interpretations from it; to create a language from the object focus. I am concerned with seeing if a language can be made from an aspect of clothing.[2]

'The cuff' and 'the turn-up' are examples of components of dress.[3] The feature which is the subject of this paper is a characteristic, rather than a component, of fashionable clothing, which became increasingly evident from 1986. Initially I termed it clothes that are 'too small', as it applied to numerous garment types, for example T-shirts, trousers and sweaters. Not clothes for small people but clothes which include in their design an element of 'smallness', and are within the reference system of Fashion.[4] This becomes most obvious when the garment is being worn because it is the relationship between the 'size' and 'fit' of the object with the size and shape of the human body that allows us to 'see' the element of smallness. By 1986 the characteristic seemed to be a minor aspect of the stylistic language of clothing, but increasingly it became appropriated into a wider fashion framework, i.e. more types of garment, and therefore more conspicuous.

Smallness creates an impression of a garment in the process of being outgrown. In some ways (but not in all ways as the item would then be unwearable) the garment is insufficient in the fabric quantity and/or the size.[5] A typology of when, where, and how the trait manifests itself, reveals parameters or a framework or a system on which to base hypotheses. In terms of manufacture, there appear to be two distinct means of production. Both are constructed to achieve the same reading (smallness) but their means of manufacture can be external or internal. By this I mean the former type is part of the industrial production system of Fashion, while the latter exists within a framework of customisation or individualisation of purchased

A man's sweater customised by the female wearer. The sweater body has been shrunk and now closely fits the female figure. The sleeves are too long but serve to exaggerate the body fit. The bottom has been cut to expose the undergarments and focuses attention on the waist of the jeans and the idea of the 'natural' waist which is covered. Photograph by Lee Wright in 1990

clothing. Specific examples of the first type could be 'leggings', which are manufactured to reach the mid-calf, unlike the conventional trouser length (leggings fall into the generic category as a form of trouser) which reaches the ankle. These garments appear 'short' because we have inherent notions as to the conventions of what trousers are like; therefore the meaning and construction are symbiotic, that is, they are short and create an image of shortness. Of the second type the wearer has consciously and purposefully made, or chosen, an item with element/s which appear 'too small'. For example, within the culture of Heavy Metal, a sweater which has shrunk and of which the armholes are tight is a common piece of sartorial adaption.

Setting out the parameters which quantify the means of production allows for the separation of differences within a typology and is a useful exercise if the subject is based on 'fieldwork' (i.e. observation).[6] It is this which allows for the distinction categorised above and indicates that the motif is part of an intra-culture. However, this also pinpoints a chronic problem which besets this case study. If I were to term the feature 'smallness', then it is obviously linked to ideas of 'bigness' and to an even wider framework of ideologies concerning the concept of size. Therefore the parameters are not just concerned with a 'littleness' but with its opposite. For example, what do we consider to be the 'correct' size of garment for our bodies? Is a 'tight' sweater perceived as 'small' at one point in time but correct at another? The 'skinny rib' sweater of the 1960s[7] superseded the baggy, loose-fitting 'Sloppy Joe'. Therefore I am dealing with a shifting notion of aesthetics which may be in

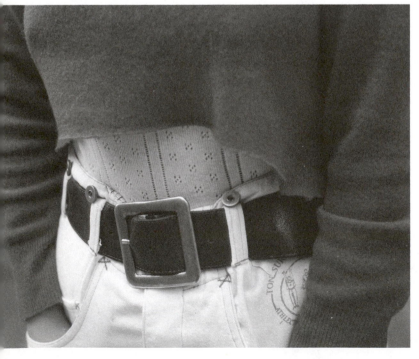

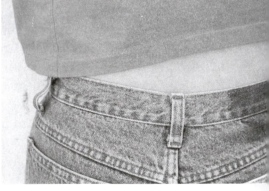

The flesh is exposed through raising the arm. This garment is long enough to cover in some situations and short enough to expose in others. The revealment/concealment issue is direct and is an external construction of 'smallness'. Photograph by Lee Wright in 1988

a far more rapid transition as a beauty and body aesthetic than, for example, the fashions of fatness and thinness. Distinctions between bigness and smallness can be illustrated by their polarities. The differentiations in the idea of 'small' lie between 'being tight', a 'smallness' and 'too small'. At the point where a garment is too small it can no longer be put on the body. Only the other two distinctions are valid in this discussion as both relate to the notion of the 'fit' of clothing. In order to observe 'smallness' in clothes there has to be one or both of two elements – too short or too tight. To be just short and/or tight is not enough to create the image of smallness. It is within the ideology of 'too' that the transaction of meaning between sufficient and insufficient (the interpretation) can be made and significance given. The degree to which smallness can be perceived is the degree to which shortness or tightness exists and to what extent they are included as traits in a garment. A garment needs only a minimum of these features to indicate the notion; for example, trousers which are short but that 'fit' everywhere else; a loose-fitting T-shirt with tight sleeves. We know the values of 'loose', 'baggy', 'tight', as Fashion has a language which allows us to play off one against the other (relativity). It has constructed a system which is inherent to our perceptions of sizing of garments based on generalities of the proportions of human form.[8] Consequently, it has systematised our perceptions of the fit of clothing; what is the 'right size' and the 'correct fit'. The predominant principle of 'smallness' is that it is visibly different from the size of other clothes. What it represents is dependent on how it has been reduced, by whom, and how it is worn. Is a mass-produced 'cropping' different from a customised one?

As a fashion form it occurs mainly between the ages of 16 and 35. This is important, as from the age of 16 the notion of outgrowness is concerned with grown-up-ness. As a motif it is worn by both male and female, which may indicate an absence of gender. However, the nature of the feature may make it an extreme example of gender-significant fashion. To explain further, by being small the motif fits the body closely, therefore indicating the shape beneath. In particular regions, for example the crotch, it begins to have readings connected to sex and sexuality, not just gender, although the two are closely related.

This type of framework, which links type, form and wearer, begins to map out the field more clearly. The use of 'grounded' research[9] enables the study of clothing to have social meaning, which in turn informs us about social behaviour.

This type of garment is concerned with its own size and how it relates to body shape.[10] The link between the two forms – the body and the object placed upon it – is crucial to the understanding of how 'smallness' can be linguistically deciphered. Of course, all clothing when worn acts as body packaging, and the process of wearing demonstrates that there is a relationship between the two. However, some forms and aspects of clothing appear to be a more conscious and obvious display of this than others. Sometimes 'covering' is not the only issue; there is a secondary level of meaning which creates an interaction. It is not an exchange from one to another but one is mapped on to the other (a layering) and 'builds' on an existent sartorial language to create another. I suggest outgrownness is one of these, as smallness relies on ideas of non-fit on the body, of only just covering it. This is demonstrated when the garment is next to the skin. A further method for illustrating smallness is in the relationship to other clothes when a short or shrunken part of a piece of clothing is put with garments we understand to be the correct size. In both cases it makes itself 'known' by its differences. It visually throws the norm into slight disarray by mismatching notions of size and fit within the conventions of garment wearing. It is through this contradictory role that it relays images connected to self-identity. It identifies parts of the body for display and/or attention which may be part of a sexual politic; for example, a short sweater which is cropped in order not to meet the waistband of the lower garment exposes part of the torso. At the same time it can construct what I call 'focused anarchy', that is, a signal of disobedience against the hierarchical language of fashion. The 'incredible hulk' syndrome, in which the body appears to be larger and the garment stays the same size, illustrates that smallness cannot completely disregard a system but works within its confines. It works as a meaning because it works within a language pushing the parameters in only one or two ways. The contradiction between being totally anarchistic and being

Leggings are purchased as a 'small' garment as they are short in terms of conventional trouser length. The wearer is creating an even greater impression of smallness by wearing them with a skirt which implies that they are 'tights', yet we know them to be leggings. The skirt also covers the gender significant area of the hips and therefore displaces the issue of sexuality on to femininity. The Doctor Marten boots, co-opted from a male sartorial system, continue the discourse as they create an impression of largeness and focus attention on the lower part of the leg which remains uncovered. Photograph by Lee Wright in 1989

anarchical only in a small number of ways, of being conventional and unconventional within the one garment and the wearing of it, sets a dualistic pattern of meaning.

1 Small but not too small
2 Fits but not quite fits
3 Short but not too short
4 Tight but not too tight
5 Conventional garment with unconventional aspects
6 Covers the body but not totally

The smallness continually places emphasis away from itself on to the body, therefore constructing a language which is not about Fashion but about the wearer. This is the point at which Body politics and Self-identity are realised through the vehicle of Fashion.[11] The smallness of a garment not only accentuates the body size and shape but can create an image of it being bigger. The iconoclasm is that smallness equals more not less, i.e. one gesture or detail can resignify the whole, and as such is a powerful and manipulative motif. It raises two issues: Is it reclaiming a sense of the past in terms of age and body growth? Or is it emphasising one of the basic expectations of clothing, which is to cover and fit? Is 'small' ageist? These clothes have been reduced in some way, i.e. miniaturised in order to achieve a discourse centred on body culture. It accentuates the adult body by conjuring up the child experience of growing

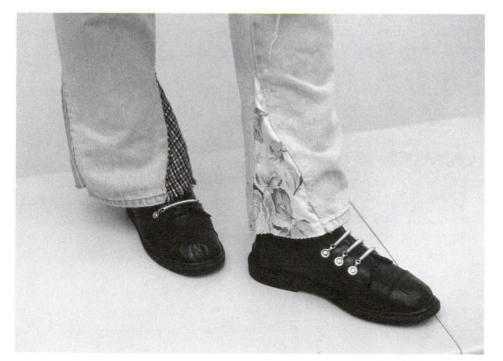

Making a garment smaller is based on the concept of correct sizing. In this case the garment has been made bigger by inserting fabric into a seam. This motif is interrelated to the culture of 'smallness' and continues the theme of individuation. Photograph by Lee Wright in 1990

out of clothing. 'Little' clothes on an adult point out the differences between the growing, the maturing and the fully grown physique (the child, the adolescent and the adult), demonstrating a display of power and control but also a sense of defeat. [12]

'Smallness' may be a way of imaging the Victim. The wearer becomes subjected to the characteristics this motif inflicts upon it. To what extent it victimises is in the control of the wearer. Anthropology calls clothes which directly inform the body of restricted mobility, 'movement shapes'. This aptly describes some of the elements of outgrownness as it can physically restrict movement and simultaneously be a representation of restriction. To explain further I will use the example of a cropped and tight (through shrinking) T-shirt. The tightness of the armhole prevents free arm movement; this is a physical connection between the armhole, its size and the arm. The cropped aspect enforces the message by inflection; that is, it introduces an element of danger, where the higher or more vigorous the arm movement, the greater the exposure of the torso. This secondary level represents rather than constructs the restriction, and supplies an indirect control on to the wearer. So the system is:

ARMHOLE – SMALLNESS – ARM
SHORT – EXPOSURE – BODY

Tightness can restrict the body and determine that movement is confined to less energetic gestures. Shortness exploits this, as body movements such as bending over increase the shortness. The mini-skirt is an example of this. It is both a small item, i.e. a miniaturisation of a 'real' size of skirt, and cropped and tight. [13] Exposure and the potential for revealing parts of the body is inbuilt into the notion of smallness and can be of three types:

a) exposure of the body THROUGH clothes, e.g. tight jeans
b) exposure of the REAL body, e.g. leggings
c) exposure of OTHER CLOTHES, e.g. underwear

The expectations of shortness are therefore both explicit and implicit. The degree to which it covers, and the part of the body it reveals (the midriff, for example) adds to the social significance. On one level outgrownness is a Body Specific Form and the secondary level makes it a Gender Significant Form.

The tight variety can achieve both, as it clings to the body, therefore insisting that it covers it, yet the extent of the tightness also exposes, by making known the physical shape beneath. Conversely, it disallows total exposure because the integral function of clothing is to cover. The motif is interacting with the difference between acceptable and unacceptable behaviour patterns by shifting notions of revealment and concealment. It can be simultaneously chaste and boastful. The revealing and concealing element is achieved through the reduction in size of the garment. Its smallness can be seen to be in opposition to excesses in terms of both the fabric and demonstrative opulence. In some instances it can be interpreted as symbolic of a minimalist approach to garment construction in a purely Modernist aesthetic of Form follows Function. The varying degrees of reduction of shorter and tighter, parallel the degree to which the garment represents an opposition to wastefulness and conspicuous consumption.[14] It is signalling an opposition to excess and the tighter and shorter the garment, the greater the demonstration and the more it illustrates outgrownness. This possibly explains its use within student fashions and subcultures.

However, it can also be a tool in order to illustrate waste in other garments, so that it is not just a meaning applied to itself but shifts on to the whole image. The example cited earlier of wearing it with or over 'normal-sized' garments pinpoints similar and dissimilar aspects. The fashion content of 'smallness' seems to be so important that price is not dictated by the reduction of size. Cropped sweaters are often more highly priced than their less fashion-conscious sisters. The material content is overridden by the monetary value

These jeans are tighter in some areas on the body than in others and tacitly display both gender and sexuality. This is an example of a garment which becomes gender significant via the wearer as the garment without the body could be non-specific. Photograph by Lee Wright in 1989

The 'small' feature is conveyed through a form-fitting shape which is tight in specific areas. Paradoxically, with the more wrinkled parts of the jeans (and therefore there is more fabric) greater predominance is given to their smallness. The thin body is exaggerated by a closeness of the clothing, simultaneously implying the 'Incredible Hulk' syndrome where the body has nearly outgrown the garment. Photograph by Lee Wright in 1989 of a recognisable fashion motif. The minimal content in the industrially produced item is little more than a fashion, but the rejection of excess in customised clothing may be a stronger social statement concerning necessity and/or allegiance to a particular subculture. Ironically, the same motif is upholding capitalist principles of fashion from one type to the other, which through poverty can easily be conveyed. The collapse of financial sustenance ('I can't afford anything else') of the customised version can be distinct and powerfully portrayed by such details as not hemming the 'cut-off' edge, thus rejecting the mass-produced aesthetic of neat finishing. Therefore there can be a split of meaning depending on the type even with the same feature, where one becomes part of a fashion system while the other implies the rejection of it. It is obvious that in one case the wearer is a 'direct' consumer, in the other an 'indirect', as the original garment has been recycled through change.

In this sense the 'small' motif has created a *new order* distinct from the manipulation of an ordered fashion system. It has achieved this by creating a disruption in the normal pattern of the way we wear clothes and the size of clothing. In all types it is a *contrived* disorder within the conventional language in clothing shapes, as for many people an item which is too tight or too small is the sign that it should be discarded. The 'outgrown' impression, whether 'built-in' or 'applied' (mass produced with the feature or customised to create it) challenges the 'ideal' or 'universal' system of Fashion Language because it contradicts many of its rules. However, because the 'small' feature is just a PART of a garment, it can only disrupt the established fashion system and not wholly change it. Therefore it can be argued that it embraces an existent interpretative culture of clothing and can never be hegemonic. [15]

Fieldwork of this sort has its limitations in that it isolates the activity of the focus of study from the culture to which it belongs. But this was one of the initial intentions: to see if theories could be made from an a-historical and a-cultural perspective. Although isolationist, it has allowed for a case study which can now be slotted back into wider parameters of motifs and meanings in a fashion system.

Notes and References

1 The method is constructed through 'participant observation' which means that the wearers define the terms rather than other determinates such as the manufacturers. It tries to make sense of social phenomena and attempts to *build theory* rather than *test hypotheses*. This is useful in an area such as Fashion Theory and Discourse which is at present underwritten. As Qualitative Research embraces both the *deductive* and *inductive* (i.e., one informs the other in an integral process) it allows for a dualistic study of Popular Culture which simultaneously deconstructs representations and constructs new languages based on data collection. In this case study there were the visual manifestations of 'smallness' in fashionable clothing.

2 See A. Lurie *The Language of Clothes*, London, 1981. This is one example among many which accepts that styles of clothing in general have significance and meaning.

3 For example, D. Colle, *Collars, Stocks and Cravats*, London, 1974.

4 1990 fashions for women such as 'the body' (an all-in-one form-fitting garment) indicate that the 'smallness' feature has progressed into a 'second skin'. I see this as a linear development from aspects of 'outgrown'.

5 This excludes those wearing 'outgrown' as a necessity for purely economic reasons.

6 See R. Ellen (ed), *Ethnographic Research*, London, 1984, for an excellent introduction to the subject and method.

7 This is an interesting example of terminology as it gives the type of construction, i.e. 'rib', *and* the meaning, i.e., 'skinny'. Another example is 'tights'.

8 The UK sizing for women's clothes (8, 10, 12, 14, 16) is based on statistical research of body proportions. It is a universal system based on averages.

9 Anthropological term meaning research carried out 'on site' or 'in the field'.

10 This is an area I have worked on before using a different type of methodology. See my essay entitled 'Objectifying Gender', in Attfield and Kirkham (eds), *A View from the Interior*, London, 1989.

11 See E. Goffman, *The Presentation of the Self*, London, 1969.

12 See M. Douglas, *Purity and Danger*, London, 1966.

13 Miniaturising was a part of the 1960s pop culture. The car 'The Mini' is another example.

14 See T. Veblen, *The Theory of the Leisure Class*, London, 1957. (Originally published in 1899.)

15 This theory indicates that the motif of smallness is useless in the construction of 'revolutionary' garment design. The point at which Fashion Design might engage with a political discourse is a redundant notion *if* it utilises the outgrown feature for anything other than a systematic visual language.

Identity, Design and Ethnicity

NASEEM KHAN

Asian Women's Dress

From Burqah to Bloggs –
Changing Clothes for Changing Times

Few fashion shows cause general furores. More often it seems as if mere *frissons* of shock – such as at the bodily exposures paraded in Paris in 1990 – had run around the salons.

When Zandra Rhodes showed her collection in New Delhi in 1982, however, it precipitated a shock of a different order. Rhodes had been commissioned by the Indian government to produce a set of clothes that would take Indian fabrics and styles as their inspiration (and would hopefully catapult Indian textiles into the consciousness of world designers). What caused outrage, though, was her treatment of the garment that has become the hallmark of the Indian woman – the sari. Ripped, shredded at the edges, scattered with strategic holes, it constituted, people felt, not a design but an assault.

Any account of Asian women's dress has to start with the sari, if only because it is such a stereotype of Western perception. Ask anyone in the street what Indian women wear, and the sari will almost invariably be the response. So far as it goes, this response is not wrong. The sari indeed is a *lingua franca* of dress. It changes with the regions of the sub-continent. There are the great saris – the gold embroidered ones of Benares or Varanasi, the silk weaves of Conjeevaram in the south, the *ikats* of Orissa, *jamdani* of Bengal. There are regional variations in the ways of tying it. But it is to be found throughout the sub-continent – in Bangladesh, India and Pakistan: namely pre-Partition India.

The sari throughout is one simple and unchanging entity – six yards of material that goes around the body from waist to ankle, ending with one end – the *pullu* – hanging loose over one shoulder. Timeless, it has shrugged off minor forays on its position: the flighty, hipster sari of the sixties, for instance, or the absurd mini-sari sunk without trace. The sari, like a stately swan, swam on. Inherited, in its finest state, from mothers by daughters, it was the object of veneration, care and respect.

In addition to symbolising continuity, it also symbolised – for many people – correct female attitudes. Pull the *pullu* over your head – as traditionally you should in the presence of a man – and you are decorously isolated from the eyes of the world. In Islam covering the head has religious connotations; inevitably Benazir Bhutto took to covering her head with her *dupatta* or shawl in public so as not to give the wrong messages. (The *burqah*, with its top to toe cover, is an extreme version of the same principle.) It was of course the ultimate violation for the evil Kuruvas in the *Mahabharata* to try to strip their rival's wife, Draupadi. This heinous act inspired divine assistance. The god Krishna so arranged it that as they tugged and tugged at her sari, the material just went on and on and on unwinding: there was no end to it.

So it is not surprising that the Zandra Rhodes experiment provoked such an outcry – one more on a par with protesters burning the American flag than to be expected from similar experiments on, say, Britain's classic twinset.

What is surprising, however, is that less than a decade later, the sari is being interfered with again, and this time from within the sub-continent. 'Many people think it's sacrilege to touch the sari. I think they're just stuffy', said Tarun Tahiliani recently. One of India's top designers, he and colleagues have forged ahead with saris that take little for granted. The so-called 'nouvelle saree' may replace the *pullu* with a length of dissimilar material, or decorate itself with environmentally conscious natural substances like bits of wood or bone, or create a turtle-neck for itself, or thread its *pullu* through a slit in a matching blazer. One designer suggested tucking the sari not into a petticoat but into *churidars* or tight trousers instead. Or why not reverse custom and have a fine organza sari over a heavily embroidered petticoat? And its *choli* or blouse might have holes nipped in it.

Why, you might wonder, should a foray on the sari now apparently be legitimate while less than a decade ago it constituted heresy?

In fact the sari is the last, or the most recent of the unexpected changes that have overtaken Asian women's dress in the sub-continent and in Britain. For though, to Western eyes, the sari may have seemed a constant, in actual fact it has been anything but that. The last decade has seen an extraordinary phenomenon – the arrival of commercial fashion, with all that that implies.

The outward signs of the change on the sub-continent are very clear. The 'colonies' of Delhi, for example, are now stuffed with boutiques, their rails filled with the work of a steadily growing army of designers, many of them women. The *shalwar* suit is the reigning force. It is made up of three components: a variety of trouser (baggy *shalwar*, either wide or tight at the ankles; wide, straight-legged *pyjamas*; narrow *churidar*) with a tunic-like *kameez* (or shirt-like *kurta*), and co-ordinated *dupatta*, or stole worn with both ends hanging loose over the shoulders at the back. Once considered teenage wear (and with very strong north Indian Muslim connotations), the *shalwar* suit has broken out of its old restrictions. Its outfits may be as grand as you please, overwhelming with glitz and glamour. They can reject grandeur for ethnic regional simplicity, using rural motifs, detail and decoration. In its new form, the *shalwar* suit can be found in Dacca as well as in Delhi, in Karachi as well as in Calcutta. It has even dented the traditional sanctum of the sari, Tamilnadu, in the conservative south.

The reasons for the change are largely economic. Although recent years have seen little change in the situation of the rural peasants who form the bulk of the population, the middle-class has undoubtedly prospered. Delhi and Bombay's contemporary art book, for instance, stands witness to this, as does the growth of absurdly lavish theme parties (with large hotels being turned, for a small fortune, into versions of Disneyland or Star Wars worlds). The new haute couture answers the same need.

The phenomenon of Hauz Khas village, for example, fits snugly into this scenario. There is something distinctly unreal about Hauz Khas. A bona fide village, it has been swallowed alive by land-hungry Delhi – bullocks, drainless gullies, drying dung-cakes and all. More to the point, its traditional old houses – cool and thick-walled, windows opening out on to the amazing thirteenth-century reservoir created when the area held a bustling university – have been taken over too. Boutique owners have moved in, to co-exist chic cheek by jowl with village life.

At the last count there were seventy boutiques in Hauz Khas village, plus other ancillary concerns like art galleries, restaurants and interior design studios. You can easily spend in an hour what the bemused farmers, sitting in groups around their hookahs, would not earn in a year; and then finish off your spree with a little light salad and mushroom quiche at the Art Bistro in the heart of it all.

It would be wrong, however, to assume that the demand for the new fashion labels comes from the very rich. Certainly their desire for an international look that could carry them from Karachi to Manhattan has added fuel to the top end of the market. But this has been reinforced by other, ground swell changes.

Above all, a female, professional middle class has emerged: the result of education, pressure and slowly liberalising mores. When, for example, I tried to get a staff job in the Bombay print media in the 1960s, the doors were closed to me (behind these doors worked literally hundreds of male journalists). I was told the work would not be suitable for me, because I could not go home on my own – as the job required – late at night. Nowadays, there are women journalists, as there are women designers and entrepreneurs of almost every type. From its genesis in the 1970s, an articulate women's movement has grown and has attacked some of the more glaring signs of female inequality – the flaccid official response to the phenomenon of bride-burning; the sub-porn images of women on billboards.

With that influx has come a more assertive and questing demand on style. The first signs were apparent in the student population of the late 1960s. Western flares triggered off a response in the East – long *kurtas* over co-ordinated, bell-bottomed trousers. It was also the time of the *lungi* and *kurt*: a simple length of cloth (around two yards long), the *lungi* is a male garment. It is tied at the waist, its extra length gathered in shallow folds tucked in on one hip. Folded up by workmen, it becomes effectively a mini-*lungi*. It is surely no accident that female urban youth adopted essentially male fashions that allowed physical mobility, eschewing the more restrictive and decorous sari.

The fashion explosion of the 1980s was to provide them with even wider horizons and possibilities. While the cosmopolitan set asked for clothes that would cater for the international scene, sober people were looking more searchingly at their identity: at the contradictions between privilege and the lack of it, urban and rural, Third World and First World. Colonialism had left its residue of double standards. The arts – including fashion – needed reconstruction. Theatre, for example, had been chugging along on a diet of Western and Western-style plays. In the 1970s, groups like those of Habib Tanvir and the Theatre Company of Poona discovered and pioneered the use of indigenous folk forms. Interior decorators and designers discovered the fantastic wealth of Indian handicrafts. And fashion benefited too. Clothes evolved which were based on regional variations: Aligarhi *pyjamas*, Patiala *shalwar*, Bhopali *kurtas*. These used the skills of local weavers, dyers and embroiderers, skills that had been threatened with decline. The old, heavy, village jewellery, inches of lacquered bangles, decorative, 'third-eye' *bindi* on the forehead reinforced the vivid and lively 'ethnic' look.

The fight to retain the old, subtle, vegetable dyes, in the face of cheaper and cruder machine dyes, sprang from this background, and was largely carried forward by women. So, more recently, has been the less successful fight in India to protect silk weavers, at risk because of government subsidising of the large mills, which churn out far cheaper synthetic textiles. (It must be remembered, however, that mill fabrics have been a boon to the very many poorer counterparts of these middle-class campaigners.) The movement that has helped craftspeople to develop their goods and market them has also been largely the doing of urban middle-class women.

Cynics may be amused by the huge popularity of so-called 'ethnic fashion', and may make reference to Marie Antoinette and the milkmaids. But the rapid increase of fashion houses has had a beneficial effect on the lives of women. In many cases it has enfranchised them.

The myriad new small ventures have been largely set up by women. Furthermore, few of these women have any previous business or work experience. A boutique, or a modest line of clothes, has proved a gentle, uncontroversial entry into the male world of work. After all, people argued, what was entailed? Little more than what respectable women had always done – conferring with their tailor at home over clothes designs. And the little shops started by some women would not deal with the *hoi polloi* and certainly not with men, but with women, and women of a similar social background. A respectable and safe step, in short, to liberation. 'Our husbands don't mind', said two sisters-in-law, who design clothes for their own new boutique in Ahmedabad.

While for some fashion might be a genteel hobby, for others it has opened the doors to entrepreneurship. Enterprise exists at a number of levels. Consider, for example, the so-called 'suitcase collections'. The clothes appear, as the name suggests, out of a suitcase and are the result of sharp-witted forethought by Asian women living in Britain. When they return to the sub-continent for a winter break, they get as many outfits made up as possible by the cheap and

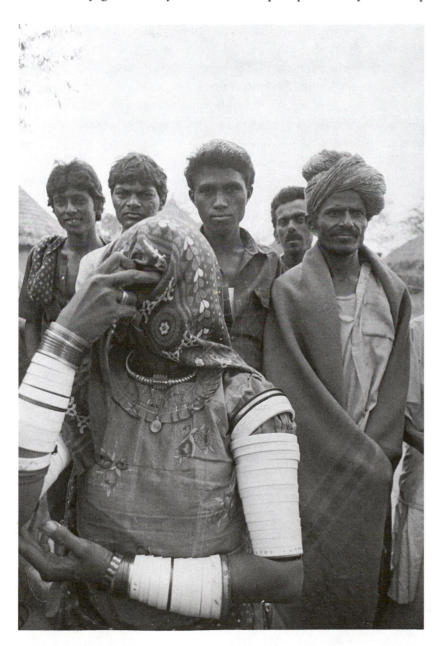

Traditional
Craftsmen,
*photograph by Amita
Prasher (courtesy of
the photoghrapher)*

efficient local tailors. Back in Britain they send the word out on their local network. A sale in their front room can significantly underwrite the cost of a trip.

The level of local entrepreneurship differs across the sub-continent, with the greatest range and energy to be found in India. Women designers are also important in Pakistan; the clothes of women like Sehyr Saigol and Faryal are also sold in Britain.

Bangladesh's less affluent middle-class has produced a more limited fashion world, though here too the sari has given way to the *shalwar* suit (or Western dress). The steady increase in education and opportunities for girls has led to new market demands. As in India, the 'ethnic look' has swept the board.

At the same time, the effect of the West – who has increasingly sought a foothold in the sub-continent – should not be forgotten. Both Benetton and Levi-Strauss have established factories there, producing their distinctive clothes for the local market. Jeans are the uniform of the urban, middle-class young. And Western fashion houses, such as Pierre Cardin, fly out collections to show to select audiences.

The West's involvement with the East has also been affected by trade restrictions. In the early 1980s, production quotas were imposed on countries like Sri Lanka and Hong Kong who had previously been very active in producing clothes for the Western market. At that time, wholesalers turned to Bangladesh, finding there a ready pool of labour. At first, reported one researcher, this labour was male, but 'men are more bolshy. They won't sit still, and get involved in union activities.' Women have taken their place and now make up the bulk of the machinists (though the more skilled and better-paid cutters are still male).

The effect on these women of the Western clothes that they make in such large quantities is of course a matter only for speculation. Stringent trade regulations prevent the clothes from being released on to the local market. Indeed, the factories and workshops that now exist in such large numbers in Dhaka and Chittagong can look like fortified stockades. Surrounded by high walls and secured by gates, they aim to prevent women smuggling garments out. If overtime is necessary, the women are locked in and have to spend the night inside.

Although this is appalling, it must also be remembered that the clothing factories in very many cases represent freedom: the first job that women have been able to get outside the home. The very act of earning and being partly independent has led to changes of attitude and improved morale. By all accounts the women are not cowed. Because of the number of workshops, they can take their labour where they want; and an informal straw poll found at least half of them enthusiastic about leaving the confines of the home to go to work.

So, on the face of it, the influence of fashion could be argued to be healthy, vigorous and diverse. The infrastructure offers a range of possibilities for women to establish themselves as independent beings in a range of images that express a contemporary Asian identity. The fashion industry has also patronised, legitimised and supported previously unregarded rural crafts and village culture.

However, there are aspects of these changes that must cause reservations. What has occurred is the growth of commercialism in an area it did not previously dominate. Until relatively recently, ready-made clothes occupied an insignificant place in the market. The initiative for creating styles remained with the wearers. Considerable thought, expertise and personal creativity went into the devising of an outfit. Magazines were pored over, old pictures studied. Each outfit was highly personal and certainly unique. Nor could anyone easily tell exactly what the outfit had cost.

The arrival of boutiques and designer labels has brought snobbery and status into this world. Outfits now recognisably issue from one or other exclusive label. Tahiliani's saris, for example, cost over 10,000 rupees (about £300), a fabulous sum for India. Look at copies of the glossy fashion magazine *Libas* (on sale in Britain and ten other countries) and you can see clothes that make no bones about their aspirations to the expensive world of haute couture. Keeping up with the Joneses, Kapurs or Khans now has a price tag on it, and it is high.

The situation in Britain may appear to mirror the sub-continent. Here too the 'outfit' has swept all before it, enjoying a similar range from the youthful and snappy to the grand and glitzy. As in the sub-continent, these changes have affected women with money and mobility – the business and international set, and the emerging, Westernised middle class. Less well-established communities stick to the old ways – saris for special occasions, day-time wear that follows the traditions of the region from which they originally came: the wide, countrified *shalwar-kameez* for Punjabis from both sides of the India–Pakistan border, saris for south Indians, Gujaratis (who often drape the *pullu* not in the usual way over the left shoulder and down the back, but from the back and forward over the right shoulder) and so on.

While initial fashion moves in the sub-continent coincided with greater independence for women, a more complex scenario developed in Britain.

The traditionalism of immigrant communities is well-established. While societies in their own countries continue to evolve, their people overseas cling to what gradually become more and more the old ways. The pressure on their youngsters not to change can be extreme and is countered by another pressure, from white society, to conform to its ways. The words 'crisis of identity' are often glibly and too easily used. But Asian girls who grew up in Britain in the earlier days of immigration will know very well, and painfully, what such words mean. They mean – to speak subjectively – the hatred of having one's hair oiled and tightly plaited, the fury of not being allowed to have it cut like one's friends, the embarrassment of wide Punjabi trousers. Small acts of attrition, they added up to conflicts of loyalty, a subtle undermining. As a result, young women tended not so much to reject their culture as to keep it discreetly to themselves. British on the streets, Asian at home; one behaviour at school, another at home.

Asian clothes occupied that same secret, private area for many young people in the early years of immigration. As late as the end of the 1970s businessmen like Mayur Shah, director of the well-regarded Variety Silk House in Wembley, were worried. The younger generation, he recalled, had its sights firmly locked into Western clothes and the sari seemed certain to dwindle in popularity. The few ready-made *shalwar* suits to be found in Britain's fabric and sari shops offered little inducement to stay dressing Asian. All too often they were the least attractive Indian imports: shoddily made, of poor quality material, and in all ways inferior to that great Asian staple, the home-made 'suit'.

But in the early 1980s all that changed – at least for the Westernised middle classes. Several factors were involved. Firstly, visitors to the Indian sub-continent came back with evidence of the creative fashion explosion there: vivid, imaginative clothes that explored and celebrated Indian roots. Secondly, a new generation of women was making itself felt, making its way through education into the professional job market. And thirdly, a distinctly new mood was abroad.

Anti-racist demonstrations, the Anti-Nazi League, Rock Against Racism all demonstrated signs of a new consciousness – or a new expression of an existing consciousness. National Front activity and attacks on black people – often specifically Asians – thrust Asian youth into action. Campaigning groups burgeoned, like the Newham Monitoring Group which was set up to fight for the right of the threatened Asian community in East London. Tara Arts Group came together, galvanised by the murder of Gurdeep Singh Chaggar in Southall. A collection of young people from various Asian backgrounds – in itself a radical act – it aimed to find a theatrical form for the unexpressed sharp realities of being Asian in Britain. The Minorities' Arts Advisory Service (MAAS), of which I was the first Co-ordinator, brought practitioners in all the cultures based in Britain together, united by a determination not to be ignored or remain behind closed doors any longer.

It cannot be accidental that the first signs of local Asian designers and clothes boutiques became apparent soon afterwards. Nor can it be accidental that their clothes aimed for an East–West synthesis.

The patterns which emerged were diverse and experimental. Geeta Sarin dreamt up 'Rivaaz' (or 'Trend') at the end of the 1970s, though it was not incorporated until 1984. She targeted the newly fashion-conscious trendy young, designing one-off outfits that she then had made up in a thriving workshop, with thirty-six employees, which she had established in New Delhi. Back in Britain, they were retailed in Sarin's Wembley boutique, a far cry from the bustling and crowded fabric shops that had once been the mainstay of fashion. Zaineb Alam, on the other hand, started from a different hypothesis. Her firm Zee Zee set out to attract both Eastern and Western women with a good income. Significantly her two outlets are in mixed and upmarket communities: Kensington and St John's Wood in London.

Alam's idea hinged on the existence of a phenomenon – the ingenious and extraordinary Asian tailor who can, it seems, cast his eye over a design, a photograph or even a scribble and in no time at all have it run up on his reassuringly old-fashioned sewing machine. Zee Zee's customers, planned Alam, would come to her with an idea and the fabric. Her two (Western) designers would then 'couture-ise' it and her Asian tailor would make it. But it was not, she discovered, a practical plan. An idea passing through so many heads (not to mention hands) ended up as far from the customer's original idea as if they had been playing Chinese Whispers.

'An atmosphere of haute couture reflects a certain art of life,' photograph by Shahid Zaidi (courtesy of Faryal, Lahore, Pakistan; evening wear in pure embroidered silk by Faryal)

Instead, Alam developed her own line based essentially on the Punjabi/north Indian *shalwar-kameez*. Glamorous, strong and decidedly glitzy, the fashions looked in spirit to both East and West, and were pitched at a level that was deliberately high. Other fashions made their way into a similar moneyed and international market. Libas, with which Zee Zee had first been associated, was set up as an outlet for the designs of Pakistani Sehyr Saigol. 'Poised, charming and clear-headed', says her own press release, quoting a feature in Pakistan's *Nation*, 'Always simply yet elegantly attired, Sehyr exudes the unmistakable strains of limitless drive and boundless energy rippling under a cool and almost languid exterior.' Her Belgravia shop caters for the wealthy members of the international jet set.

From whatever different sources they emanated, the clothes found ready acceptance; indeed, they were welcomed. At last, said the middle- and upper-class women who bought them, here were clothes that could take in both East and West, that didn't involve them in a choice between two different worlds, and that mirrored their own confidence in presenting themselves on their own terms as Westernised Asian women.

Harshinder Sirah's first collection with its Euro-Asian outfits (courtesy of Bristol United Press)

Where haute(ish) couture led, others followed. When in the mid 1980s *Network East* (the BBC's Birmingham-based Asian television programme) announced its competition for new designers, hundreds applied. The atmosphere was bullish, optimistic. After years in which a career in fashion had seemed, said Mayur Shah, to offer young people simply the dull option of designing saris or selling fabrics, all had changed. His own business – visited by people from across the country – responded by stocking lines from the sub-continent: Xerxes Bhadena's flamboyant clothes (designed for the starry denizens of Bombay's silver screen), for example, and Dia from Bangladesh. And he and his wife began to create their own designs. Their clothes, sold under the Rani label, were made up in India and sent back to Britain.

Other ventures emerged; often these were the ideas of women who saw a chance to become independent. Young students at art college, like Harshinder Sirah at Salisbury, explored the concept of East–West fusion, developing 'the sort of clothes I wear myself as an Indian living in a Western society.' Her first collection – appropriately launched in a nightclub, and followed by a Bhangra Rock disco – used Indian colours and fabrics for trousers and leggings, and detail like embroidery on knitwear. Fascinated by movement she designed a number of garments with swirling asymmetrical skirts; she incorporated hoods into her *kurtas* rather than keeping the traditional head cover, the *dupatta*.

The politics of the new movement appeared to make good sense. When Rekha Prashar started the label Peepul, she saw it as essentially extending her work with the pioneering Tara Arts in searching for a strong Indian/Western statement.

However, not all is as buoyant as it might appear, and this raises uncomfortable questions. Who is the new fashion for? How can it survive economically in a world inhabited by sharks and giants? And why is there a lack of an indigenous 'British Asian look'? For all the zappy work of individuals like Sirah, a uniquely British–Asian line has yet to emerge. Clothes like those of Zee Zee and Libas lean heavily on the original formula; they are variations on a familiar theme. Peepul rings a few changes, notably in the search for day clothes (a problem with other lines). But none are yet breaking into truly new imaginative territory. The point of fusion culture is not that it should be a compromise between its constituent elements, but that it should be an utterly new statement. A sense of caution still informs the clothes made (or designed) here, and this is particularly apparent when you compare them with some of the sub-continental designs. Consider, for example, Satya Paul's innovative sari where the *pullu* has been replaced by a fan-like arrangement covering the bust.

This problem may, however, be endemic in the very structure and nature of things. A number of constraints, mostly economic, militate against the emergence of an independent and adventurous line. For a start, the market is not a large one. Two million Asians include many – men, the elderly and young children – who are irrelevant to fashion. And of those who remain the price will deter many. Rivaaz's clothes start at £20 for an outfit, but the upper level is £2,000, and many are beyond the reach of straitened pockets. Again, a certain percentage will refuse to buy what they regard as over-priced commodities; there is a huge disparity, sometimes 600 per cent or more, between the price of an outfit in India and the identical outfit imported here; let us wait, says this section of opinion, until we go back on the annual trip to India (or Pakistan). Pirates account for another nibble at the potential market. Sketches of the new models find their way to deft tailors or to the hordes of women who are accomplished with the needle. Cut-rate products result, to the fury of the couturiers. And too whacky designs, as some shopkeepers explain, carry their own dangers: 'The parents will not allow their daughters to wear them.' This is not all. Any locally based label has to contend with the big guns of the sub-continent, where the fashion industry is second only to diamonds as an export earner. India's huge market lowers the unit cost; and both labour and materials are comparatively cheap. There is also an established network of retail outlets – Britain's sari and fabric shops.

The shrewdest businesswomen have recognised and responded to this scenario by extending their appeal. Inevitably this means they will have to blunt the distinctiveness of their clothes' appeal. Rivaaz, for example, looks increasingly to the United States and the Middle East for orders. Zee Zee herself has opened up a market in the United States with a mail order catalogue that reduces the line to three items – trousers, top and cape. In Britain her attempt to appeal to both Asian and white customers has led to a 20 per cent non-Asian clientele.

This is higher than the ratios reported by other outlets. Rivaaz and Geeta Sarin, for example, reckon that 10 per cent of their customers are non-Asian, while for Variety Silk House the figure is only 1 per cent. Interestingly, both are now using a new sales technique. In 1988 Sarin was the first to embrace the wholly Western concept of mail order. Her catalogue has become steadily thicker and more expensive over the years. Now costing £10, it contains 210 full-colour pages featuring clothes that range from watered-down 'fusion' fashion to the most traditional sub-continental styles (including spanking white silk marriage suits for men). Orders from her catalogue form, she estimates, 60 per cent of her total sales. The effect of the Variety Silk House's change of strategy has still to be seen since 1990–1 was the year of their first catalogue.

The existence of the catalogue and, therefore, bulk lines, has led to more thinking about the distinctive nature of the British market. Britain is not just India, or the sub-continent, writ small. Certain things just will not succeed here. The quality of the West's crisp, cold light is unkind to the vivid colours that suit the sub-continent. And general attitudes, said Mayur Shah, favour a certain measure of British restraint: orange – so popular until recently in India – has never sold well in Britain. Lines, reported Geeta Sarin, are more important in the West than fabric, detail and decoration.

In an ideal world, it would make more sense to employ local Asian designers who are close to the pulse of the times and the customers. Few, however, have made their way into the fashion arena. Even those stimulated by *Network East*'s competition have mysteriously faded away. Harshinder Sirah has still to find backing for her own collections. When Rekha Prashar contacted art and fashion colleges, hoping that Peepul could form a platform for young Asian design talent, not a single person responded: her clothes are consequently now designed by Faryal in Pakistan and made up there.

What are we to conclude from this? Have young people been defeated by the ferocity of a savage world, or – as some believe – have they opted instead for safer areas? Certainly that is the case with other art forms. There are many learning Indian classical dance, for example, but few Asian professional dancers in Britain, and few in the ancillary (but underpaid) areas of arts administration and management. Accountancy and dentistry, it seems, still win hands down. But other factors are relevant too. When Harshinder Sirah took her designs to (male) Asian clothing manufacturers, they laughed in her face, preferring the safer and more traditional approach of the sub-continent. And an era of recession has closed the doors of Western houses to her undoubted talent.

The example of Shammi Ahmed might offer some clues. A millionaire while still in his twenties, Ahmed's success has come from fashion – but not from Asian fashion. His Manchester firm – perkily called 'The Legendary Joe Bloggs' – has made its name with its young sports and leisure wear: the unmistakable Joe Bloggs T-shirts, the improbably baggy, wide-bottomed jeans that led fashion pundits to point to a new dawn emanating from Manchester (and other people to shudder, 'Flares!'). The ambitious might see a lesson in this. 'I am determined', said Ahmed (who named his firm to sound 'common . . . and truly British'), 'that Joe Bloggs will do for England what Gucci has done for Italy.' Is this the ultimate destination of confidence? The final point that Asian fashion, escaped from the living room of the past, can reach? Or is Joe Bloggs just a red herring?

There can only be speculation about the answers. For what fashion is really about are all those issues involved in the shifts and squeezes that go on when one race locates itself in the midst of another. The nature of the accommodation changes, and will continue to change as the self-images of women themselves change. Walk along any street in a so-called 'Asian area' and you can see the range of allegiances now represented: saris and home-made *shalwar*, designer 'suits' and jeans. Mobility and choice are far greater than only

Fanfare – a dramatic fan bodice in steel grey silk, Image International *Spring 1989 (courtesy of Geeta Sarin and* Image International*)*

ten years or so ago. The rails of the Variety Silk Houses of the land are the litmus paper of change. When they begin to stock a British-Asian line, produced by the Sirahs of the future, then horizons will have broadened.

HILARY O'KELLY

Reconstructing Irishness

Dress in the Celtic Revival, 1880–1920

A COAT

I made my song a coat
Covered with embroideries
Out of old mythologies
From heel to throat;
But the fools caught it,
Wore it in the world's eyes
As though they'd wrought it.
Song, let them take it,
For there's more enterprise
In walking naked.

W.B. Yeats 1914

Naked aggression and bald contempt may describe the mutual regard of the Irish and English during the early years of English colonisation in Ireland. Nothing so simple, however, could be said of the situation in 1900. Seven hundred years of living at close quarters on a small island is a long time and naked aggression can tame to passive acceptance, bald contempt to a grudging admiration, even respect. By early this century people like Maud Gonne MacBride who danced at the Viceregal Lodge by night, by day were active on the side of the nationalist cause, while Douglas Hyde, a Protestant member of the Ascendancy, led the movement to re-establish the Irish language, customs and traditions.

The social and political structure of the colony had broken down by 1880 with the Protestant Ascendancy, no longer English but Anglo-Irish, being increasingly undermined both socially and politically. Irish-Catholic peasants, re-enfranchised since the 1840s, were growing in social, economic and political strength. The air was charged with a sense of change and the country was alive with images and aspirations for a new Ireland. Each group of Irish society had its own ideal. Those groups included not only the Anglo-Irish and the nationalists but the nationalist Anglo-Irish and the loyalist Irish Catholics, the nationalists who rejected violence and those who were militant. These groups can be broadly divided under three headings: the Gaelic League, the Castle-Set and the literati. Many people, of course, were active in more than one of these groups but most had a predominant interest in just one. Each group built its image of the New Ireland on a selective vision of the country's history. Irish history had been a fashionable subject among the wealthy and educated since the Romantic 1840s. Their interest

> was not just the condescension of a governing class amusing itself with quaint native antiquities. Their concern with the ancient civilization was perfectly genuine, though it was not wholly disinterested. Few of them seriously contemplated the restoration of the Irish language as part of the common currency of educated people, but they did see in the revival of Irish studies in general a means of attaching themselves to their native country and at the same time of holding at arm's length the English connection which the more perceptive of them already sensed to be both dangerous and unreliable.[1]

By the 1860s research findings from Irish mythological and historical sources had been codified by Eugene O'Curry into what was essentially a reference book – *The Manners and Customs of the Ancient Irish*. It included tracts on the subject of dress, the relevance of which will be seen later on. Its three volumes were of considerable importance in the cultural reconstruction of Irishness.

While the enlightened few studied the ancient annals and archaeology of Ireland, the majority proclaimed their nationality in the application of shamrocks, round towers and Irish wolf hounds to all forms of produce and publication. More actively, however, they rallied behind Charles Stewart Parnell and the cause of Home Rule. Parnell's charisma and the optimism of the 1880s was a major force for that decade in Irish society but with the political demise of Parnell in 1890 that force lost its political direction and civic energy was subsumed into other separatist causes. Nationalism grappled with the issue of national identity; shamrocks would no longer suffice. In 1892 the Irish Literary Society was founded, in 1893 the Gaelic League and in 1894 the Gaelic Athletics Association. Membership of these societies was initially small and culled equally from middle-class Catholics and Protestants. Together they rallied in the name of Gaelicism and Nationalism in support of an Irish Ireland. They were reacting primarily against England: it was her manners and modes they wished to eradicate. The Irish language, names, music, literature and sport were to live and breathe again. Irish dress was included in this list but how 'Irish dress' was to be interpreted was another matter.

The immediate options must have seemed inappropriate to the urban middle class of the late nineteenth and early twentieth centuries. Neither the Galway shawl and *bán ín knits* of contemporary west coast peasants would have held much appeal, nor the famous and far traded shag-lined rugs of the sixteenth century. O'Curry's descriptions of the flowing gowns of the heroes and heroines of ancient tales must have lacked a certain 'gravitas' to a society bred on dark colours, starched linens and solid corsetry. But Irish dress had been outlawed by Henry VIII in the decree that 'no man or manchild [should] wear no mantle in the streets, but cloths or gowns shaped after the English fashion'. [2] Irish dress should therefore be revived along with all the other casualties of English rule in Ireland. The variety of interpretations of Irish dress that emerged seem to reflect closely the more subtle attitudes of their respective creators towards both the old and the new Ireland.

The Gaelic League or Irish Irelanders, as they were also known, were determined to see their country vigorous, majestic and separate in the twentieth century. Their attitude can be summed up in the words of Jonathan Swift who advocated that Ireland should 'burn everything British except their coal'. To create this Ireland distinct from England they fostered the language, music, sports and literature; those elements of Irish culture that had been almost eradicated under English rule.

While not questioning this group's real commitment to their ideal it is reasonable to point out that when it came to the question of dress the issue was, for the most part, fudged. Their interests, actions and proclamations set them apart as distinctly Irish while their fashionable sartorial appearance rooted them firmly in their social class. Having a body and a voice is a great advantage, making it possible to speak two languages at once and even to say two different things simultaneously. To espouse the cause of nationalism and to dress in a national costume would have left this group quite divorced from the established society of 1900 and wholly committed to a classless and structureless system, because the new Ireland was not yet a reality, and how any such reality would be structured was not at all clear. For the vast majority of the Gaelic League, Irish dress was interpreted as being fashionable dress made of Irish fabrics. They could, in that way, maintain their social and economic position while still helping to regenerate the textile industry on which Ireland's erstwhile economy had largely been built.

It was in their accessories that some Gaelic Leaguers ordinarily made their most committed sartorial statement. A replica of the Tara Brooch might be worn by women, or a shamrock tie-pin by the men. This jewellery created the right tone as it was not eccentric and decoratively alluded to the glorious Celtic past and the great artistic skills once alive in Ireland. At the same time if its message inconveniently offended, the jewellery could easily be dismissed as mere ornamental frippery. Why, even the Princess of Wales wore a shamrock brooch of emeralds to an Irish Fair in London in 1906.

In Ireland at the turn of the century the majority of urban costume made a paradoxical statement. In its cut and style it loudly proclaimed a social structure and philosophy introduced to Ireland by a colonising England, while in its fabric it rejected England and the English destruction of the Irish national economy. The choice of fabric, however, was a relatively mute sub-clause in that one would need a well-trained eye to identify confidently a material as Irish, as opposed to English, German or Italian, for example. These middle-class Gaelic Leaguers wished to make a strong avowal of their Irish nationality. Their nationality, however, was an accident of birth; their social status had been fought for and was now established; it was not to be let slip.

Equally, the Castle-Set had several delicate issues to keep in mind which affected their response to both costume and the Celtic Revival. The Castle-Set included all those people who regarded themselves as the legitimate reins of English rule in Ireland; if Home Rule were granted, their position would become untenable. Their efforts, therefore, were directed towards rebuilding the Irish economy while not encouraging the nationalism that was being fed from all sides, including – most strongly – religion and politics. The thinking was that if the Irish economy were stronger, perhaps the struggle for autonomy would be less imperative. If the status quo was upheld then the Ascendancy might retain their position at the top of the social hierarchy.

It was important that the Castle-Set be seen to work for Irish regeneration but the sort of support they lent had to be closely monitored. Even moral support could be dubious as the Vicereine Lady Aberdeen discovered, when, on her first appointment to Ireland in 1886, she decided to dress her children in green for a procession through Dublin. Organising officials heard of the proposal and were aghast; the green coats were put aside and cream poplin ones were worn instead. On a separate occasion, though, it was thought sweet and charming to have the same two children painted as two little Home-Rulers, dressed in leprechaunish outfits of breeches and tailcoats sitting in a wheelbarrow filled with and surrounded by potatoes.

A suitable area to support were the cottage industries on which the early Irish textile industry had been based. The Congested Districts Board had established a scheme which offered the wives of the Lord-Lieutenant and other high-ranking officials the opportunity of active charity without becoming involved in anything contentious.

Lace, linen and wool were the primary cottage industries, lace becoming the most established due to the demands of current fashion and the promotion it received in magazines and on occasions like Lady Aberdeen's Charity Lace Ball of 1907. Considering that lace was the high fashion fabric from the 1880s until the First World War, the Castle-Set was not entirely disinterested in the support they lent to such occasions. It was the height of fashion in London and Paris, let alone in Dublin, to appear bedecked in lace flounces, skirts, jabots, sleeves, collars and trimmings. So occasions such as the Charity Lace Ball allowed these ladies to win on all sides; they could build the economy of their own country while legitimately feasting on high fashion and still receive words of praise, not only from that unknown quantity, the 'Oirish', but also from London's *The Queen Magazine*, who praised their 'charming function' and their 'efforts to inspire the humble lace-makers of Ireland'.[3] This white lace reached across the greatest divide in Irish society. It was made by barefoot women in unlit, unclean cottages along the coast of Ireland to be worn by English and Anglo-Irish ladies at Dublin Castle. There was certainly a degree of circumspection required at this level of society where to dress a child in green was not to be tolerated, but adults dressed from head to toe in Irish lace were utterly laudable.

An occasion which more clearly revealed the condescending attitude of the well-meaning Castle-Set was another charity do, a garden party; on this occasion the Aberdeens

> . . . desired a fancy character should be imparted by ladies who attend it appearing as far as possible in the costumes of peasants of different countries, however, whether in such costume or not all ladies should wear dresses of Irish manufacture. All children should appear in peasant dress. It is desired that gentlemen should wear suits of St Patrick's blue. Both ladies and gents should wear Irish gloves exclusively.[4]

While the *Irish Textile Journal* announced the affair, *The Freeman's Journal* also discussed it and supplied nineteen drawings of possible outfits.[5] Everybody, however, arrived in fashionable dress of Irish-made material, except for the children who came dressed as the Irish peasants who were ultimately to be the beneficiaries of the event. The suggested drawings are interesting though in that none of them refer to the ancient garb of the Celtic past. It must have been regarded as an image unlikely to appeal to those attending the garden party.

The first suggested costume is that of 'An Irish Peasant' (right); the drawing, however, is an utterly fanciful creation based largely on rococo porcelain shepherdesses. The only possible relationship to an Irish peasant is in the plaid scarf around her shoulders. The shamrock-shaped bunchings of the kilted-up skirt are purely pantomime. It does, however, offer the chance of a new lace flounce and a lace parasol.

The second drawing (overleaf) bears quite a close resemblance to a real Irish peasant. The image has however been disinfected by being called the 'Colleen Bawn', which in Irish means the 'Fair Girl'. The title immediately romanticises the image and relates it to the contemporary play by Dion Beuciault in which the title role was that of the Coleen Bawn. What little fun it would be to suggest

*'Irish Peasant
costume of White
Beige and Guipure
Lace'. Illustrations
from* The Viceregal
Garden Party,
How to Dress in
Irish Materials, *a pamphlet reprinted
from* The
Freeman's Journal,
*May 1868 (courtesy
of the National
Library of Ireland)*

going to the garden party looking like an Irish peasant and calling yourself an Irish peasant.

The suggested male costume (far right), which seems an inappropriate counterpart for either of the females illustrated, is 'The Irish Gentleman'. The irony of the title is fairly plain. Any man warranting the appellation 'gentleman' in 1880 would have been part of the establishment and would have dressed accordingly. The costume of this conceptual character is again a disinfected version; but this time it's 'Paddy' from *Punch* magazine who is portrayed. *Punch* regularly featured 'Paddy' wearing tails, breeches and top hat in varying states of inebriation, thuggishness or wiliness. No Irishman in 1880 who was in a position to buy new tailored clothing would have chosen this outfit. Tail-coats had been out of fashion for almost fifty years by that stage. Even in 1860 a group photograph of Donegal peasants shows almost nobody wearing tails.

The contrivance and condescension of the male costume suggested to the Castle-Set is made clear when the image is contrasted with one in which peasants are being personally addressed. The British army needed men and recruiting posters were billed in Ireland. To stir up nationalistic vigour, the potential recruit on the poster is not dressed in leprechaun gear or as a tidy version of 'Paddy' but realistically, in a shabby version of the fashionable lounge jacket and trousers.

By dwelling on these images of Irish peasant girls translated into porcelain dolls or 'Colleen Bawns', and thuggish 'Paddys' translated into 'Irish Gentlemen', the Castle-Set presumably sought to focus attention on the less glorious aspects of Irish society, and thereby to legitimise its role and justify its continuing presence in Ireland as a sophisticated and 'civilising' influence.

Pageantry also played an important role in the 'gala occasions' of the middle-class Gaelic League, who recalled in their dress on these occasions the great and glorious past of Ireland before the English suppressed the country's rich and varied culture. According to O'Curry's book, *The Manners and Customs of the Ancient Irish*, Irish dress comprised a *brat* and *léine*. A *brat* is a cloak and a *léine* a shirt or chemise. In the ancient texts the word *léine* was spelt two different ways and O'Curry translated these two variants as two distinct garments: the shirt and the kilt. The Gaelic-League men could therefore adopt, with apparent legitimacy, the *brat* and the kilt as their national costume. The kilt had spurious connotations of antiquity and masculinity which had developed in the country of their Celtic kinsmen.[6] This costume was worn on 'gala occasions' in a colour scheme of saffron and green; Henry VIII had outlawed the colour saffron in Ireland and a late nineteenth-century song declared that 'they were hangin' men and women for the wearin' of the green'. Predictably this costume was worn with a black jacket, white collar and black tie to maintain an establishment appearance alongside that of the Celtic Hero.

'Colleen Bawn Costume' (courtesy of the National Library of Ireland)

Heroines of Ireland had also worn the *brat* and *léine* which for turn-of-the-century women was correctly interpreted as a cloak and chemise or gown. These would naturally be made of Irish material and adorned with Irish brooches and Celtic embroidery. Photographs of middle-class women thus adorned are rare, however, presumably because the attitude expressed in this article of 1917 was widely held:

> But dearly as every lover of Irish National characteristics, and every admirer of womanly decorum must wish to see these distinctive costumes preserved, we must face facts. In the pressure of modern life, especially in urban districts, it is impossible to secure the general wearing of these picturesque costumes. The most we can hope for is that on gala occasions the daughters of the women who once wore National costume will produce their treasures. The memory of the romance and beauty of the past will thus be kept alive.[7]

The safe conservatism of this vision contrasts with the actions of an ordinary middle-class family in Cork. Mr and Mrs Ryan, who ran an umbrella business in the city, were to be seen wearing 'Irish costume' every day and on all occasions from 1918 until Mr Ryan died in 1925 (below). The manufacture, retail and continual wearing of the costume was their response to the Easter Rising of 1916 with which they had initially felt little sympathy. It was the secret execution of its leaders that appalled them and impelled them to make an obvious statement of their allegiance to a strong and living Ireland. They wanted to create employment; they could 'see no point in men dying for Ireland with an English fag in their mouths and an English cap on their heads'.

'Irish Gentleman in Lucan Cloth, Poplin and Fine Linen' (courtesy of the National Library of Ireland)

Mr and Mrs M.A. Ryan of Cork with their four children, c.1920. The family is dressed in 'The Irish Costume' which comprised a Brat and Léine, i.e. a cloak and gown for the women and, erroneously, a cloak and kilt for the men (courtesy of Mr Ryan Senior, Cork)

The pragmatic approach of the Ryans contrasts with the romantic vision of the artistic and literary circles who felt an ethereal attachment to dressing in Celtic finery. The literati, unlike the Gaelic League, were not overly concerned with middle-class values or with England's activities or presence in Ireland. Their concern was with a literary and artistic revival drawing on Ireland's mythological past. Women who were attached to the Abbey Theatre could be seen walking through Dublin in long dresses and flowing cloaks with fish sellers calling out that 'them Irishers are going daft, look at them trying to look like stained-glass windows'. The literati were aware that their costumes were not particularly Irish except in the fancy Celtic fixtures attached, but they enjoyed the symbolism and romanticism of the costumes which brought them into line with European artistic movements. Ultimately historical accuracy did not matter; the costumes represented an ancient, pure and glorious Ireland. It summarised their vision of their country's past and their aspirations for it's future.

The most gloriously artistic costumes were made by the Dún Emer Guild which was set up in an Arts and Crafts spirit by two sisters of W.B. Yeats, Lilly and Lolly, along with Miss Evelyn Gleeson. The 'historic' costumes of *brath* and *léine* were made of Irish silk poplin lavishly adorned with Celtic embroideries worked in brightly coloured silk threads. The desirability of such expensive and beautiful expressions of Celtic Ireland in an age of pageantry cannot be doubted. Though created in an 'artistic' environment they were worn proudly to 'gala occasions' by the wives of high-ranking persons who would certainly be numbered among those so ascerbically described by Seán O'Casey as

respectable white-collared, trim-suited Gaelic Leaguers snug in their selected branches [of the Gaelic League] living in Whitehall, Drumcondra, Rathgar, Donnybrook and all the other nicer habitations of the city. [8]

These were the attempts made by the different groups of Irish society to express subjective visions of history and ill-defined group aspirations in the symbolic language of dress. Dress, for the most part, is an uncodified and highly personal language; the wearing of uniforms is an attempt to make a clear and collective statement. The 'Irish Costume' never became a strict uniform; each group, and individuals within each group, wished their expression to reflect or conceal their particular social, economic and political history. It would seem that the various expressions of condescension, aspiration and contempt that are part of these costumes are so complicated and so open to interpretation and misinterpretation that they are, in fact, quite representative of Anglo-Irish relations.

Notes and References

I am very pleased to have the opportunity to thank those people who helped me at various stages with researching this piece: James Ryan and my family in Dublin, Jeanne Sheehy in Oxford, Aileen Ribeiro at The Courtauld Institute, and the Ryan family of Arbutus Lodge in Cork.

1 J.S.L. Lyons, *Culture and Anarchy in Ireland 1890*-1939, Oxford, 1982, p. 28.
2 E.F. Sutton, *Weaving: The Irish Inheritance,* Dublin, 1980, p. 14.
3 'Society in Ireland', *The Queen Magazine*, March 1907.
4 *The Irish Textile Journal*, 15 April 1886.
5 *The Viceregal Garden Party, How to Dress in Irish Materials*, A pamphlet reprinted from *The Freeman's Journal*, May 1886.
6 C. Hobsawm and T. Ranger (eds), *The Invention of Tradition*, Cambridge, 1983; cf. 'The Invention of the Highland Tradition' by Hugh Trevor-Roper.
7 Mary Butler, 'The Ethics of Dress', *The Irish Monthly*, vol. XLV, April 1917, pp. 222–8.
8 Ruth Dudley Edwards, *Patrick Pearse: The Triumph of Failure*, London, 1979, p. 21.

CAROL TULLOCH

Rebel Without a Pause

Black Street Style & Black Designers

The world has made being black a crime . . . I hope to make it a virtue.[1]

Yesterday we were black and oppressed; today, our blackness is a tool for our liberation.[2]

And to see the youth of our culture be able to pick up the bits and pieces of life as it is lived and transform mess into a message.[3]

Britain enjoys a unique phenomenon. Two valuable contributors to Britain's cultural make-up have emerged from what has been termed an 'alien culture' – black street style and black fashion design (in the 'very traditional sense').[4] Their approach to image-making is different from each other, they produce in general for different markets, yet they have one common denominator – black culture. Their colour is of course important, but is not the primary factor in this instance. What they share, consciously or subconsciously, is their black history. The question is what place of importance does it hold in their attitude to style and design? In order to understand their development and ideologies, it is necessary to map out the history of black culture, style and street style in Britain.

Black style, the embodiment of dress, music, language and mannerisms, is a complex commodity to define; since its voluntary arrival in Britain over forty years ago it has proved to be a coveted elusive enigma; secretive and defensive whilst flirting with ostentation.[5] Black style is not attributed to tangible elements, but requires a quality born from within the courier, be they 'born again' or 'outside in the world'.[6]

Black style has always played a starring role in the development of black culture, which emerged in direct opposition to the dominant cultures practised by a fraction of fellow countrymen within the black diaspora. It should not be viewed simply as cool, or as just another arbiter of style. A far more seminal theme, as in any fashion story, lies behind its expressive exterior; as does its ally – black street style – belonging to the 'Extra' extravert, the 'Natty Rebel', 'U' Roy exclaimed, '. . . I'm a rebel, rebel in the morning, rebel in the evening'.[7]

There is no attempt at delusion here as to the origins of Britain's black culture. At its conception there was no sanction from a sovereignty; rather it was manufactured as a form of survival against the unnecessary barbarism of the African slave trade practised in the West Indies, beginning with the formation of a distorted form of English, the Creole language. It was a culture of resistance 'which had been forced in its very inception, to cultivate secrecy and to elaborate defences against the intrusions of the Master Class';[8] its style became a rather ostentatious armour in order to create an exclusive identity for a people who desperately wanted to achieve a sense of community following the abolition of slavery and 'acceptance' into the free world.

On the home front the seeds of black style were sown in the late forties, germinating throughout the fifties with the arrival of black immigrants from the West Indies. Their original, underground lifestyle, in a spectrum of colours, was made more vibrant against the backdrop of endless shapes of grey that engulfed 'never had it so good' Britain. The women on the whole dressed relatively conservatively, diversifying only through a courageous use of colour and prints. Black men conversely (the 'Classic Dandy')[9] (below) must be

Greyhound Bus Terminal, New York, 1947, photograph by Esther Bubley (courtesy of the University of Louisville Photographic Archives)

credited for upsetting Britain's dress status quo. They set a new pace in picture ties, and 'Tropical' lightweight, vanilla-tinted, Scottish tweed or 'Rainbow' mohair suits, so devilishly cut by fellow cottage bespoke tailors they appeared to move in rhythm with the wearer's easy stride. Hats expertly perched on the head completed the look. It was an ensemble so sharp that these purveyors of style appeared to slice their way through the smog of Britain's major cities. It was a potent, capricious mode of dress worn *en masse* by black, working-class immigrants, accompanied by a deep-rooted love affair with hot calypsos, sensuous Latin-American sounds and temperamental jazz. A rhythmic patter laced with fresh, intoxicating words and phrases, was an essential accessory. This cocktail of energy was catered for by black-owned underground clubs and *shebeens* (house parties), a life-support for these 'new people' who had become disillusioned and displaced due to the onslaught of the so-called colour bar system that relegated them to the rank of Britain's underclass.

> Want a drink in the pub you're told you're not drinking in here. The Prince of Wales on Brixton Road was one of them . . . We were young, you had to enjoy yourself and house parties was the only way we could meet. [10]

> In some respects those days were better than now. We were closer. We met every weekend for parties travelling from Doncaster to Birmingham or Bradford to see friends. [11]

The jazz scene which was prominent in the basement clubs of Soho and the American ghettos had a massive impact on the dress code of that period. Why do you think Jack Kerouac hung around with his mate, jazz guitarist Slim Gaillard? As the man said:

> At lilac evening I walked with every muscle aching amongst the lights of 27th and Welton in the Denver coloured section wishing I were a negro, feeling that the best the white world has offered me was not enough ecstasy for me, not enough life, joy, kicks, darkness, music, not enough night. [12]

The infatuation with and gleaning of black style and culture virtually began as West Indian immigrants stepped off the boat. By the mid to late fifties white teenage subcultures, such as the Jazz Fiends, Beatniks and West End Boys, who wanted to slip the constricting noose of adult, post-war Britain, believed the 'Black Man' to be, among other international influences, the 'Quintessential Subterranean', [13] injecting danger and excitement 'into their cautious ordered lives', [14] the likes of which had lain dormant since the hedonistic days of the

Roaring Twenties. The result was the birth of street theatre performed amid the debris of war-torn Britain. As an alternative lifestyle to the legitimate English culture, they preached non-conformity and freedom of expression in the face of what both black and white camps saw as the *alien* culture. In 1961 Mary Quant, while trying to keep pace with and catering for the Modernists ('mods'), as a market growing in size and influence, confessed that 'It was the Mods who gave the dress trade the impetus to break through the fast moving, breathtaking, uprooting revolution'.[15] Quant presented Britain and the world with the 'Look' in 1963, receiving *The Sunday Times* international award for 'Jolting England out of its conventional attitude towards clothes'.[16] A year later authentic mods, obsessed with their pursuit of 'image', looked to West Indians for reassurance in their desire for individuality:

At the moment we're hero-worshipping the spades – they can dance and sing . . . We have to get all our clothes made because as soon as anything is in the shops it becomes too common. I once went to a West Indian club where everyone made their own clothes. It was fantastic, everyone was individual, everyone was showing themselves as they really wanted to be . . . They were just expressing themselves as everyone should be entitled to do, be it in homes or private clubs or in the streets.[17]

Subcultures, such as the skinhead and racially harmonious two-tone movements, stand as glowing testimonies to the reliance on the nattier side of black style – black street style – which developed in the late sixties with Jamaica's first authentic subcultural street style, the cocksure, delinquent Rude Boy. His answer to Jamaica's deteriorating socio-economic problems was to 'Loot and Shoot',[18] taking to the streets and *shebeens* of West Kingston, Jamaica on motorcycles of light, stripped-down chrome, dressed to rule the night in cropped, slim pants, bum-freezer leather or tonic jacket, intense shades and skiffle hair cut. The pork pie hat was an optional extra (overleaf). The Rude Boy was the Jamaican equivalent to the perpetually impeccably dressed black American hustler, or 'Cool Cat', as he was more endearingly known; 'A poet of cloth . . . a clothes-wearing man, a man whose trade, office and existence consists of wearing clothes'.[19] This 'Sportive Dandy' was seen back in the fifties as a positive role model for the Rudie, whose priorities of subversion, materialism and a little violence for diversity were the same. The comparison is further cemented through dress and disregard for hegemony:

The cat revolts against the low paid work of the ghetto . . . he lives on his wits by hustling. Cool and aloof, ridiculing the 'square', he is an 'operator' completely cynical about the motivations of others . . . costume is used to convey an essential symbolic class and ethnic message.[20]

CAROL TULLOCH

The American soul-element was reflected most clearly in the self-assured demeanour; the sharp flashy clothes, the 'Jive-Ass' walk which the street boys affected . . . the Rude Boy lived for the luminous moment, playing dominoes as though his life depended on the outcome – a big-city Hustler with nothing to do, and all the time Rocksteady, Ska and Reggae gave him the means with which to move effortlessly . . . Cool, that distant and indefinable quality, became almost abstract, almost metaphysical, intimating a stylish kind of stoicism – survival and something more.[21]

Men in Pork-pie Hats, photograph by Red Saunders (courtesy of the photographer)

The mainstay of many a Ska tune then was a loveable rogue.

Initially it was the Hard Mods, fathers of the skinhead movement, who drew heavily on the subversive style of the Rudie 'street boys' and hustlers, adopting the 'stingy-brim' (pork-pie) hat and the crop trouser so unproportionately cut,

the length appeared 'to have been measured inna flood'.[22] They found that the non-conformist, rugged style of ska, with its saucy lyrics and outlaw comic-book-type songs, matched their wayward, deviant desires. The popular culture in full swing at that time held no interest at all, a little too squeaky clean for their proletariat taste. Towards the end of the sixties, along with the first reggae tracks, skinheads who partook of midnight rambling stomped frenetically to beats pumped out of sound systems (no black underground movement is legitimate without them) reserved for a black only audience;[23] ultimately they were rewarded for their loyalty with a personalised reggae signature tune – 'Skinhead Moonstomp'. In just over twenty years of black presence in Britain, history was being made in the working-class areas of south London where these two camps lived, congregated and socialised. It was an unprecedented, voluntary convergence between black and white; the first phase, alas short-lived, of some kind of cultural integration. In Hebdige's study of Britain's blossoming black street culture he stresses the skinheads' dependency on its style:

> The long open coats worn by some West Indians were translated by the skinheads into the 'Crombie' which became a popular article of dress amongst the more reggae-orientated groups . . . even the erect carriage and the loose-limbed walk which characterized the West Indian Street-boy were (rather imperfectly) simulated by the aspiring white negroes.[24]

The divergence between black and white youths shone all too brightly through the inequalities taking place in the world outside the clubs. In 1968 *The Observer* reported that black youths leaving school faced the demoralising fact that their white equivalents from the same depressed areas would be 'almost five times more likely to get skilled jobs'. Second-generation black British youths were having none of this, no longer wanting to be called British, considering themselves West Indians, considering themselves black.

While Britain came to terms with its new cultural elements James Brown begged fellow black Americans to 'Get into it and get involved', referring to the objective of promoting black people and their culture; and encouraging them to fight inequalities and racism through either the Civil Rights' or Black Power movements. A fervour of pride in being 'black' was instilled throughout the black conscripts of the 'urban reserve armies'.[25] In 1968 Maulana Ron Karenka, a spokesperson for black nationalism, commanded brethren to *Think Black, Act Black, Create Black, Buy Black, Vote Black, Live Black* – a global revolution with black expressionism as ammunition.

Along with this cultural awakening, black style changed its tone. The 'dress for success' approach, adopted by first-generation black immigrants on entering Britain, rapidly metamorphosised into a striking, wild-style mien worn by black people of all age groups, whether or not they were aware of the coded messages transmitted, for example, in the millions of afros that exploded around the world. The afro was cool for Black Panthers in cuban heels, black polo neck. The 'leather-clad urban guerrilla image was one of the most effective manifestations of black power'.[26] The Soul Sisters' participation was fundamental, with a crowned queen of soul, Aretha Franklin; and their feminist views and style were embodied in the militant persona of equal rights defender and political activist, Angela Davis.

The Rastafari religion came up with a stark, no-nonsense radical culture to jolt the masses.[27] Its goal the ostracisation of Western culture, it looked to Africa, the 'Promised Land', for inspiration and guidance. Its concept perhaps was expressed most significantly in cultivated dreadlocks (antennae to Jah), signifying the wearer's commitment to the movement. By turning to the subculture, Britain's disenchanted black youths believed they had finally found their true identity, distancing themselves further from British culture, and adopting patois as their native tongue.[28]

Rastafari spread throughout Britain in two phases. The original guise was as underground cult; humble, natural dress was seen as a far more effective means of protest than the mystical words set to reggae played within the sanctity of 'Blues' (a strictly no-go area for non-blacks). A dread in fatigue dress (red, gold and green embellishments and millinery) strode defiantly through the concrete jungle 'striking fear in the hearts of Babylon'.[29] Out of obedience to the doctrine, Rasta Queens covered their locks at all times in public, swathed themselves in draped fabric and wore humble sandals, as in the African tradition. By the mid seventies the movement and its music had dropped its guard, becoming a major international counter-culture on the back of musical freedom fighter Robert Nesta Marley, who endorsed dreadlocks to idolatory status, while the tracksuit became *de rigueur*. The same messages were put to rhythms less loaded with a dread drum beat and heavy base line. Marley and his aides converted hundreds on thousands of both sides of the Equator, achieving through music what Kurt Weill described as a 'Revolutionary use coming about through the listeners' sympathy, not by forcing them against their will'.[30] They cleared the way for a more radical cultural change in Britain. Peter Tosh implored that we 'Don't Look Back'. Syncretism proved to be the only way forward.

The first signs of syncretism amongst black youths came in 1981, when Smiley Culture's popular chart success 'Cockney Translation' introduced a counter-culture which was in effect the marriage of the Rude Boy and loveable Cockney expressed through clothes and language. Spruce, smooth and working class, donning Farah trousers, sheepskins, gold chains, a selection of rings, stingy brim or Kangol hats, slim-fit silk shirts, the skiffle returned with razored side partings, crocodile skin, or even worse, pastel-shade shoes. 'Daughters' were just as slick in silk blouses or dresses, Gucci bags, Bally shoes, pleated skirts, slacks, permed, straightened hair or the *Sade* ponytail – we're talking quality items.

The seventies, although subculturally dramatic and exciting with punk, Rastafari and two-tone, was still a complex subcultural era, with a plethora of what Peter York described as 'Style Wars'. Yet during this period two reggae-based sound systems were operating: in 1973 Jamaican DJ Kool Herc in the West Bronx, New York, and circa 1976 Jah Rico in north London. The former was responsible for the birth of rap and its hip-hop culture; the latter changed its name to Soul II Soul (representing spiritual soul and musical style) – aka the Funki Dreds. Both movements originated from the 'street' and remain loyal to it. They are based on the same cultural phenomenon of black expression and have the same goals as previous black movements, successfully packaging an *attitude* and offering it to the nation in order to deal with daily narrow-mindedness. The dress and musical styles over the years have merged and may well appear subversive, but to black youths within the various foster countries around the globe they are the epitome of black street style, continually articulate in making visual statements and capturing a multi-racial, multi-class worldwide audience. Youths of the Bronx have an even stronger allegiance with London Posses, who identify with kids in Jamaica and Soweto; sympathising with each other's day-to-day, socio-economic problems that contribute to the ideologies behind the styles they create.

> Black hairstyles teach us about being pluralistic, about being black. To actually cherish the symbolism that we grow our hair in all sorts of different ways – to me that is a very powerful symbol of the changes. It says that we are able to accept that we have a very highly complex and differentiated identity. In a sense being able to escape from being what I call either/orism. If you are not one thing you are another, when actually all different things at once. It's a question of being able to inhabit them all into a framework without it being a problem.[31]

The above analysis, therefore, is perfectly expressed in the hair sculpture amongst young black men and women. The Funki Dred image of dreadlocks and shaved back and sides created by Jazzy B and Aitch for the Soul II Soul crew 'incorporates the roots of their reggae culture and the style of the urban dance scene'[32] and spread like wildfire amongst non-members of the band. An alternative for the broader clubbing contingent are the scores of awesome variations made possible by combining either the Philly Cut or skiffle with shaved inroads of single diagonal lines at the sides, or a myriad of furrows around the head, and/or bleaching and perms.[33]

Hip-hop dress is erratic and eclectic. During its ten-year reign as an inter-

CAROL TULLOCH

national style, it has undergone numerous shifts – Teenybopper to Home Boy to hard-rocker to Afrocentric; Hustler to Superfly to Daisy Age to Cosmic – the latter courtesy of Rifat Ozbek and back again. But the basis of all these looks was founded in the United States where the originators got rid of all the flim-flam surrounding previous black styles and gave a new dimension to the fashion terminology, casual dress. Rich and famous Americans immersed themselves in leisure-wear, with designers like Norma Kamali doing wonderful things with sweatshirting. Home Boys and Fly Girls shared the same garments and turned this respectable style into something ragga, tuff and ready. Designer tracksuits and straight or customised flying jackets (below left) developed into the laid-back, sloppy tubular appearance of long covetable T-shirts, sweat pants or

Girl with Bomber Jacket, The Face, July 1987, photograph by Sheila Rock (courtesy of the photographer)

Four men in baseball-influenced sportswear, The Face, July 1980, photograph by Paul Lawrence (courtesy of the photographer)

cropped shorts and 'pin-tucked' baggy jeans with elaborate high-tech status symbol trainers and the indispensable baseball cap. The look was formally glamorised with the odd gold tooth, a multitude of rings, obligatory gold chains, Dukie Ropes and/or medallions – the latter then discarded by any self-respecting hip-hopper in favour of leather pendants in protest against South African gold. Deadly female rappers like Salt 'N' Peppa and Neneh Cherry (overleaf) added a robust sexuality to the style.

Soul II Soul's image is club-based, and started out with the now classic Funki Dred 'T'-shirt designed by Derek Yates, which was primarily intended as a means of identification for its DJs. Its success with clubbers led to an extended range based on the easy style of sportswear-dominated street culture, incorporating the Soul II Soul logo with a wide range of printed T-shirts designed by partner and art director, Nicoli Bean. It was a street style that was being incorporated by the more, so-called legitimate fashion designers, and in a sense belonged to Soul II Soul through the group's affiliation to the hip-hop subculture via music, culture, colour and history.

> . . . the objects, the 'gear' used to assemble a new subcultural style must not only already exist, but must also carry meanings organised into a system coherent enough for their relocation and transformation to be understood as transformation. [34]

What makes the Soul II Soul concept unique is that it has proved Cohen's notion, that in 'subcultures . . . there are no career prospects as such . . .', [35] to be null and void. They have built up a legitimate subcultural organisation, stressing at every stage that they are black, British, and in total control of their business ventures – be it the sound system, designing and purchasing of merchandise, shops, records and videos. They have consciously promoted themselves as a positive cross-cultural tangram bent on world domination. Basically the Soul II Soul team has designed a movement. For example, the video 'Soul II Soul' is an introduction to their ideology of what it means to be black and British at the close of the 1980s. It is a fusion of black history, music and their own brand of black British culture. It is a concept that has been an inspiration to British black youths, reassuring them that they can be proud of their mixed culture and 'an asset to the collective'. [36]

> As the expressive culture of young blacks has continued to evolve into new, organic and uniquely British forms, the impact of the black presence on British life has become more widespread and profound. The populist appeal of black culture and music has made it a central reference point for the struggles of other young people, creating an important space for dialogue between black and white. [37]

I would suggest that the bombardment of sports-inspired style accompanying Rap, Soul II Soul and Ragga music styles,[38] plus the entire club and street scene, has contributed greatly to the demise of the 'designer wear' syndrome. With the opening of a new decade, 'street stylists' have played a crucial part in influencing the more avant-garde fashion designers' work.

In the run up to the nineties the world of fashion reviewed its position. It no longer took the stance of dictator but opted for the 'gentle persuader' approach of democratic stylist. Designers contributed to a 'style of success' as depicted in *Vogue*, *The Face*, *Marie Claire* and *Arena*. Obviously it is imperative for fashion designers, regardless of their cultural background, to broaden their outlook for influences in order to expand their sketchbook of ideas. This latter point goes some way towards explaining the division that has occurred between black fashion designers, some of whom argue that their skin colour and cultural heritage are 'incidental' to their work, while others believe them to be vital and worthy of broadcast.[39]

> I think of myself, for professional reasons, as just a designer, not a black designer. That is the only way to progress. Once you start selling yourself as a black designer you're holding yourself back a bit . . . [fashion is] one of the areas where it doesn't matter if you are green, yellow or black, but there are always problems.
>
> Joe Casely-Hayford

> I was born in England so I think like an Englishman. Colour is incidental. It doesn't change the way I think, I think like an Englishman because I went through the school and college system.
>
> Charlie Allan

> Like accessories (being black and your sexuality), they are not important. They colour your personality, but ultimately you want to see the part of you that is completely unique and put that first . . . The essence of me is more than any colour. To limit ourselves and think well I'm a man and that is it and you identify with that totally and absolutely is crazy because I think whatever we are is beyond sex and colour and all that.
>
> David Phillips

I think you have got to ask yourself, as a black person, how you perceive yourself. I mean I am in a situation where my mother is black and my father was white and I would say he had just as much of an influence on my early life as my mother did, and I do not think it would be right to negate that side of my family and I think I perceive myself very much as English, and English to me means you could be black, you could be

Neneh Cherry, record sleeve for her debut album More Like Sushi, *1989. Photograph by John Baptiste Mondino, style by Judy Blame, t-shirt and shirt by Body Map, bra by Judy Blame (record produced by Booga Bear, Circa Records)*

white, you could be a mixture, you could be a lot of things because I think that is the England of the 1990s . . . Africa for me has about as much relevance to what I actually do in my design work as any other country. It doesn't mean that people should deny their background or origin in any way, shape or form. My everyday reality is that I grew up in London, I went to school here, all my early experiences were here in England, so that is what essentially shapes the way I perceive things. So I think being a black designer is for me very incidental . . . Being black is not . . . any more relevant than anything done by a white person.

Darlajane Gilroy

I will not have my name put in a book or magazine without them knowing I'm black . . . I think it needs to be done. I'm not just British, my parents are from the West Indies and it plays a major part in my life.[40]

Nicoli Bean

When I design . . . I do take parts of my culture and heritage . . . My heritage is still a very important part of me.

Robert Lewis Stephenson

The division was inevitable. These designers are, after all, artistic individualists. What I dispute fundamentally is the notion that skin colour and cultural heritage is a hindrance. *No, it Enriches.* For example, Joe Casely-Hayford belongs to that school of designers who aim for a market where the priorities are not those of a cultural street style. This is not a critical analysis of his work, simply an observation that as a result of his traditional training at St Martin's School of Art in London his approach would be more sophisticated and the influences on it far more varied than those of street style inventors.

Yet despite his declaration above, Casely-Hayford does draw on his cultural background, as was demonstrated exquisitely in his 'One World' spring/summer 1991 catwalk show. He proved that one need not be an overt black expressionist in order to filter segments of one's cultural heritage and views into designs whilst capably delivering the goods to a non-black clientele to incorporate into their own lifestyle: 'locksed up',[41] barefooted white models in waif-like slip dresses shielded themselves with giant silk scarves (hand-painted by David Phillips) depicting a world map of three globes – Africa being the focal point – held in black hands and incorporating the slogan, 'No more first, second and third world, just one world'. This is Casely-Hayford's contribution to cross-cultural dressing.

Robert Lewis Stephenson, another St Martin's graduate, received rapturous media response to his final degree show, 'Law and Order'. He cheekily united judicial wigs and navy pinstripe – British Establishment regalia – with leopard and zebra prints and West Indian crocheting techniques. In one fell swoop Stephenson practised what he preached, that cultural heritage is important and relevant to his design work.

Paul Gilroy has the final word:

We have talked about subculture and dominant culture and there is a struggle between them. Different groups articulate their different experiences through culture and these cultures come under a hierarchy. The arts we were given instead of freedom we can expand and define as a vehicle to be able to talk about the complexity of our lives as a whole. Of course it's art and of course it's important, but it comes from a tradition which doesn't separate art from life ... which doesn't separate artefact from experience ... we are in a kind of dialogue with the performer and together we will create a performance that will satisfy us both and give us pleasure.[42]

Notes and References

Special thanks goes to Karen Falconer for starting the ball rolling, and to Syd for his role as critic, unflinching support and making nourishing meals!

1 Marcus Garvey quoted in *A Political Dictionary of Black Quotations*, collected and edited by Osei Amoan, Oyokoanyinaase House, 1989, p. 127.

2 Eldridge Cleaver quoted in *A Political Dictionary of Black Quotations*, op. cit., p. 13.

3 Jesse Jackson as quoted on *The Media Show*, October 1990.

4 Darlajane Gilroy, in interview with the writer, at the Dome, King's Road, March 1990.

5 Dick Hebdige, *Subculture: The Meaning of Style*, London, 1979, p. 45.

6 Religious terminology used to describe sinners.

7 'Natty Rebel', Virgin Album, 1976.

8 Dick Hebdige, 'Reggae, Rastas and Rudies: Style and the Subversion of Form', Stencilled paper 24, Centre for Contemporary Cultural Studies, University of Birmingham, 1974, p. 26.

9 Michael and Ariane Batterberry, *Fashion: The Mirror of History*, New York, 1982.

10 Mr H. Simpson, in interview with the writer at his home in Stockwell, London, December 1986.

11 Mrs C. Thomas, in interview with the writer at her home in Doncaster, South Yorkshire, November 1986.

12 Jack Kerouac, *On the Road*, London, 1958.

13 Hebdige, op. cit., 1979, p. 44.

14 Colin McInnes, *City of Spades*, London, 1957.

15 Barbara Bernard, *Fashion in the Sixties*, London, 1978.

16 Ibid.

17 David Holborne, a 19-year-old mod, interviewed for *Generation X* by Charles Hamblett and Jane Deverson, Library 33, 1964.

18 'Shanty Town' by Desmond Dekker.

19 Batterberry, op. cit.; Thomas Carlyle quoted in John Clarke, *Leisure and the Working Class in Resistance Through Rituals*, Stuart Hall and Tony Jefferson, (eds) London, 1976.

20 Michael Brake, *Comparative Youth Culture*, London, 1990, p. 128.

21 Hebdige, op. cit., 1974, pp. 22–3.

22 West Indian expression for severely cropped trousers.

23 Hebdige, op. cit., 1974, p. 25.

24 Ibid., p. 38.

25 Brake, op. cit., p. 118.

26 Dylan Jones, *Haircults*, London, 1990, p. 58.

27 Rastafari evolved in Jamaica during the 1930s.

28 'Patois' is the official name for the Jamaican-based Creole language.

29 Hebdige, op. cit., 1979.

30 Quoted by I. Macdonald in 'What is the Use of Music', *The Face*, March 1986.

31 Paul Gilroy in interview with the writer at his home in London, 18 September 1987.

32 Taken from Soul II Soul History given by Jennifer Lewis.

33 The Philly Cut is a hairstyle based on the 1930s Tapered Cut favoured by Philadelphia Muslims. See Jones, op. cit.

34 Clarke, op. cit.

35 Quoted by John Clarke in 'Style', op. cit.

36 'Get A life', 10 Records, 1989.

37 Simon Jones, *Black Youth, White Culture*, London, 1988, p. 56.

38 1990 saw the re-emergence of reggae as a driving force in musical style in the form of Ragga Music; the style is natty, infectious and fresh.

39 For the purpose of this article a significant amount of this information was acquired through personal interviews with designers: Joe Casely-Hayford (August 1987); David Phillips (February 1990); Darlajane Gilroy (March 1990); Charlie Allan (June 1990); Robert Lewis Stephenson (June 1990); Nicoli Bean (aka Jennifer Lewis, November 1990).

40 At the time of interview, Nicoli Bean announced that Soul II Soul would be stocking their first own-label, designer womenswear collection for spring/summer 1991.

41 'Locksed up' refers to hair that has been twisted into dreadlocks.

42 Paul Gilroy, in interview with the writer.

Haute Couture
versus
Popular Style

ELLEN LEOPOLD

The Manufacture of the Fashion System

INTRODUCTION

'Fashion' industries are often depicted as being in the grip of forces beyond their control. The notion of an industry that is passively responding to rather than actively creating the conditions which guarantee its survival has made it possible to develop a history of fashion which is entirely demand-led, based on the view that 'it is fashion that makes the industry rather than the industry that makes fashion'.[1] This inherent bias is reflected in a literature which, until recently, consisted on the one hand of straightforward histories of costume and on the other of behavioural theories that address the psychology of fashion and patterns of consumption.[2] Both imply that *consumer demand* is the determining force in the creation of fashion. Totally absent from this tradition is any consideration of the determining role that might be played by clothing production and its history.

Supply-side history, for its part, has focused on the development of labour organisation in the garment industry and on the central role played by a variety of immigrant groups. Though the literature has incorporated demand for clothing, it is viewed primarily as a consequence of the rise of disposable incomes created by factory employment. The specific pattern of demand that has emerged in women's clothing and its role within a unique configuration of distribution and supply, have not been addressed.

In other words, the history of clothing production has made little contribution to an understanding of the 'fashion' system. Loosely defined as the inter-relationship between highly fragmented forms of production and equally diverse and often volatile patterns of demand, the fashion system is a hybrid subject; it incorporates dual concepts of fashion: as a cultural phenomenon, and as an aspect of manufacturing with the accent on production technology. This dual aspect has made it difficult to accommodate within a tradition in which the histories of consumption and production plough largely separate furrows.

A consequence of this division is that the history of fashion has overlooked the slow but sustained development of mass markets for cheap standardised clothing (largely associated with the history of production) and has concentrated instead on the differentiation and diffusion of production emanating from a much narrower segment of the market which, despite its limited scope, has none the less attracted a disproportionate share of media attention. The result has been a tendency to view the history of fashion from the top down, rather than from the bottom up – as the history of haute couture, in other words.

This paper attempts to explain the origins of this extreme contrast in historical traditions by examining the supply-side history of the women's dressmaking industry in the early twentieth century. It interprets the evolution of fashion as a consequence of the specific historical development of a distinct branch of clothing production and as a response to a particular set of constraints on that development. More specifically, it argues that the seemingly anarchic and rapidly changing proliferation of style in women's clothes, a feature that has distinguished it not just from other industries but also from other branches of the clothing industry, has served as a substitute for technical innovation, arising not in response to a rise in incomes or to changes in consumer preferences or to the exhaustion of possibilities arising from early mass production, but rather from the industry's failure ever fully to embrace mass production techniques.

This explanation is offered as a more plausible alternative to those which treat fashion as an emanation from the innate drive of all women to consume. The mutual exclusiveness and incompatibility of these views are succinctly illustrated by the belief that 'categorically, man is always the producer . . . woman the consumer' [3] espoused at a time when four-fifths of the producers of women's apparel were themselves women working in dangerous conditions for extremely low wages. The starkness of the contradiction between the world of high fashion and the sweatshop reveals the weakness of a framework which, in denying any link between consumption and production, dismisses any historical consideration of the class relations which have determined them and their relationship to one another.

AN ALTERNATIVE FRAMEWORK

Karl Marx predicted that the arrival of the 'decisively revolutionary sewing machine' would, in combination with other progressive forces, help to do away with 'the murderous, meaningless caprices of fashion', while 'the development of ocean navigation and of the means of communication generally' would sweep away the 'technical basis on which seasonal work was really supported'. [4] Over a century later, despite many far-reaching changes in the clothing industry, both of these brakes on large-scale mass production remain, particularly in branches of the women's apparel industry. This is in itself a good indication of the limited extent to which the revolutionary changes, which transformed other industries and led to the dominance of the Fordist production line, bypassed the clothing industry.

The apparel industry is composed of several wholly separate branches, each with its own pattern of historical development. A distinction has first to be drawn between the development of ready-to-wear and factory-made clothing. The former grew out of bespoke tailoring[5] which allowed for the build up of stock dresses during seasonal periods of slack but which did not imply any changes in the methods, organisation or location of manufacturing. English guild records and stock inventories indicate that making clothes in advance of purchase was well established by the sixteenth century.[6] Factory production, which came later, implies the investment in and co-ordination of labour and machines in a designated workplace for the purpose of increasing the productivity – and profitability – of manufacturing. The earlier spread of many ready-to-wear garments (particularly those which were loose-fitting and simply cut) means that in a limited sense, mass markets preceded mass production.

In the United States, both ready-to-wear and factory-made clothes for men appeared first, at least partly encouraged by demand for clothing for sailors (with only 24-hour turnarounds in port), and by demand for military uniforms at the time of the Civil War. The earlier demand for standardised work clothes (particularly shirts) for men, coinciding with their earlier mass participation in paid labour, also contributed to the earlier development of large-scale markets in some of these goods.

Women's factory-made clothes did not begin to appear until the beginning of the twentieth century, corresponding to (though not entirely the consequence of) their later entry into the labour market. Yet even at the close of the First World War, the industrial development of women's clothing continued to lag behind men's, displaying characteristics increasingly at odds with those conducive to the spread of mass production.

Dressmaking in particular failed to conform to the orthodox pattern. It is also the branch of the clothing industry most closely associated with the evolution of 'fashion', i.e., with the rise of the role of demand as an active and transforming agent on its own. The link between these two attributes is revealed most clearly in the history of dressmaking in the United States in the decade immediately following the end of the First World War: this is the period commonly cited as triggering off the fashion phenomenon in its twentieth-century mode.[7]

BEGINNINGS OF INDUSTRIAL DEVELOPMENT

The most important distinguishing characteristic of clothing in the twentieth century was its continuing dependence on the individually-operated sewing machine. Introduced in the middle of the nineteenth century, this remained at the core of factory production a century later. The central dynamic at work in most incipient mass production industries, that is, the progressive subordination of the worker to the machine and his or her eventual displacement by large-scale capital equipment, simply did not occur in the clothing industry at a comparable state of development.

The introduction of rigid and interchangeable parts in other industries reduced their dependence on the highly skilled work of the precision engineer.[8] This set the long process of industrial deskilling and technological unemployment in motion. By contrast, the development of machinery in the clothing industry neither displaced labour on the same scale nor stripped it completely of its skills. Such transformation as did occur from the hand-sewing to the manufacturing of clothing was based on the mechanisation of tailoring practices rather than on the wholesale transfer of the production process to machinery.

Based in New York City, the entry point for literally millions of skilled and unskilled immigrants from Europe, the fledgling clothing industry faced none of the skilled labour shortages that would act as a spur to earlier innovation in Detroit and elsewhere. Until the advent of immigration restrictions in 1923, labour was so plentiful and competition for jobs so cut-throat that employers could often pass on some of their overheads to the workforce, insisting, on occasion, that workers supply their own machines and thread. Despite technical innovations which occurred before the mid 1920s, technological unemployment remained low as aggregate demand for clothing continued to rise.[9] Nevertheless, while the incentive to replace labour altogether was much attentuated, the drive to reduce the skill content of sewing jobs was clearly in evidence.

In the move towards mechanisation, though the multiple skilled tasks formerly provided by a single skilled worker (tailor or seamstress) were broken down into separate processes, most still required the use of a distinct if limited skill applied by an individual machine operator to garments handled individually on his or her own machine.

Early innovations that reinforced this relationship include an automatic button-holing machine invented in 1862 and a button sewer patented in 1875.[10] These were followed by blind-stitching machines, which allowed for invisible stitching by pricking fabrics rather than sewing through them; over-edgers, that could wrap thread around the edge of a fabric in order to produce a finished appearance; and, early into the twentieth century, new pressing machines and irons that could generate live steam directly. These inventions all speeded up the pace at which the tailoring task could be carried out,[11] but they did not increase the number of garment pieces that could be worked on simultaneously.

An early exception to this one-to-one link between the individual garment or segment of a garment and the individual operator was the introduction in the 1870s of the steam-powered cutting machine followed in the 1890s by a portable and electrically-powered rotary knife. These enabled an individual worker to cut up to twenty-four layers of cloth at one time.[12] Offering clear advantages in accuracy, efficiency and ease of manoeuvring over hand tools, the new machines rendered obsolete the use of the short-bladed knife and scissors. With the loss of the hand-tooled craft came the rise of a clearly demarcated, highly productive, and hence lucrative source of employment. Women who had been cutters alongside men up to this point, rapidly disappeared from the newly enhanced trade.[13]

All clothing workers in the apparel trades shared the problem of dealing with soft and shapeless raw materials which therefore required – and still require – a great deal of individual handling before being submitted to machinery. As recently as the 1970s, a survey estimated that only 20 per cent of a sewer's time was spent in actually sewing, with the rest spent in garment handling.[14] So industrial development, which adds an increasing assortment of specialist operators – and machines – to an increasingly subdivided sequence of production, must inevitably generate additional dead time between operations, which might or might not be offset by the increased productivity of the operations themselves.

This trade-off between gains in productivity and increases in complexity echoes at the industrial level the ambiguity surrounding the impact of the sewing machine on the home production of clothes. Though advertised as a labour-saving device, it has been argued that the sewing machine served rather to increase expectations of dress (and hence of the dressmaker) leading to the production of ever more elaborate clothing, requiring more seams, trimmings, drapes and ruffles,[15] and enabling 'her to put a hundred tucks where once she put three'.[16] The tendency towards increasing complexity of dress facilitated by the sewing machine exemplifies the more general contradiction between the avowed labour-saving attributes of mechanised forms of housework and the countervailing rise in labour-consuming expectations which such equipment brings in its train.

In the factory, new machinery paved the way for an extraordinary extension in the type of specialist operators which included fellers, basters, snappers, folders, gaugers, etc. All of these facilitated the closer approximation of ready-to-wear clothes to the complexity of hand-sewn clothing rather than tending towards the evolution of distinctly different, more standardised products reflecting newer modes of production.

In such a context, the sequencing of production is obviously critical. Not only does an increase in the subdivision of labour increase the overall time lost to handling by a growing number of participants, each working on one piece at a time. It creates further problems in co-ordinating the pace of each operation and the transfer of garment segments between one work station and the next.

Solutions to the problems of assembly in the clothing industry in the first quarter of the twentieth century more closely resembled the workings of Adam Smith's pin factory of the eighteenth century than they did the production line at Ford's. Assembly methods did improve; switching from the 'bundle' system to the 'straight line' system did shorten the process time for an individual garment, but the scale of productivity gains so generated were modest.

The apparel industry remained one of the least mechanised of all industries. In 1913 at least one third of the 25,000 workers in the waist and dress industry (as the shirtwaist and blouse industry was called) were still engaged in hand operations, and a similar proportion of operators in the coat and suit section of the industry were finishing garments by hand as late as 1921.[17] In 1923 the average horsepower per plant across all industries was 169.0; for men's clothing the corresponding figure was just 11.4,[18] but this was still almost three times the level of power achieved in the women's clothing industry, 4.0.[19]

But even this very modest consumption of power is in a sense misleading. Most of it was used to support an increasing number of individually operated machines. Though these increased in sophistication and speed of operation, they essentially propped up an unchanging production system still firmly based on tailoring. Referred to as the 'whole garment system', it was based on individual operators carrying out all the separate specialist tasks needed to put together an entire garment. Though the manufacturing system had been subdivided into several basic crafts – cutting, operating, finishing and pressing – the skilled operator remained at the heart of what was a largely unspecialised division of labour.[20] Under this system, every garment produced was essentially unique.

Efforts to break the grip of the whole garment system, to subdivide the sewing of a garment into separate operations, led to the development of the 'section work' system. Under this system, one operator would, for example, work exclusively on sleeves, another on collars, a third on cuffs, etc. This system encouraged both the development of standardised garments and of larger production runs. It made possible intra-process inspection to which the whole garment system did not readily lend itself and so led to the possibility of greater quality control.[21]

However, section work did not find easy acceptance within the industry. It did not offer the flexibility in production characteristic of the whole garment system that made it possible to respond immediately and frequently to changes in style. With a premium on fast turnaround, a whole garment shop could turn an order around in three to four days compared with a much more sluggish three weeks required by a section workshop. Such a system naturally encourages those productive activities that have the capacity to exploit this competitive edge. Of all the main branches in the women's clothing industry, dressmaking, based on the simplest sequence of operations, lent itself most easily to the whole garment system. With the entire dress under the control of one operator, changes in style could be implemented instantly. Once set in train, this short cycle of demand and supply would be hard to break.[22]

CHANGES AFTER THE FIRST WORLD WAR

The post-war rise in industrial employment, together with growth in the population, lifted the level of disposal incomes (and hence effective demand) to new heights. National transportation and distribution networks began to emerge after the First World War, and these helped to smooth the way for new patterns of consumption.

Although the apparel industry did not play a central role in raising the scale or pace of post-war markets for consumer goods, it was none the less caught up in its consequences. Unprepared for the sudden expansion in demand in the immediate post-war period, the industry remained undercapitalised and undeveloped, made up of a large shifting mass of small and intensely competitive firms too small to wield market power or to reap the economies of scale arising from increasing concentration of capital. The great majority of these clothing firms were very small – in 1929, 96.5 per cent were still single-unit establishments – which made large production runs of standardised products impossible.

Poorly organised and lacking any concentrated leverage, clothing producers were out-manoeuvred by the emergent retail and distribution agencies that gained the upper hand in the 1920s. Their coming together was more a confrontation between unequal partners than a mutually-reinforcing spur to development and the accommodation that ensued retarded the further development of the apparel industry.

THE RISE OF THE JOBBER

The rise and consolidation of the power of the jobber was the response of the dressmaking industry in the first decade after the First World War. When manufacturers first began to farm out some of their excess production to outside firms at the end of the nineteenth century, it was the jobber who organised newly arrived immigrant labour for contract work. By the 1920s, he had transformed this middleman role into a much more powerful position, which widened the gap between the production of clothing and its marketing. The jobber (also referred to as the 'stock house') now took over from the manufacturer all decisions about what was to be produced, how much and when, designing garments, supplying raw materials to contractors, and later, selling the finished products but subcontracting manufacture to outside firms.

The jobber, freed from the technical and labour problems arising in the factory, was able to concentrate his attention on styles and sales. The capacity to commandeer and direct production enabled him to sell to retailers from an exceptionally wide range of stock which could quickly adapt to changes in demand. The emergence of jobbing activity was to some extent a mark of the increasing leverage of retailers who now insisted on both delaying the placing of orders until the last possible moment and on minimising the length of time any merchandise took up prime selling space in their shops.

The consequences of this change for the production of clothing, particularly women's clothing, were almost entirely negative. The new 'hand-to-mouth'[23] buying practice adopted by retailers led to the rapid decline of advance orders on which manufacturers had previously depended to help them plan and smooth out production over a longer period. With increased uncertainty and decreasing production runs, manufacturers (now contractors) could only survive by underbidding each other, through either lowering the quality of work or lowering wages or both. Not surprisingly, there was a very high turnover of firms. Of 2,000 dress manufacturers in existence in 1929, 709 were new entrants and 478 went out of business. In 1931 a further 621 new firms entered the fray while 504 abandoned it.

With so little capital required for entry into the business, it was almost as easy to enter the industry as to withdraw from it. As *Fortune Magazine* put it in 1939: 'with $2,500, a few customers and a colossal amount of nerve, almost anyone can go into the dress business'.[24] Strong family connections in many clothing shops allowed family members to pool savings to elevate one of them up to contractor status, only to see him return the next year to the shop floor. The composition of and boundaries between participating firms were constantly shifting; winners in one year's round of activity might be forced in the next 'to sell off equipment to last year's losers. Under these circumstances, every employee could become a subcontractor, every subcontractor a manufacturer, every manufacturer, an employee'.[25] In effect, dresses were really financed more by the lost savings of contractors, unpaid indebtedness to workers, and many defaults to landlords and power companies than by any kind of planned or dynamic accumulation.[26]

The rise of the jobbing system represented an increasing fragmentation of industrial production at a time when other industries were moving rapidly towards increasing integration and concentration. The loss of direct control over markets, product design and levels of output deprived producers of important stimulants to technical change, contributing instead to delays in further development.

The fact that the industry became vulnerable to this form of reorganisation is itself a mark of the limits to growth inherent in the preceding generations of technical change. It had not been conducive to the amalgamation of smaller firms into larger units or to heavy investment in dedicated machinery to produce high volume output of standardised goods. Its taking instead what appears as a retrograde step also points to the continuing co-existence of variable modes of production within an economy moving increasingly towards mass production technologies.

The specific path that mechanisation took in this industry preserved the possibility (and hence embodied a preference) for the traditional made-to-measure product over a machine-made one. This led to a potentially open-ended system of product differentiation. As a strategy to widen markets, it would not be more different from the market widening consequences of mass-production which were based on very large-scale output of a very limited number of products. The women's clothing industry could not achieve these economies of scale and so pursued a form of market fragmentation as a means of increasing the volume of sales.

THE HIGH FASHION HOUSE

The haute couture end of the market producing the most expensive dresses depended for its survival on the notion of exclusiveness, i.e., on the preservation of the privileged relationship between a bespoke tailor and his or her client. Dresses were presented as one-off style 'creations' that enhanced the originality and individuality of the consumer in a world of increasingly mass-produced goods.

The survival of this pre-industrial service relationship kept alive its desirablity; it had a profound impact on the imagery of advertising which sought to play down if not conceal entirely the contribution of machinery to the production of clothing while emphasising the individuality of the product. At a time when the superiority of factory over hand-made goods had been decisively established for many other garments purchased by women (stockings, brassières, trousers, etc.), a lingering preference for the designer original dress was propped up and encouraged by the fashion houses.

In France, the home of haute couture, the image of the hand-sewn designer dress was almost literally true. In many fashion establishments, the only machinery ever used was the simple sewing machine. Yet many firms grew to an astonishing size. The House of Chanel employed over two thousand people in twenty-six workrooms, each presided over by its own 'première', in charge of the sketching and sewing of his or her own staff.[27] These firms pushed the co-ordination of craft work to its limits, mimicking the growing concentration occurring in factory production at the same time but without achieving any of its economies of scale or increases in productivity. They were modern only by virtue of their scale and marketing sophistication but the increased visibility they gained from these attributes conferred a renewed legitimacy on their mode of production which percolated down through all price categories of dress production.

Paradoxically, it was inter-war improvements in air transport and mass communications (giving such a boost to other consumer industries) that enabled French couture (and the attitudes it embodied) to be transplanted to the United States. The practice of presenting the latest Paris and Italian fashions to American buyers was introduced on an experimental basis in the 1930s and had become an established promotional device ten years later.[28]

Their arrival in the United States coincided with the introduction of 'line-for-line' copies,[29] i.e., designer models sold to department store buyers for the explicit purpose of copying. These were often sold at twice the price charged to private clients. They were then reproduced for sale in large numbers at a fraction of their couturier price. In this way, couturier fashion has had a profound effect on both the demand for and supply of dresses. It forces the dressmaking industry to adapt hand-sewn garments to machine production, i.e., to mimic the very techniques of manufacture it was designed to replace. This inhibits the reverse process, in which the capacity of machinery is pushed to the limits to open up possibilities for technical innovation. The dominance of couturier design, therefore, can be viewed as perpetuating a retrograde orientation in production which permeated all layers of dressmaking. (Yet see Valerie Steele's article in this volume, which suggests that Chanel's designs did contain the potential for a mass produced style.)

WIDENING DIFFERENTIATION

The general tendency towards product differentiation in clothing became more marked during the post-war period, taking new forms which were quickly adopted as standard features. A few of these are briefly described below (large-scale, made-to-measure outlets, special order firms, price lines and the substitution of 'little ticket' for 'big ticket' items). Almost all of them left the basic productive techniques unchallenged and unchanged. The persistence of static and inefficient production methods was to some extent disguised by significant cost reductions that were achieved during the same period in the manufacture of women's clothes, particularly dresses. These were due to external factors, such as the introduction of versatile yet cheap new fabrics, rather than to any changes in the production process itself.

THE DOMINANCE OF THE MADE-TO-MEASURE ETHOS

In the 1920s the jobbing/contracting system placed a premium on the rapid and repeated turnover of stock, reinforcing a demand that was increasingly fragmented and less and less tied to traditional seasonal buying habits. With decentralised production under the thumb of an increasingly centralised marketing network, it became both possible and necessary to extend markets by massive differentiation of the garments on offer. The organisation of the industry, with its proliferation of specialist operators each perpetuating a single tailoring skill, made this approach still feasible.

It is hard to over-estimate the extent to which manufacturers went during this period to minimise risks by extending their markets at the margin of production. A firm with an output of 400,000 suits a year produced them in average lot sizes of twelve.[30] (Astonishingly, many lots were as small as three or four.) Although over 90 per cent of sales were based on variations of just eleven basic models, fear of losing ground to competitors prompted this manufacturer to 'conduct a ready-to-wear business almost on a make-to-measure basis'.[31] Essentially, the strategy pursued was to make up suits only in response to orders, what was then called a 'sell-then-make' policy.

The practice had a predictably destabilising effect on attempts to introduce – and sustain – rational production processes or long-range planning. The organisation of production – which still required from 80 to 150 separate operations to make a sack coat – continued to be dominated by an implied preference for the made-to-measure over the mass-produced garment. The constant switching of styles and fabrics (to which the flexible sewing machine readily lent itself) created havoc on the shop floor with some operators absurdly overworked and others kept idle or waiting for their next piece of work.

Despite these drawbacks, the dressmaking business did offer the possibility of considerable profits. Dress firms, on average, turned over their capital seven or eight times a year.[32] Occasionally a firm offering a particularly 'hot' style could reap windfall profits over a very short period. But investment remained pitched to the short term; capital was almost universally financed by credit rather than by retained earnings. Under these conditions, long-term planning was impossible.

SPECIAL ORDER FIRMS

The emergence of special order firms represents an attempt to stabilise production in some firms by hiving off the highest-risk elements of demand, i.e., those catering to late-flowering elements of consumer preferences. It represented an attempt to push out the limits of the market, by extending differentiation at the margin.

Special order firms were offered impossible deadlines at very short notice one month and the next would find no work at all. Given the feast or famine framework in which these firms operated, it was inevitable that wage payments would continue to depend on piece rates, i.e., that attempts to win a weekly wage would fail.

In the ready-to-wear branch of the industry in Chicago over the period 1923–1930, the minimum payroll, i.e., for the least active week of the seasonal cycle, reached 48 per cent of the payroll for the maximum week while in the special order branch it was only 25 per cent.[33] In other words, wages associated with peak activity in the special order branch were four times higher than payments made during periods of slack compared with wages in the ready-to-wear branch that were, at their peak, just double those achieved at the slowest point in the seasonal cycle. This points to a great deal of idle capacity combined with high overheads which of course must be carried over the full year.

Special order firms or special order departments within retailing outlets persisted well into the second half of the twentieth century. The English firm of Montague Burton specialised in made-to-measure men's suits on a massive scale. Set up in Sheffield in 1900 as retail clothiers, at their peak in 1950 they were responsible for providing employment for more than 100,000 people.[34] The Bergdorf Goodman store in New York City did not abandon its custom operations until 1969, after seventy years of continuous operation.[35]

PRICE LINES

Another important strategy for diffusing risk was the introduction of price lines. Widely adopted in the dressmaking branch of the industry, this practice segmented the market for dresses into rigid price categories which allowed for a varying proportion of skilled labour to be applied to similar styles and fabrics, according to circumstances.

'Price lining' led to a reversal of the usual relationship between cost and price in which the former, under conditions of competition, determind the latter. Under 'price lining', dresses could be 'built' up or down by manufacturers to given price categories, thereby squeezing the gross margin of retailers.[36] Retailers meanwhile benefited from price lines because the practice allowed them to carry smaller stocks in each category which could be turned over faster. However, while serving to limit risk to both manufacturer and retailer, this practice acted as a further disincentive to both cheapening and standardising production.

THE EMERGENCE OF THE 'LITTLE TICKET' ITEM

Another change which encouraged a higher rate of turnover in apparel stocks was the gradual emergence of 'separates'. Ready-made suits and dresses had traditionally been thought of as major purchases, like many other consumer durables. They involved a major outlay and were expected to be used over several seasons, if not years. The 1920s eroded this approach to clothing, encouraging the idea of obsolescence in fashion and design. Manufacturers had been left with unused capacity in a depression which followed a sudden surge in demand in the immediate post-war period.

They turned to the production of separates, promoting the substitution of jackets and trousers for suits, and sweaters and skirts for dresses. Each of these so-called 'little ticket' items was cheaper to produce – and to buy – than the 'big ticket' item which it replaced. Wardrobes could be infinitely extended by the incremental addition or substitution of relatively inexpensive individual garments. Items which quickly became unfashionable could be discarded without guilt. Small-scale clothing purchases could be made continuously.

By this means, clothing was transformed from a consumer durable to a non-durable good. The changeover was accompanied by yet another form of differentiation, an emphasis on the versatility of separates. An article in the *Atlantic Monthly* (1953) cites their ability to provide 'a greater variety of effects for a given outlay. For instance, three skirts and three blouses, waists or sweaters are capable of nine different combinations, whereas three dresses are still only three dresses.'[37] Between 1929 and 1950, the number of dresses as a proportion of the total production of women's 'outwear' garments declined from 86.9 per cent to 53.1 per cent, while the share of blouses and skirts over the same period rose from 2.7 per cent to 37.9 per cent.[38] The switch to co-ordinates pushed up the total volume of purchases at the expense of individual profit margins which declined. It also to some extent further facilitated deskilling, as the subdivision of outfits into their separate components led to a subdivision of the tasks involved in their manufacture. It did not, however, generate any significant changes in production techniques.

THE INTRODUCTION OF NEW FABRICS

The failure to adopt mass-production techniques in dressmaking was masked to some extent by significant advances in the production of textiles, the raw materials of clothing. In the strongest possible contrast to the apparel industry, textiles – having got off to an early start – showed all the classic features of mass production. The industry was heavily capitalised, highly concentrated and operated large-scale production units. By 1918, it was surpassed only by the iron and steel industry in the total volume of capital invested.[39]

Particularly important for the dressmaking trade was the emergence and rapid diffusion of synthetic materials, especially rayon. Introduced in Britain at the end of the nineteenth century, rayon was first known and worked as 'artificial silk'. At the beginning of the 1920s, top quality rayon cost $2.80 a pound compared with $8.65 for raw silk.[40] Over the next two decades, its price fell dramatically. By 1940, an improved rayon cost just 53 cents a pound. Consumption in that year was twelve times higher than it had been in 1923.

The take-up of rayon enabled the dressmaking industry to reduce the prices of finished products without having to undergo any changes in technology or organisation. Furthermore, the improved rayon of the 1940s allowed for widening of the market for the cheapest grade of dress, which now was able to reproduce on a larger scale styles of dress traditionally made in small batches of more expensive fabrics. Since the greatest scope for standardisation already lay at the bottom end of the market where skilled labour and design costs were minimised (in the so-called 'dozen-priced' dress category), the introduction of rayon in effect facilitated a quantum leap in the production of mass-produced garments.

THE DECLINE OF THE NEW YORK GARMENT INDUSTRY

The rise of the cheap dress corresponds with and was in large measure responsible for triggering the decline of the specialised industrial district that was the New York City garment centre. The increasing substitution of unskilled for skilled machine operators, which accompanied the spread of synthetic fibres and the development of improved freight transport, enabled manufacturers to relocate outside New York City, in areas of cheap labour, beyond the grip of the city's high wages and closed shops.

The nub of the industry left behind continued to depend upon the same organisation and technical base established generations earlier. It made a virtue of necessity by concentrating increasingly on the margin of markets, increasing differentiation of products as it has decreased their volume of production. Rather than cheapening its products, it has turned more to the custom-made end of the spectrum, relying more heavily on those aspects of design which increase the cost differentials between its own products and those mass-produced in the hinterlands. It has then exploited this reputation by using its top-of-the-line activity (which is largely unprofitable for most firms) as a loss leader for designer brand, ready-to-wear price lines pitched to lower income groups.

Taking the long view, it is clear that differentiation in apparel has been incontrovertibly – and almost uninterruptedly – the norm, from the days when all clothing was hand-made. The mechanisation of tailoring skills did not replace this attribute of clothing with an alternative idea of apparel as a consumer durable designed to be worn until literally worn out. Instead, it preserved the possibility for a high turnover of an unlimited elaboration of styles. Constant renewal of designs substituted for high levels of output. The industrial organisation that emerged in the dressmaking sector exploited this open-endedness, first by continuously maintaining a large and constantly shifting pool of compliant and competing small-scale contractors, and secondly by rooting transactions and market strategies exclusively in the short term. In this way, dresses came to be marketed more like perishables, 'like milk that spoils and citrus fruits that decay'.[41]

Finally, this active strategy for survival was recast as a passive response to changes in consumer demand. The fickle consumer, and by extension, the retailer, were charged with responsibility for encouraging the increased differentiation and turnover in fashion goods. Set against this tradition, the longevity of truly popular garments like Levi 501 jeans bedevils the industry – and contradicts the classic 'consumptionist' explanations from Veblen onwards – because it suggests an underlying receptivity to genuinely mass-produced clothing that contradicts what has been accepted as orthodox behaviour. Indeed, outside the dressmaking sector, it is possible to discern a clear development in the mass-production of clothing growing out of ready-to-wear markets for simple goods selling at modest prices. Levi 501s embody the dynamics of this opposing tradition which is based on a widening of markets through a trickling *up* of demand for machine-made garments with their distinct qualities. This contradicts the tradition discussed here of a 'fashion system' which takes the hand-sewn product as the ideal form and which tolerates the sewing machine because it allows the original to trickle *down* in cheapened form into more profitable volume production.

Notes and References

I should like to thank Ben Fine for his help and the Leverhulme Foundation for their support.

1 *Working Party Report on the Light Clothing Industry*, HMSO, London, 1947, Chapter 6, pp. 25–8, and Appendix I, pp. 87–99.

2 The descriptive history of costume is exemplified by the many volumes of Phyllis and Cecil Willett Cunnington. The works of René König and James Laver among many others offer psychological explanations for changes in taste. More recent writers have moved towards an analysis of the social construction of fashion in the context of economic and cultural change. See particularly, Elizabeth Wilson and Lou Taylor, *Through the Looking Glass*, London, 1989.

3 *Advertising Age*, 12 July 1937, pp. 14–15, quoted in Roland Marchand, *Advertising the American Dream: Making Way for Modernity, 1920–1940*, Berkeley, 1985, p. 162.

4 Quoted in Louis Levine, *Women's Garment Workers: A History of the International Ladies' Garment Workers' Union*, New York, 1924, p. 382.

ELLEN LEOPOLD

5 Alison Beazley, 'The "Heavy" and "Light" Clothing Industries 1850–1920', *Costume*, vol. VII, 1973, p. 56.

6 Ibid.

7 Roy Helfgott, *Made in New York: Case Studies in Metropolitan Manufacturing*, ed. Max Hall, Cambridge, Mass., 1959, p. 54. The idea that the 1920s witnessed 'the birth of the idea of clothing obsolescence' is also put forward in Claudia B. Kidwell and M.C. Christman, *Suiting Everyone: The Democratization of Clothing in America*, 1974. Though the history of dressmaking in Britain closely parallels the US experience in most important respects, the United States was the source of most technical innovation that occurred during this period. Factory production of dresses in Britain lagged behind its US counterpart, dating from about 1930 (Margaret Wray, *The Women's Outerwear Industry*, London, 1957, p. 41).

8 David Gartman, 'Origins of the Assembly Line and Capitalist Control of Work at Ford', in *Case Studies on the Labor Process*, ed. Andrew Zimbalist, *Monthly Review Press*, p. 192.

9 Robert James Myers, 'The Economic Aspects of the Production of Men's Clothing (with particular reference to the industry in Chicago)', part of a PhD dissertation submitted to the Department of Economics, University of Chicago Libraries, Chicago, 1937, p. 43. Subsequent slackening of demand and further productivity gains *did* push out large numbers of mostly male workers from the industry.

10 O.E. Schoeffler and W. Gale, *Esquire's Encyclopaedia of 20th Century Men's Fashions*, 1973, p. 512.

11 The earliest sewing machines could sew 800 to 900 stitches per minute. The application of electric power increased their speeds to between 2,000 and 4,000 stitches per minute. (Helfgott, op. cit., p. 38.)

12 Kidwell and Christman, op. cit., p. 81.

13 Levine, op. cit., p. 11.

14 Louise Lamphere, 'Fighting the Piece-Rate System', in *Case Studies on the Labor Process*, op. cit.

15 Ava Baron and Susan E. Clepp, 'If I didn't have my sewing machine . . . Women and Sewing-machine Technology', in J.M. Jensen and Sue Davidson (eds), *A Needle, A Bobbin, a Strike: Women Needleworkers in America*, 1984, p. 37.

16 See Margaret L. Brew, *American Clothing Consumption 1879–1909*, University of Chicago, PhD thesis, 1948, p. 424.

17 Roger Waldinger, 'Another Look at the International Ladies' Garment Workers' Union: Women, Industry, Structure and Collective Action', in Ruth Milkman (ed.), *Women, Work and Protest*, London, 1985, p. 94.

18 In a typical, large, men's clothing factory in the mid 1930s, though fifty to seventy-five different types of sewing machine might be in use, no commonly used machine occupied more than a few square feet of space, or cost more than $1,000. Up to three hundred different operatives might be employed in the production of a single suit. Myers op. cit., p. 12.

19 Helen E. Meiklejohn, *Dresses – The Impact on a Business*, New York, 1938, p. 316.

20 Nathan Belfer, 'Section work in the women's garment industry', *Southern Economic Journal*, October 1954, vol. XXI, no. 2, p. 188.

21 Ibid, p. 191.

22 As late as 1950, just 1 per cent of workers and less than 1 per cent of shops in the women's dress, coat and suit industry in Manhattan worked on a section work basis. Ibid, p. 192.

23 This phrase is echoed today by Benetton's 'sell-then-make' strategy, a variant on the more general 'just-in-time' system that seeks to reduce

inventories by closing the gap between demand and supply.

24 Meiklejohn, p. 324; and Roger Waldinger in Milkman, op. cit., p. 103. Fifteen years later, in 1954, it was still possible to start up a dress or blouse firm in New York for as little as $15,000 in capital. (Helfgott op. cit., p. 30.)

25 Michael J. Piore and Charles F. Sabel, *The Second Industrial Divide*, New York, 1984, p. 29, referring to clothing workers in Italy.

26 Meiklejohn, op. cit., p. 351.

27 Barbara Yu, 'The Fashion Industry: A Compromised Technology', Harvard College Honors Thesis, 1978, p. 95. Even in the 1960s, the sewing machine was used to carry out just 2–3 per cent of the work in high fashion houses; it still took at least four workers 65–90 hours to make a simple dress or suit. (Bernard Roshco, *The Rag Race: How New York and Paris run the breakneck business of dressing American women*, New York 1963, p. 179.)

28 Roshco, op. cit., p. 153.

29 Ibid, p. 153. The phrase 'line-for-line' is attributed to Macy's department store in New York City.

30 The Committee on Elimination of Waste in Industry of the Federated American Engineering Societies, *Waste in Industry*, 1921, p. 96.

31 Ibid., p. 96.

32 Helfgott, op. cit., p. 31.

33 Myers, op. cit., p. 21.

34 K. Mudron, *The Archaeology of the Consumer Society*, 1983, p. 68.

35 Jeanette A. Jarnow, Beatrice Judelle and Miriam Guerreiro, *Inside the Fashion Business: Texts and Readings*, New York, 1981, p. 279.

36 Meiklejohn, op. cit., p. 380.

37 Fessenden Blanchard, 'Revolution in Clothes', *Harper's Monthly*, March 1953, p. 60.

38 Market Planning Service, division of National Credit Office Inc., *The Apparel Manufacturing Industry*, New York, 1952, p. 12.

39 The Committee on Elimination of Waste in Industry, op. cit., p. 240.

40 Drake and Glasser, op. cit., p. 78.

41 Meiklejohn, op. cit., p. 325.

VALERIE STEELE

Chanel in Context

Gabrielle 'Coco' Chanel is the most famous woman in the history of fashion, and one might legitimately wonder whether there is anything new to be said about her. Yet, ironically, the myths surrounding Chanel have actually concealed her true significance.

Chanel herself was responsible for much of the mythology that surrounds her life and career, since, in the course of her long life, she 'wove such an elaborate tissue of lies about herself . . . that hard facts are . . . hard to come by'.[1] As a result, much of the enormous body of literature about Chanel more closely resembles hagiography than history. Even when scholars have attempted to separate fact from fiction, their essentially biographical approach has limited the nature of their inquiry. By placing Chanel back in her historical context, however, we may obtain a more accurate picture of her contributions to modern fashion.

The popular image of Chanel is of a unique genius who created her personal style in isolation from the work of other fashion designers. Yet style is a social phenomenon, not merely a reflection of the individual creator's personality. Even stylistic innovations occur within a particular cultural context: a fashion that bore no relation to the other fashions of the day could hardly be influential.

Clearly, we cannot simply take Chanel's word that she originated all the important new sartorial ideas of the twentieth century. We need to compare her life and work with the lives and work of her contemporaries.

Chanel was born in 1883. At this period in French history, an army of women worked in the needle trades, and it would have been quite normal for a working-class girl like Gabrielle to become a seamstress. Her contemporary, Madeleine Vionnet, for example, was apprenticed at the age of 11 to a dressmaker, gradually working her way up, until she opened her own couture house in 1912.

By contrast, Chanel had an abortive career as a café singer, during which time she seems to have adopted the vulgar nickname 'Coco'. It was a milieu in which prostitution was common, and Chanel always drew a veil over this part of her life, admitting only that she became the mistress of at least two wealthy men. But Chanel's early years as a *demi-mondaine* were crucial to the development of her style.

Courtesans and actresses were among the most fashionable women of the *belle époque*. Vionnet's most avant-garde, corsetless dresses were popular with just such a clientele. Unconstrained by issues of modesty or propriety, perhaps also motivated by hostility towards the established order, they pioneered the newest styles. Sometimes they even broke the taboo against women wearing trousers. Chanel, too, was a fashion iconoclast. But rather than dressing in the ultra-feminine clothing that most courtesans favoured, she created her own personal style, based on the attire of her male protectors. [2]

'Chanel always dressed like the strong independent male she had dreamed of being.' [3] So Chanel told Salvador Dali, and although both of them frequently fabricated stories, this has the ring of truth. Of course, tailored suits with skirts were already an accepted fashion when Chanel was still a child, especially among English and American women. But Chanel was no middle-class feminist in a man-tailored business suit. When Chanel 'took the English masculine and made it feminine', she did so in the spirit of a female dandy.

Dandyism is 'a cult of the self', wrote the poet Charles Baudelaire. The dandy is 'in love with *distinction* above all things [and] the perfection of his toilet will consist in absolute simplicity', which is symbolic of his 'aristocratic superiority of mind'. All this is very much in accordance with Chanel's philosophy of style, which had little to do with functional dressing for work and everything to do with the symbolic power associated with, for example, black clothing and upper-class male sportswear.

As yet, however, Chanel was still only a kept woman with a certain style. Her career in the world of fashion began in 1910, when she convinced two of her lovers to set her up in business – as a milliner, and then also as a sportswear designer with boutiques in Deauville (1913) and Biarritz (1916).

In the *belle époque* it was almost a cliché for a man to set up his mistress in the hat business, so that she would be financially independent when he tired of her. The caricaturist Sem depicted Chanel holding a giant hatbox and clinging to the neck of a horse ridden by her polo-playing lover, 'Boy' Capel. Chanel herself once told Dali, 'I was able to open a high fashion shop, because two gentlemen were outbidding each other for my hot little body.' [4]

Professional dressmakers like Vionnet dismissed Chanel as merely a milliner, but Chanel's early sportswear designs were genuinely innovative, often made of jersey, with relatively short skirts and no armature of corsetry. Nevertheless, fashion historians who exaggerate Chanel's role conveniently forget that Paul Poiret rejected corsetry, slashed skirts and even pioneered the idea of trousers for women several years before Chanel began working.

Vionnet also claimed that she had abolished the corset as early as 1907: 'I have never been able to tolerate corsets myself', she recalled. 'Why should I have inflicted them on other women? Le corset, c'est un chose orthopédique.'[5] No one person, of course, was responsible for abolishing the corset. But it is significant that the period from about 1906 to 1916 was characterised by such radical experiments in dress and behaviour as to constitute a true fashion revolution.

In the early years of her career, Chanel knew little about the technical aspects of dressmaking (and relied heavily on her ill-paid *premières*). But her strengths lay elsewhere: in concept and image. She designed radically simple sportswear priced extremely high: as much as 7,000 francs for a dress in 1915 – approximately £1,000 in today's currency, and far more than most couturiers of her time charged. The second important point to note is that, although Chanel was not yet famous as a designer (her name was misspelled, for example, in *Les Elégances Parisiennes* in 1917), she was already well-known as a fashionable personality: a woman of style. The fact that she was her own best model would prove extremely important for her subsequent career.

Fashion histories give the impression that Chanel single-handedly invented the style of the 1920s. But if one actually looks through the pages of fashion magazines from the 1920s, it is clear that *many* designers, both male and female, were creating simple, comfortable clothes. Indeed, it is virtually impossible to identify which clothes were designed by Chanel without reading the captions under the fashion illustrations.

Jean Patou, for example, designed sportswear that was every bit as streamlined and modern as Chanel's. But Patou had the misfortune to die early, whereas Chanel lived to tell generations of journalists that she alone was responsible for putting women in skirts and sweaters. Moreover, he was a man, and this was not necessarily an advantage in the 1920s, as we shall see.

The well-known tennis player Jane Régny also specialised in designing fashions for sport and travel, receiving much attention in the fashion press of the 1920s. As one shopping guide of the period put it: 'Jane . . . saw the inevitable conquest of her world by the new idea of sports for women, of a freer life, with different demands on the couturiers.'[6] Even Jeanne Lanvin, who was most famous for her pretty mother/daughter dresses, also designed frocks for flappers.

Chanel's *image* as a modern woman has strongly influenced our perception of her contribution to fashion. Jeanne Lanvin was 'a great great designer', says Karl Lagerfeld, but she has been neglected by posterity, because by the 1920s she was 'a nice old lady' – not a fashion personality like Chanel.[7] A working-class woman who began as a milliner and founded a great couture house all by herself, Lanvin was certainly as independent as Chanel. Yet even apart from

her age, Lanvin's public image focused on 'the miracle of maternal love'[8] – and this has not appealed to subsequent generations.

Because Chanel seems to epitomise the liberated woman of the 1920s, it is easy to think of her 'liberating the leg'. And, indeed, as British *Vogue* noted in 1923, 'The very short skirt at once suggests that the lady is dressed by Chanel who makes all her skirts short, whether for morning, afternoon or evening.'[9] We need to remind ourselves, however, that almost everyone raised hemlines in the 1920s, and there is no evidence that they were simply copying Chanel – who did not become really famous *as a designer* until the mid 1920s.

Everyone today knows about Chanel's little black dress, which in 1926 *Vogue* described as 'a fashion Ford'. But others were also thinking along the same lines. In 1922, for example, 'Premet's designer' (unnamed, but statistically probably female) 'turned out a plain boyish-looking little slip of a frock – black satin with white collar and cuffs'. Named 'La Garçonne' after the best-selling novel, the dress apparently achieved 'the most sensational success reached by any individual dress model of recent years . . . counting both licenced and illegitimate reproduction, a million Garçonnes were sold over the earth'.[10]

The boyish look would almost certainly have been fashionable even had Chanel never been born. Similarly, the idea that 'less is more', and that ornamentation was unnecessary and even ugly, affected all the decorative arts, not only fashion. In this sense, Chanel was typical of the entire modernist movement. To the extent that she stands out, it is because she most successfully synthesised, publicised and epitomised a look that many other people also developed.

At the time Chanel was born, male couturiers, like Charles Frederick Worth, had only recently invaded the feminine realm of fashion and begun to transform the couture from a craft into high art and big business. Although women continued to form the overwhelming majority of fashion workers, in the new climate of opinion it was widely believed that men were, by nature, *creators*, while women were merely *technicians* who performed the necessary but mundane tasks associated with transforming the ideas of the male genius into actual clothes.

But by the time Chanel opened her shop in Deauville in 1913, women designers had made a remarkable come-back and were competing successfully with their male counterparts. Mme Jeanne Paquin, for example, employed more than a thousand workers, and was widely regarded as the world's greatest fashion authority – at least until she was thrown into the shade by Poiret. After the First World War, when Chanel opened her *maison de couture* in Paris, women once again dominated the world of fashion.

Indeed, the period 'between Poiret's harem and Dior's New Look' – roughly the period between the First and Second World Wars – might be called 'the golden age of the couturière'.[11] In addition to Chanel, the leading couturières included: Alix (later known as Mme Grès), Augustabernard, the Callot Sisters, Mme Chéruit, Sonia Delaunay, Nicole Groult (Poiret's younger sister), Mme Jenny, Jeanne Lanvin, Louiseboulanger, Lucile Paray, Madeleine de Rauch, Jane Régny, Nina Ricci, Elsa Schiaparelli, the incomparable Madeleine Vionnet, and many more.

Naturally, there were male designers too in the years between the wars, but 'the excitement lay among the regiment of women'.[12] Jean Patou told *Harper's Bazaar* that *he* did not believe that to be a woman was 'an advantage for a dressmaker', because she would only design for herself.[13] But many other people apparently assumed that female designers (from Jane Régny to Chanel) were more in touch with the changing needs of the modern woman.

The *femmes créatrices* of the 1920s came from a wide range of social origins and professional backgrounds. Whereas women like Vionnet had followed the traditional path from *arpète* to *première* to independent *couturière*, both Chanel and Lanvin were representative of women whose career showed a spectacular rise. For the first time middle-class women began entering the workforce in great numbers. Not surprisingly, they often gravitated towards traditionally 'feminine' fields such as fashion.[14]

Germaine Barton, for example, came from a typical bourgeois Parisian family; her parents were horrified that she wanted to become a sculptor, but they reluctantly permitted her to study fashion. As Alix Grès she became famous for the sculptural beauty of her evening gowns. Even upper-class women, such as the Roman divorcee Schiaparelli, entered the fashion business, hitherto despised as 'trade', but now in the process of being redefined as 'artistic' and even fashionable. Indeed, the first of many 'socialite' designers appeared at this time.

Chanel, though, was the woman that other women wanted to look like. In this sense, she represented the *new type* of fashion designer, who combined in her person the hitherto masculine role of the fashion 'genius' with the feminine role of fashion leader (not the dressmaker, but the celebrity). Vionnet always denied that a clever man like Poiret or a stylish woman like Chanel could ever equal professional dressmakers like the Callot Sisters, and in technical terms this was probably true. But in terms of mass popularity, it was irrelevant.

As the 1920s gave way to the 1930s, however, Chanel entered something of a creative slump. Photographs of Chanel *herself* show the continued development of a striking dandiacal persona: we see her in a crisp navy blue suit edged in white, or in a chic black dress covered in real and costume jewellery. But photographs of

Coco Chanel in one of her own suits, 1929 (courtesy of the Hulton Picture Library)

124

VALERIE STEELE

her clothes in the fashion magazines of the day show more conventional long evening dresses, even tea-gowns. The fashion press increasingly extolled the amusing Surrealist designs of Elsa Schiaparelli, whom Chanel angrily described as 'that Italian artist who makes clothes'.

Meanwhile, the lingering effects of the Depression pushed many designers out of business. Even a major figure like Vionnet was in 1938 'making only half the number of dresses she had been making ten years earlier'.[15] The outbreak of the Second World War, followed by the German occupation of Paris, further damaged the French fashion industry (see Lou Taylor's article in this volume). In 1939 Chanel closed her couture house. So did Vionnet. Schiaparelli fled to America. The golden age of the couturière was over.

If Chanel's career had ended then, she would probably be remembered now only as one of the many women designers who flourished in the period between the wars. That Chanel was able to begin again in 1954, at the age of 70, and make a success of it, was something of a miracle.

It was the era of the New Look, and the new generation of Parisian couturiers was overwhelmingly male: Dior, Balenciaga, Fath. The reasons for this are complex, involving both social attitudes, which once again favoured the male 'genius', and a new economic environment. Haute couture had evolved from

Chanel evening dress from L'Art et La Mode, *1939 (courtesy of Archives Hachette)*

the atelier to the global corporate conglomerate, and Chanel was one of the few women with access to substantial financial backing, based on the profits from Chanel perfumes. (Almost the only other woman to reopen her couture house after the Second World War was Alix Grès.)

In the 1920s Chanel had epitomised the modern woman, and her image, although tarnished in France (because of her collaboration with the Nazis), remained strong among Americans. In 1954 when French and English periodicals laughed at Chanel, American *Vogue* proudly presented 'the story of the original Chanel Look'.[16] Not coincidentally, many American women were uneasy with the rapid changes in post-war fashion, and Chanel's little tailored suit offered an acceptably Parisian alternative to the confusing array of new lines. Moreover, Chanel herself seemed to provide an alternative – female – model of the fashion 'genius'.

'Ah, no, definitely no, men were not meant to design for women', Chanel insisted. 'Men make dresses in which one can't move.'[17] Accustomed to a pre-war fashion world populated largely by women (most of whom, admittedly, she detested), Chanel now saw the propaganda value of proclaiming herself as the one woman in a fashion world increasingly populated by men. Her genius, she implied, was to liberate women.

All the vicissitudes of her career were glossed over in the creation of an ahistorical – mythic – unity: if she was the single most important woman designer of the 1950s, then she must *always* have been the one great woman designer; if Chanel Number 5 was a best-selling perfume now, then it must have been the *first* designer perfume, and so on. The Chanel suit of the 1950s was significantly different from the ones she had designed in the 1920s and 1930s, but she pretended that it had always looked that way.

As her contemporaries gradually died, young journalists credulously repeated Chanel's most self-serving anecdotes. Moreover, each successive generation reinterpreted her (heavily fictionalised) life story: in the 1950s and early 1960s it was the romantic story of a 'fiery peasant girl' and her lovers that caught the popular imagination, while in the 1970s and 1980s she was reincarnated as a feminist heroine.

Yet Chanel did not 'invent' the little black dress, designer perfume, costume jewellery, trousers for women, and the myriad other fashion items for which she has received credit. Indeed, to focus on such phenomena trivialises her true significance, which involves an *attitude* towards style.

Chanel's attitude was always complex and she related dress to the circumstances in which it was to be worn. Hers was very much a woman's style, for example, but it was based in large part on a masculine model of power and freedom. In the 1920s, although not necessarily the first or the greatest influence on fashion, Chanel epitomised the modernist aesthetic, which was defined in opposition to the past. In the 1950s Chanel was no longer on the cutting edge of fashion, but she seemed to provide an alternative to fashion's relentless juggernaut – timeless style versus trendy fashion. Again, she was in opposition, both to the dominant look in women's clothes and to male fashion dominance in the couture.

In the context of today's fashion world, it is surely significant that many, very different designers admire Chanel. For Vivienne Westwood, Chanel was an iconoclast, even a 'street fashion designer'. It is the early, avant-garde Chanel who inspires Westwood. By contrast, the relatively conservative designer, Carolyne Roehm, admires Chanel's classicism, which she contrasts to Schiaparelli's outrageous antics. Karl Lagerfeld, of course, has combined elements from both Chanel and Schiaparelli in his 'postmodernist' interpretation of the Chanel look.[18] It is perhaps this subversive ambiguity which has continued to inspire her many admirers over the years.

Notes and References

1 Ernestine Carter, *Magic Names of Fashion*, Englewood Cliffs, New Jersey, 1980, p. 54.

2 Caroline Evans and Minna Thorton have a fascinating chapter on 'Chanel: The New Woman as Dandy' in their book, *Women and Fashion: A New Look*, London and New York, 1989.

3 Salvador Dali as told to André Parinaud, *The Unspeakable Confessions of Salvador Dali*, New York, 1981, p. 212.

4 Quoted in Salvador Dali, op. cit., p. 211.

5 Quoted in Bruce Chatwin, *What Am I Doing Here?*, New York, 1989, p. 89.

6 Thérèse and Louise Bonney, *A Shopping Guide to Paris*, New York, 1929, pp. 29-30.

7 Quoted in *Chanel, Chanel*, a film by Eila Hershon and Roberto Guerra, RM Arts, 1986.

8 *Le Pavillon de l'Elégance.* A special issue of the *Gazette du Bon Ton*, 1925.

9 Georgina Howell, *In Vogue: Sixty years of international celebrities and fashion from British Vogue*, New York, 1976, p. 45.

10 Robert Forrest Wilson, *Paris on Parade*, Indianapolis, 1924, second edition 1925, p. 53.

11 Cecil Beaton, *The Glass of Fashion*, London, 1954.

12 H. W. Yoxall, *A Fashion of Life*, New York, 1967, p. 57.

13 Quoted in Meredith Etherington-Smith, *Patou*, New York, 1983, pp. 71-2.

14 See the catalogue *Femmes créatrices des années vingts* for the exhibition of the same name at the Musée Richard-Anacréon Grandville, Paris, 1988.

15 Madeleine Ginsburg, 'The Thirties', in Ruth Lynam (ed.), *Couture: An Illustrated History of the Great Paris Designers and Their Creations*, Garden City, New York, 1972, p. 93.

16 American *Vogue*, 15 February 1954.

17 Quoted in Frances Kennett, *Secrets of the Couturiers*, p. 57.

18 See Valerie Steele, *Women of Fashion*, New York, 1991, for more on contemporary reactions to Chanel.

Paris Couture 1940–1944

The Occupation of Paris in June 1940 brought the whole giant international fashion system to its knees – a crisis which lasted until 1946–7. In France haute couture and the work of the Chambre Syndicale de la Couture Parisienne was considered the lifeblood of the country: in 1938 the French clothing industry's turnover was 25 billion francs.[1] Paris was home to an international mixture of couture talent, which included Schiaparelli from Italy, Molyneux from Britain and Mainbocher from the United States. Balenciaga, who opened his salon in 1938, was Spanish. New, home-grown talent emerged with the work of Marcel Rochas, Balenciaga and Jacques Fath. The financial empires of long-established salons such as those of Patou, Chanel, Vionnet and Lanvin had, by dint of careful management, recovered by the late 1930s from the shockwaves of the Wall Street crash. Although they now had a smaller private clientele, their successful wooing of foreign department stores and ready-to-wear manufacturers had once again placed the Paris fashion industry at the forefront of the French export drive. This achievement was recognised by the government which supported the couture industry in various ways.

By the late 1930s the great salons were becoming much more commercial, marketing perfumes and ranges of luxury accessories. Some of the more astute houses, such as Lelong, were already producing cheaper *prêt-a-porter* collections.[2] Increasing numbers of Paris designs were also being sold for direct copying at many different levels of quality by ready-to-wear manufacturers. So, as the Second World War approached, Paris wore the crown of fashion style leadership; with no serious contenders or rivals within sight.

When war was declared in September 1939 there was an immediate mobilisation. In Paris, trenches were dug through the Tuileries gardens and general panic set in. Many of the male couturiers were called up, but, during this *Drôle de Guerre* or 'phoney war' period, the French government, conscious of the vast sums of money and thousands of jobs dependent on the success of their collections, granted designers leave (*permission*) to return to their studios. Thus the autumn collections were nicknamed '*Les Collections des*

Permissionnaires'. They featured two distinct ranges of clothing: practical, designer, bomb shelter/cycling clothes for their regular French clientele, and the usual glamorous fashion styles for the export market, particularly for North and South America.

By the spring of 1940 the political situation had become much more critical, but somehow the shows were held, for the few foreign buyers brave enough to come to France. The elegant wife of a French fascist leader helped obtain export permits for them before it was too late. The *Vogue* photographer Durst took a series of now famous shots of models, sitting on packing cases in their couture clothes as the salons were abandoned. Alison Settle, the English fashion journalist, wrote that the buyers were keenly aware that this was likely to be their last visit to Paris for the foreseeable future.[3]

On 14 May 1940 German tanks and paratroopers swept through the 'impregnable' Maginot line and one million French officers and soldiers were taken prisoner. The terrifying, chaotic and frenzied *Exode* began, as thousands of French refugees clogged up the roads and trains, fleeing desperately in front of the advancing forces. Paris was abandoned. The government escaped to Bordeaux, burning petrol supplies and records as they left. The city was depopulated and shrouded in acrid smoke. On 14 June the first Nazi forces arrived, dressed in the smartest of uniforms to dazzle the residents.

The Nazi authorities arrived in France with a detailed plan for governmental control already drawn up. France was to be allowed to continue its basic manufacturing and agricultural industries, although both the products and the profits were thereafter destined for Germany and the Third Reich. By August 1940, they announced that all businesses in the occupied zone were to be reopened immediately, or be taken over by the Germans. By 1942 (some months later than in the 'free' Pétainist zone), anti-semitic regulations had been enforced, forbidding Jews to work in public occupations, to own businesses or to teach.[4]

The Nazis envisaged a special role for Paris. Rather than obliterate its culture they determined to take it over – to embrace the city's reputation in the arts, theatre, entertainment and tourism as their own. The provision of luxury '*articles de Paris*', amusements, and gourmet food was therefore allowed, but the Nazis intended that these should be turned to the benefit and pleasure of the Third Reich and their friends.

Haute couture fell into this category of protected luxury trades, although, as the couturiers were soon to discover, the Nazis had specific plans in mind for their future too. Along with all other major industries they were faced with the prospect of deciding their own fate. Meeting at Bordeaux, they agreed that their Chairman, Lucien Lelong, should be asked to intercede with the Nazis in an effort to salvage what they could.

Yet what place was there for luxury clothing in a conquered, demoralised, occupied and chaotic country? What role could couture play in such black times? These were the questions designers and their business backers asked themselves. Although haute couture continued to be exported to the United States until 1940 (gorgeous, camellia-laden hats from Schiaparelli),[5] it rapidly became clear that they could no longer engage with the international export market. If they were to survive at all, the couture houses would be forced to operate in a completely different way.

The Nazi leaders took a serious interest in the Paris couture trade, not surprisingly, because its long-established international reputation far surpassed that of the German fashion trade. The French had long mocked what they saw as German women's lack of style – a situation the Nazis could not allow to continue. The headquarters of the Chambre Syndicale de la Couture Parisienne were raided so that the Nazis could discover for themselves what profits might be appropriated from the trade. Lelong was summoned before the Nazi authorities and told that the Paris couture industry was to be moved to Berlin or Vienna, where the companies would continue their work under the banner, name and auspices of German fashion. Though Lelong was compelled to visit Germany, he managed to prevent the Nazis enforcing their plan.

Alison Settle discovered later that over the four years of the Occupation, Lelong had been forced to attend fourteen official conferences with the Nazi authorities.[6] They declared four times that the business was to be totally suppressed.[7] On one occasion they demanded that 80 per cent of couture staff should be re-employed in war industries. The eventual figure was 3 per cent; 12,000 employees remained in the couture trade for the war's duration.[8] Mme Grès, Balenciaga and Molyneux had their showrooms forcibly shut down, but sixty out of ninety-two houses remained open.[9] When Alison Settle arrived in August 1944, she believed that about a hundred were in operation.[10]

Every aspect of the business came under Nazi scrutiny. The Paris office of American-owned *Vogue* was raided. The journalists decided to shut the magazine down rather than operate under Nazi press censorship.[11] *Femina* was another fashion journal that closed for the same reason.[12] Other fashion magazines were less principled and continued to publish throughout the war.[13]

The first consideration for many of the designers was their staff. A couture salon can employ as many as a thousand people, from the grand *vendeuses* (saleswomen) through to the skilled tailors and midinettes. The luxury clothes trade also needed hundreds of specialised, supportive, industrial trades, crafts and artisans – embroiderers, silk, lace, wool and linen designers, manufacturers and weavers, printers, and knitters. The products and assistance of the most creative milliners, artificial flower makers, shoemakers, belt and handbag manufacturers, *corsetières* and jewellers were essential to the collection's success.

Most salons kept the same staff year after year and even generation after generation. The designers were genuinely afraid that if they closed their salons, their workers would be unable to find alternative employment, and, later in the war, might be sent as forced labour to Germany. To remain open was to keep thousands in employment – Balmain wrote that Lucien Lelong employed about four hundred staff throughout the war.[14]

With these practical considerations in mind, most of the top couturiers continued to produce luxury clothes for their clients throughout the Occupation. All foreign clients had vanished, along with many of the elegant women to be seen in pre-war Paris. Many fled south to the Mediterranean. Others sat out the war on their estates in the countryside. A few remained, but even within the quiet rooms of the salons, times were dangerous. At one show the Aryan wife of a member of the Rothschild family refused to sit next to the wife of a Nazi official, moving her seat rather ostentatiously. The next day she was sent to Ravensbruck concentration camp.[15]

The clientele who remained were an odd mixture of a few old customers, a phalanx of French movie and theatre stars and the wives of popular male stars such as Sacha Guitry. They had to obtain special permission from the Germans to purchase these clothes, over and above the usual rationing that applied to the mass of French women. According to Dominique Veillon, in 1941 a total of 20,000 women did so. For the next few years the number of German women buying French couture clothes remained at two hundred, clearly only a small percentage of clients.[16] The French called the typical German women seen in Paris at that time 'Les Souris Gris' (the grey mice) because of their dowdy clothes. Those with savoir-faire ordered their clothes under the intimidating roofs of the great salons, sitting at the collections alongside a cluster of the well-off wives and mistresses of French fascist leaders. 'Les Dames du Marché Noire', 'the black market women' (nicknamed the 'Butter, Eggs and Cheese women', or BOF – the initials of beurre, oeufs and fromage) were a completely new type of customer. They produced wads of dirty banknotes which they thrust into the hands of the vendeuses while their husbands offered the salon black market butter at the back entrance.[17] They sat awkwardly in the chic salons, showing their red knees, and Dior commented that they would be shot after the war in their little black designer robes.[18]

Lucien Lelong negotiated special concessions on yardage and fabric, more generous than the rationing endured by the general public. Compared with pre-war conditions these allowances were still restrictive but they just about allowed the couturiers to cope. They even managed to take their collections on tours, aiming to reach the dressmakers and boutique owners in the Vichy-controlled provinces, who could no longer visit Paris themselves. Madrid was another popular centre. Under the rule of Franco, fascist Spain was still an international meeting point, and the French held large trade exhibitions there, hoping to persuade international buyers to visit their collections and place orders. In 1942 the young Balmain, working for Lelong, was sent to the

Barcelona International Exhibition, though he had first to swear that he would not try to escape to London or New York.[19]

The fate of the great couturiers was as varied as their nationalities. Some took to their new customers and the social life of the new collaborationist '*Tout Paris*' with aplomb. Jacques Fath, Nina Ricci and Marcel Rochas in particular were to be seen at many social gatherings, mixing with the socialites and military in Nazi-ruled Paris. Others, like Mme Grès, whose action in opening her salon with a parade of tricolour clothes met with the fury of the German authorities, were temporarily closed down.[20] Jacques Heim, who was Jewish, went into hiding for part of the war, but managed somehow to keep his business running in Monte Carlo.[21] Molyneux returned to Britain where he chaired the Utility dress design committee whilst his Paris salon remained open. Schiaparelli fled to the United States where she raised huge sums of money for medical aid for French children. Her salon also remained open. Mainbocher was forced to abandon his rue Faubourg St Honoré establishment and to start afresh in New York. His salon in Paris never reopened. Others designers kept their doors open for the duration of the war – Lelong, Piguet, Patou, Jeanne Lanvin, Nina Ricci, Worth and Rochas.

Chanel, however, refused to run her business. She stayed in the Ritz throughout the war in the company of a handsome and well-known Nazi secret serviceman. There was nothing very surprising about this as she had always held very right-wing views. She tried to exploit anti-Jewish legislation to take her financially successful perfume business out of the hands of two Jewish brothers, the Wertmullers, who had run it for many years. With her influential British contacts (she had been the mistress of the Duke of Westminster, the richest man in Britain) she also dreamt up the idea of trying to persuade Churchill to sue for peace with Hitler.[22]

STYLE EVOLUTION

From 1940 to 1944 French couture style evolved as usual despite the extraordinary circumstances of its manufacture. Waists grew smaller and hems and hips wider and fuller, with more emphasis on drapery. Medieval, rural, peasant and classical influences were strong. Alongside these styles, the Victorian mood – so prevalent in Paris in the late 1930s – continued to inspire the couturiers, with bustle effects and fuller skirts. Shoulders remained large and very square. Hats above all became towering, extravagant and exotic.

Yet while Rochas and Fath worried about the trimmings for cocktail dresses, ordinary Frenchwomen struggled with their coupons, the black market and the severe clothing shortages to find a way to shoe and cover themselves and their families. Most knew nothing about the work of the couture houses until the Liberation.

LOU TAYLOR

By 1942 in Paris, the cycle of couture fashion change is on the move, with a more feminine line than in London – wide shoulders stay but are softened with drapery, narrow waists and fuller hem-lines (Modes et Travaux, September 1942, published in Paris, showing designs by Rauch, Maggy Rouff, Marcel Rochas, Raphael and Germaine Lecomte, author's collection)

FASHION TEXTILE DESIGN

The textile companies, like the couture houses, were all told to reopen and continue their trade, or else be taken over by the Germans. This they did, but they found the increasing shortage of imported raw materials extremely difficult to deal with. Many of their skilled technicians had gone. The fact that huge quantities of their products were shipped to Germany for the benefit of the Third Reich was another problem. Every level of their production was threatened. Anny Latour reported that the textile manufacturer Boussac 'came to a temporary agreement with the occupying authorities although production sank by 20 per cent and the Germans took another 6 per cent.'[23]

None the less, the production of luxury fashion fabrics continued. The manufacturers even produced designs of great beauty, quality and elegance. Some of the garments survive and can be seen in museum collections in France. Some of the top textile manufacturers, the Lyonnais *fabricants*, like the couturiers, felt that to stop this line of work was tantamount to giving in to the Nazis. The production of luxury fabrics was their trade and they were determined to continue.

In 1941 an exhibition was held in Paris at the Petit Palais of the newest designs in rayon fabric. Alongside a German company called 'Deutsche Zellwolle-und Kuntseide-Ring', a French textile group, 'France-Rayon', showed their newest creations. Some of these survive today in the collection of the Musée des Arts Décoratifs in Paris. The couturiers showed a collection of garments made up in rayon textiles, a fibre they had scorned before the war. Lelong showed a suit tailored in a rayon Prince of Wales check, Robert Piguet showed a coat and Anny Blatt some fine rayon lingerie. Lamé, jersey, and many new fibre mixes, such as angora or rabbit mixed with rayon, were proudly exhibited.[24] Designs often featured red, white and blue. Imagery frequently displayed the Vichy ideals of health, natural beauty and nationalism. Floral styles were particularly popular, but so too were portrayals of national heroines such as Joan of Arc.

Only once did reports and descriptions of couture clothes reach the world outside France, in 1943, when a copy of Michel de Brunhoff's luxury magazine *Album de Mode de Figaro* reached London and New York. It was a clandestine edition, produced with great risk in Monte Carlo. This fact, however, was not known abroad. Above all the sketches of the flamboyantly vulgar hats caused a scandal. *Picture Post* got hold of some sketches and published a shocked and hostile article.[25] Elsa Schiaparelli, touring the United States to raise funds for French charities, found herself in very deep and stormy waters. She tried to explain to the US press and public that these styles represented to the French women who wore them a slap in the face for the Nazis. They were, she said, a symbol of the indomitable, free and creative spirit of Paris. No matter how much the Nazis made them suffer, the jaunty hats remained a constant irritant to the Germans – or so she argued. She found few who accepted this view, either amongst her friends or in the US press.[26]

Apart from this one leak, until the summer of 1944 the couture world of Paris remained an enclosed circle of the Franco–German social, media and cultural society of the '*Tout Paris*'. The industry survived, but the much longed for Liberation was to bring deep problems too.

The Paris line of winter 1943, showing designs by Worth, Hermès, Germaine Lecomte, Alix, M. Tizeau, Marcel Rochas, Mad Carpentier and Jean Patou (courtesy of the Musée des Arts de la Mode, Palais Galliera, Paris)

THE END OF THE WAR

The first fashion reporters to arrive in Paris after the City's liberation in August 1944 were Lee Miller and Alison Settle. Lee Miller had travelled across France photographing the horrors of battle. Alison Settle was still deeply distressed by the condition of her only son, who had been so severely injured at the landings at Arnhem that his recovery was not at first expected.[27] The sight of young Parisiennes in their pretty summer dresses and billowing skirts and hats caused a deep shock. The discovery by Alison Settle that at least one hundred fashion houses had kept running more or less intact through the Occupation caused even more profound surprise.[28] When news leaked out about the extraordinary extravagance of designs there was an international scandal. There were whispers of collaboration, and the fate of the huge French fashion industry hung in the balance.

The American authorities tried to censor the astonishing news about Paris designer fashions. The French were now allies. Although Paris was liberated in August 1944, the war continued on French soil. Both the Free French army and the united Resistance forces had joined up formally with the Allies by the summer of 1944.

From August 1944 until well into 1947, the good name, as well as the huge, multi-million dollar international trade of French haute couture, was under question. Once again Lelong was forced to fight for the future of his trade. This time his interrogators were French, American and British. After discussion the couturiers took several courses of action.

Firstly, they altered the style of the clothes they produced for the first 'Free' collections to be shown since spring 1940. The autumn 1944 shows in Paris, which were seen by only a few foreign press and no foreign buyers, featured strikingly different designs from those made during the Occupation. Gone were the outrageous hats, fancy trimmings, and full skirts. Instead, simple tailored styles, much closer to British and American designs, were seen on the catwalks. Lelong even produced a hat made from wood shavings, a far cry from his work during the Occupation.[29] It is true that as soon as Paris was freed, the salons no longer had the special access to fabrics permitted them by the Nazis. They now had to struggle along with everyone else to find yardage and to hope that the electricity and gas would stay on for long enough to be able to keep work going in the studios.

Even with these alterations Alison Settle amongst others still found the designs extravagant and rather shocking. The stylistic change was not, however, a product only of the current shortages. Statements made both by the designers themselves and fashion journalists, revealed a sense of deep unease about the Occupation fashions.

Lelong, as head of the Chambre Syndicale, was asked to make a public explanation. In New York, the fashion press, led by Edna Woolman Chase of *Vogue*, was frantic to resolve the crisis, so that they could return to their old friends and partners with a clean slate. They were anxious to pick up again from where they had left off in June 1940. So, keeping their own interests in mind, the couturiers and the fashion journalists worked together on their explanations and justifications. Lucien Lelong issued a statement published in detail in American *Vogue* in December 1944.

He stated that the French had no idea that state fashion schemes, such as Utility, existed in other countries. He explained that he and his colleagues had fought to keep Paris couture alive in the most difficult circumstances, and that they had all struggled to keep their staff employed. He told the international press of Nazi attempts forcibly to move the whole industry to Berlin or Vienna and that this had been resisted with great difficulty. He recognised that the designs of occupied Paris seemed shocking when compared with those worn by women in Allied countries. With this in mind, he added that since French military forces were again actively fighting in the war, the Paris couturiers had all toned down their designs to more practical styles. He also explained that every yard of fabric wasted in France was seen as a yard less of fabric that could be sent to Germany. Lelong added that in the recently shown autumn collections the Paris salons had cut down the number of models from the pre-war figure of 150 in each collection to forty. Restrictions had, for the first time been imposed on yardage, with 3¼ yards allowed for a dress, 3¾ yards for a suit and 4¼ yards for a coat. These limitations did not impress Alison Settle. She commented at the time that they were: 'very generous in comparison with British rules, even by American ones'.[30]

Many in the international fashion world, however, were eager to accept Lelong's explanation. The new French government was desperate to get exports going again and loath to damage the industry with any further public talk of collaboration. No charges were ever brought against the couture houses by the committees charged with rooting out collaborators.[31]

This was not the only problem that beset the shattered industry. Between 1944 and 1946 the Chambre Syndicale was faced with a whole series of intractable practical problems. Fabric shortages were at crisis level. Stocks of silk, wool, cotton, linen and rayon were almost nil. (Most of the fabrics had been sent to Germany during the war.)[32] What stocks had been ordered from overseas were stranded due to shipping difficulties. Later, when the Allies landed, Boussac stopped selling to the Germans and provided the Allies with war supplies. Forty-five of his textile factories were soon making American uniforms. The newspaper *Nouvel Observateur*, reported that in 1944 French textile production was down to only 14 per cent of its pre-war levels.[33]

Even stylistically the designers seemed lost in these years. As they produced styles 'more suitable to the French war effort' they seemed to have lost their flair, turning out a jumble of directionless styles, some with bustles, some severe and tailored. These simpler designs produced in 1945–6 were not a success with anyone. Americans commented that there seemed little point in travelling all the way to Paris when they could buy clothes like those in the United States. [34]

In 1946 Alison Settle interviewed a French government minister about the problems facing French couture. Remembering the difficulties she had persuading the British Board of Trade to develop any meaningful understanding of couture, she was astonished at the sophistication of the minister's reply: 'You cannot divorce trade and creative art', she was told firmly. 'Dear me', she was to write later, 'if only then or now or at any time between, a British Government Minister thought in such terms.' [35]

As the fashion houses struggled to return to pre-war normality, both the designers and the French government were keenly aware that they needed more positive international publicity. The need for such publicity to avert the threat of a leadership takeover by the top designers in New York was recognised, discussed and tackled co-operatively.

The solution to all these problems emerged in the unexpected form of a fashion doll exhibition, the Fashion Theatre, or 'Théatre de la Mode'. Twelve scenes of Paris life were depicted on small sets, which were designed by famous artists such as Cocteau and Christian Bérard. Each of the sets was filled with quarter-size dolls, or *poupées mondaines*, made of wire, and dressed perfectly in miniature fashions produced by the couture houses. It was a typically sophisticated Parisian answer to a crisis.

As the international buyers were unable to come to Paris, the couture industry went to them. The show toured all the major cities where they were to be found: London to New York, Chicago and Rio de Janeiro. A chic and weighty catalogue accompanied the show; it included not only articles about the long history of Paris as an international fashion centre, but also photos of each scene. Full-page advertisements were taken out by all the great designers, to show the world abroad that they, and their perfume subsidiaries, were back in business. [36]

The plan did not evade the problem of the war years. The Chambre Syndicale explained in a foreword that all the profits from the exhibition were to go to the French 'Entraide' charity. The exhibition seems to have served its purpose well. By 1946 the orders were coming in again, though the struggle to meet them must have been prodigious.

Under the new economic arrangements in post-war France, the couture industry came under the organisational umbrella of the 'Office Professionel des Industries de l'Art et de la Création' (the Professional Bureau of the Art and Design Industries). In 1946 this committee determined to encourage growth in couture exports – 'even at the cost of restriction of goods to French customers'. Furthermore, they agreed that 'the aim must be to bring the foreign buyers to Paris to buy, not to send goods abroad on paper orders'. Alison Settle believed that 'the lure and support of the capital city increased orders out of all belief'. Home sales represented only one-fifth of annual production.[37]

PARIS COUTURIERS IN THE IMMEDIATE POST-WAR PERIOD

The fate of individual designers after the war varied. Chanel vanished into Switzerland for some years for reasons probably connected to her behaviour during the Occupation and was not much loved by the French public on her return in 1952. Heim came out of hiding and became one of the classic successes of the 1950s. Rochas, Fath and Ricci, who were a conspicuous part of the Occupation '*Tout Paris*', seem to have restarted their businesses with no trouble, although Rochas's business closed in the 1950s and Fath died in his thirties of leukemia in 1957. Elsa Schiaparelli returned from exile. Her salon had stayed open during the war years. She never did regain the wit and verve of her pre-war success and in 1957 she also closed her salon. Mme Vionnet, who relied very much on her own skills, and not on a team of supporting designers, was elderly and retired after a few years. Mainbocher stayed in New York. Molyneux returned but also failed to recapture his pre-war reputation. His house was taken on by his nephew, John Tullis. Lelong perhaps suffered most, his salon soon closing under a cloud, whether justified or not.

The new successes were Dior, Balenciaga and Balmain. Dior, with strong financial backing from Boussac, opened in September 1947, with a huge, smash hit collection named the 'New Look'. His designs were actually not so different from those of his rivals. The long, gathered skirts, hip emphasis, and general softening of the silhouette were discernible features of Parisian design from 1946, and even, in Mainbocher's case, from 1939. Perhaps it was the glamour of his presentation, and the successful wooing of the foreign buyers and press that brought him such critical acclaim.

Boussac, who survived the war in a strong financial position, provided Dior with enough yardage of fabric for him to put 50 metres into some of his dresses.[38] Boussac also experimented with nylon, with new lightweight taffetas and soft draping wools. The long frothy skirts of Dior's collection were so full that they brushed against the cheeks of the assembled crowd as the models swished down the catwalk. The audience was shocked, enraptured and captivated. Seasoned fashion journalists to this day remember that show as one of the most magical moments of their lives. Perhaps the huge quantity of Dior perfume that was sprayed over each member of the audience as they struggled to gain entrance to the little showrooms made everyone a little lightheaded.[39]

Whatever the reason for the success of this particular show, it had one important result. It re-established Paris as the international fashion leader.

Other designers contributed to Paris's success. Balmain, who also opened in 1945 (although with much less money behind him than Dior, and much less ballyhoo), and Balenciaga, were soon recognised by the trade buyers as prime sources of progressive design.

By 1948 these buyers were flocking once again to their old haunts, and the old system of seasonal shows, and seasonal visits to Paris by journalists, forecasters, buyers and manufacturers resumed. The rehabilitation campaign waged by the couture industry had been subtle and sophisticated. The French government had played its part, and the foreign fashion press, particularly in the United States, had made its contribution too. The great French empire of fashion was safe.

The reputation of Paris was safe too. The war years were swept into oblivion. No dress histories ever mentioned them in any detail. No exhibitions were held of the designs. A blanket of silence covered the whole area for fifty years. It had certainly been a campaign worth waging in economic terms. The odour of the war years was quickly buried. It was mentioned, often painfully, by some of the more honest of the couturiers in their autobiographies,[40] but until very recently the fashion historians and the fat coffee table accounts of the glamour of Paris couture mostly simply evaded the issue, as if the war had never happened.[41]

Seven years is a long time in terms of stylistic development and yet, of all periods of French dress history, it was the one that remained unexamined. Not until 1990, a full fifty years after the Nazis marched into Paris, was any detailed objective research produced on the activities of the Paris couturiers over that period. Dominique Veillon, in her book *La Mode Sous l'Occupation*, is the first to address seriously the issue of the role played by the couturiers during the four years of the Occupation of Paris.[42] Rumours of collaboration, rejected by all French dress historians and by almost everyone involved in the trade, are carefully assessed in her book, although she neglects to examine surviving garments, textiles and illustrations in any detail. In this fascinating study on Paris, she concentrates on the couture customers, on the relationship between the couture houses and designers and the Nazi and French collaborationist authorities, and on the details of the regulations imposed on the trade by the Germans.

Yet in the collections of the two great Paris dress museums, hang rails of elegant evening, cocktail and day dresses, tailored suits and even grand, full-length wedding dresses from the Occupation years. The salon of Schiaparelli produced a shocking pink twill silk suit. Now housed in the Palais Galliera collection, it was embroidered in 1942 with large ears of wheat, in gold thread, on the crowns of the sleeves.[43] Robert Piguet, also represented in this collection, continued his interest in the use of thick cord passementerie all through the years of the Occupation. It was an illustration of one of these designs which so angered *Picture Post* in May 1943. The magazine scorned its embroidered pockets, 'involving many hours of hand-work' with 'more work in the trimmings than in a whole dress in England today.'

Balenciaga continued with his Spanish look through the war years, with short matador jackets and bobble fringing. The Musée des Arts Décoratifs has a simple, bright pink satin, full-length evening dress in just this style.[44] *Picture Post* called these clothes 'Fashions for Traitors', and 'The Clothes of the New Order'. This opinion has to a large extent coloured British historians' views of the role of the Paris couture houses to this day, to the extent that any of

Catalogue of Fashions

ECONOMICAL DESIGNS PLANNED TO BALANCE YOUR WARTIME BUDGET

ADDRESS all orders for patterns to The Pattern Shop, Leach-Way Catalogue of Fashions, Tower House, Southampton Street, Strand, London, W.C.2. Sizes and prices are clearly marked on each page. When ordering, be sure to state age or size required. Quantities of material required for these designs will be found on page 2.

COAT
No. 11,488
32-40 in. busts
(Pattern price 1s. 3d.
plus 1d. for postage)

FROCK
No. 11,487
32-40 in. busts
(Pattern price 1s. 6d.
plus 1d. for postage)

FROCK
No. 11,491
32-40 in. busts
(Pattern price 1s. 6d.
plus 1d. for postage)

THE home dressmaker has come into her own, as she can plan her outfits, utilising existing garments, down to the last inch of material without wasting a scrap. Whereas the woman who has been used to rushing out to buy ready-mades is bound to have a few " white elephants " which won't " go " with anything. Real economy means careful planning, and that is where this catalogue will be such a help to you. Study its pages carefully before getting rid of those precious coupons, and make a list of the garments you really need before sending for the patterns and buying the materials. Don't you think the new short coat a good wartime idea ? If made in a fairly neutral colour it can be worn over practically any existing frock or skirt and so dispenses with the need for a new suit.

COAT
No. 11,489
32-40 in. busts
(Pattern price 1s. 6d.
plus 1d. for postage)

COAT
No. 11,490
32-40 in. busts
(Pattern price 1s. 6d.
plus 1d. for postage)

Contrasting Utility designs in London, January 1942, with scanty yardage and minimal trimmings (from a dressmaker's pattern book, author's collection)

them have taken any interest in the subject.[45] How fair is it?

De Holden Stone commented in 1946 that 'any model shown cold was bound to look queer – if sometimes strangely attractive, with its huge top, full skirts and tiny waists – to eyes which had been marking time with endless "Utility" and austerity'.[46] Thus the products of the famous couture houses were still seasonally reflecting the frivolity and essential waste of the pre-war fashion system. In Britain in the years 1944–6 this was judged as positively immoral. The hats above all caused the deepest offence. British women had long found the creations of the most famous French milliners extreme and exotic. Designs were usually watered down for English customers. The towering piles of flowers, lace and feathers, the draped and flowing turbans were condemned immediately as the clothes of 'smart collaborators'.[47]

After researching the background to the designs and studying them only from drawings, it was an astonishing experience to find all one's preconceptions and prejudices shattered on an examination of surviving garments. It soon becomes clear that they are far from vulgar, ostentatious or 'demoralised' in themselves. They are, instead, typical examples of classic Paris couture – sophisticated, understated, even simple, and perfectly skilled in cut and quality of embroidery, although the fabric is often obviously of inferior quality cloth. They are certainly stylish garments, especially those created between 1942–3, with very wide shoulder pads, narrow waists, and with the peplums of the long jackets curvaceously moulded over the hips.

De Holden Stone believed that these designs 'grew out of an intense psychological opposition to the invading Nazis', and that the ever-changing silhouettes reflected the 'progress of survival and of reaction to the rule of the Boche'.[48] The styles also grew out of the salons' determination to retain their grip on their businesses, even if this meant dressing the red-kneed wives of the black marketeers or the mistresses of leading French fascists, or negotiating special extra allowances for themselves. It is also absolutely true, as Lelong emphasised in 1944, that Paris couture saved itself from obliteration, from removal to Berlin or Vienna, and that it kept thousands in employment for the four years of the Occupation. Does all this amount to collaboration?

Our responses are, finally, personal. From the safe distance of fifty long years, and from across the Channel at that, perhaps we have little right to make judgements at all. Who knows how the British would have behaved under occupation? But it is also important not to avoid the issue as so many dress histories have done before. Perhaps it is the extraordinary juxtaposition of the continuous production of individually designed, luxury fashion for a few thousand wealthy women with the savage behaviour of the Nazis and Gestapo in Paris that is so offensive and disturbing.

Others would say, and in the end I find myself amongst them, that by the very fact of remaining open the couture houses, like the theatres, contributed to Hitler's overall plan for Paris. Like the Tour d'Argent restaurant, kept open exclusively for Nazi officers, the fashion houses kept the veneer of elegance alive. Despite protestations that their designs were 'a slap in the face to the Boche', perhaps, now, the couturiers seem more like fiddlers at work while Rome burned, however beautiful their products.

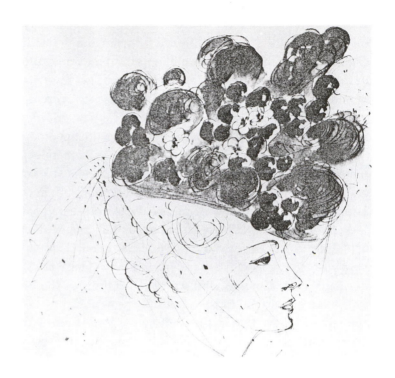

Green hat with artificial cherries, black feathers and veiling, by the milliner Rose Valois, Paris. From the 1944 special edition of Album de Mode de Figaro, *printed in Monaco (photograph courtesy of the Musée des Arts de la Mode, Palais Galliera, Paris)*

The views of French friends, with whom this research has been discussed over the last decade, have varied as much as do these two conclusions. Some have said. 'Il ne faut pas fouiller dans la merde', because it opens up wounds that have been festering in French society for fifty years. Others disagree profoundly with this view. Much new historical analysis of collaboration and resistance in wartime France has been published, particularly over the last ten years, in France itself.[49] Dominique Veillon's study of Paris fashions during the war was a development from earlier research into the Resistance press, for example.[50] Friends who worked for the Resistance are almost unable to believe that such clothes were actually made during the war years, because their lives were so differently oriented.

Perhaps the couture houses were inevitably trapped, whichever way they turned, by the very nature of their highly specialised luxury trade. It behoves historians, from both ends of the debate, at least to look closely at their work, and at the conditions under which they were forced to work, before making easy judgements.

Notes and References

1 Martine Renier, *Femina*, Special Edition, 1945, p. 93.

2 Paul Nystrom, *The Economics of Fashion*, New York, 1929, pp. 167–8; and Pierre Balmain, *My Years and Seasons*, London, 1964, p. 55.

3 See Alison Settle Archives, St Peter's House Library, Brighton Polytechnic, *Notes for 1940–1945*.

4 Jean-Pierre Azema, *From Munich to the Liberation – 1938–1944*, Cambridge, 1984, p. xxii. The Vichy Council of Ministers, in the 'free' unoccupied zone of southern France, passed its first law against Jews on 30 October 1940. It was not until 29 March 1941 that anti-Jewish legislation was established in occupied France.

5 Jessica Dawes, *Ready-made Miracles*, New York, 1967, p. 141.

6 See Alison Settle Archives, article in *Vogue* (English edition), December 1944, AS.B.44.7.

7 Dominique Veillon, *La Mode Sous L'Occupation*, Paris, 1990, p. 172.

8 Alison Settle Archives, op. cit., note 6.

9 De Holden Stone, 'French Fashion Survives the Nazis', *Art and Industry*, 1946, p. 4.

10 See Alison Settle Archives, *Notes for 1946*, B.405.5.

11 Thomas Kernan, *France on Berlin Time*, New York, 1941, p. 35.

12 See *Femina*, Special Ed., May 1945.

13 Among the popular women's magazines that stayed open throughout the war were *Marie Claire*, *Mode du Jour*, *Modes et Travaux*, *La Femme Chic*, *Silhouette* and *Album de la Mode du Figaro*.

14 Musée de la Mode et du Costume, Palais Galliera, Exhibition catalogue; *Pierre Balmain, 40 Années de Creation*, Paris, 1985, p. 225.

15 Veillon, op. cit., p. 210.

16 Ibid., pp. 204–5.

17 Ibid., pp. 212–13.

18 Balmain, op. cit., pp. 72–7.

19 Ibid., p. 77.

20 Hervé Le Boterf, *La Vie Parisienne Sous L'Occupation*, Volume: Paris Le Jour, 1940–1944, Paris, 1974, p. 54.

21 Balmain, op. cit., p. 72.

22 Jean Leymarie, *Chanel*, Paris, 1987, pp. 197–9; and see also Axel Madsen, *Chanel – A Woman on Her Own*, New York, 1990.

23 Anny Latour, *Kings of Fashion*, London, 1958, p. 251.

24 Veillon, op. cit., p. 134.

25 'In Paris: Clothes for the 2000 Wealthy Collaborators', *Picture Post*, 1 May 1943, p. 10.

26 Elsa Schiaparelli, *Shocking Life*, New York, 1954, p. 164.

27 'Alison Settle Remembers', *The Observer Review*, 1 July 1973.

28 See Alison Settle Archives, *Notes for 1946*, B.405.5.

29 *Journal de France, De L'Occupation à la Liberation – Les Années 40*, Paris, Reprint Editions, 1971, shows a photograph of a model in the autumn of 1944, wearing a Lelong suit, with a small hat made of curled wood shavings. (With thanks to Rod Kedward for letting me study these editions.)

30 See Alison Settle Archives.

31 Veillon, op. cit., p. 248.

32 'La Situation Critique de Notre Industrie Textile', *Le Monde*, 24–25 December 1944.

33 'Le Nouvel Observateur', 1944.

34 See *Picture Post*, 27 September 1947.

35 See Alison Settle Archives, *Notes for 1946*, B.405.5.

36 In September 1983 sixty of the fashion dolls from the Théatre de la Mode were discovered in the De Young Museum outside San Francisco. They were restored with the help of seventeen

Paris couture houses and were exhibited at the Musée des Arts Décoratifs, Paris, in December 1990. A book, *Théatre de la Mode*, was published simultaneously in Paris, 1990, with contributions from Edmonde Charles-Roux, Herbert R. Lotman, Stanley Garfinkel and Nadine Gasc.

37 Alison Settle Archives, 1946.

38 'Paris forgets that this is 1947', *Picture Post*, 27 September 1947.

39 Muriel Pemberton, then a fashion journalist on the *Daily Herald*, later Head of Fashion at St Martin's School of Art, London, interviewed for the BBC 2 dress history series, *Through the Looking Glass*, part 4, autumn, 1989.

40 See Balmain, op. cit., and Christian Dior, *Dior by Dior*, London, 1957.

41 See, for example, Caroline Rennolds Milbank, *Couture: the Great Fashion Designers*, London, 1985, p. 202, where she writes, incorrectly, that the House of Schiaparelli was closed during the war. She also misrepresents the activities of Jacques Fath by stating that 'after fighting in World War Two, he re-opened in more spacious quarters in 1944' (p. 262). In fact, after he was demobbed following the defeat of France in 1940, his salon ran with great acclaim throughout the years of the Occupation, and he was heralded by the Paris wartime fashion press as the brightest new talent of the period.

Another example may be found in Francis Kennet, *The Collector's Book of Fashion*, London, 1983, p. 64, where he states that 'Most of the Paris Houses had closed their doors in 1940 ... A few carried on their business in Paris'. It is indeed true that over the *Exode* period, the summer of 1940, most of the couturiers closed down, moving to Bordeaux. However, most of them were back in business by 1941.

42 Veillon, op. cit.

43 In the collection of the Musée de la Mode et du Costume, Palais Galliera, Paris, museum no. 84.1.35. Schiaparelli, August 1942, design no. 76056. (With thanks to Mlle Valerie Guillaume, Keeper of Twentieth-Century Dress, and to Mlle Renée Davray-Piekolek, Keeper of Nineteenth-Century Costume, for their kindness.)

44 *Union Française des Arts du Costume*, Musée des Arts Décoratifs, Paris, Dress Collection, no. 68.38.16, Balenciaga, 1943.

45 David Pryce-Jones, *Paris in the Third Reich*, London, 1981, p. 26, is an exception in that he does include the names of six couturiers in his list of organisations that kept running during the Occupation, but includes in them Paul Poirier (*sic*) – meaning Paul Poiret, the most famous couturier of the 1910–1914 period, who had been forced to close his couture house due to bankruptcy during the late 1920s. He died in poverty in Paris in 1944, soon after putting together an exhibition of his paintings in order to raise some funds.

46 De Holden Stone, op. cit., pp. 4–5.

47 *Picture Post*, 1 May 1943.

48 De Holden Stone, op. cit., p. 6.

49 See Pascal Ory, *Les Collaborateurs*, Paris, 1987; Henri Amouraux, *Les Beaux Jours des Collaborateurs*, Paris, 1978; Rod Kedward, *Vichy France and the Resistance: Culture and Ideology*, London, 1985; Azema, op. cit.; Rita Thalman, *Le Mise au Pas* – Idéologie et Strategie Securitaire dans la France Ocupée, 1940–1944, Paris, 1990; and M.D. Matisson and J.D. Abribat, *Psychanalyse de la Collaboration* – Le Syndrome de Bordeaux, Paris, 1991.

50 See Dominique Veillon, *Le Franc Tireur, Un Journal Clandestin de Resistance*, Paris, 1977; and Dominique Veillon, *La Collaboration*, Paris, 1984.

ANGELA PARTINGTON

Popular Fashion and Working-Class Affluence

The two women in the wedding photograph from 1951 (overleaf) called their outfits 'New Look'. What they are wearing is different from fashion history representations of the style, however, particularly with regard to the 'nipped in' waist achieved by boned corseting and hip-padding, which is usually regarded as an important feature of the New Look, but which appears to be absent from these outfits. That the clothes worn in the photograph are not particularly restrictive might be explained by describing them as 'watered down' versions of the New Look, since it is commonly accepted that cheaper or mass-produced 'copies' of designer fashion tend to dilute or otherwise 'tone down' its more extreme aspects. This notion of popular fashion, as a weaker version of couture or designer originals, appears to rest on an assumption that working-class consumers of fashion goods are less innovatory or adventurous in their preferences and choices than the consumers of designer clothing. This assumption is in turn supported by an understanding of a mass-market fashion system which is assumed to 'diffuse' middle-class tastes and preferences to a working-class market, creating popular fashions by enabling innovations in style to 'trickle down' from high-status to low-status social groups.

Such an explanation is questionable for two reasons: first, it reinforces a cultural hierarchy in which class-specific lifestyles are ranked and which endorses the presumed superiority of middle-class culture; second, it relies on a theory of fashion adoption which, I would argue, is incapable of explaining the workings of popular fashion or of providing an understanding of the mass-market fashion system. A 'trickle down' model of fashion adoption reinforces the notion that a mass-market fashion system is a feature of a consumer society in which class differences have been eroded, absorbed, or concealed, due to the ability of a relatively affluent working class to aspire to the tastes and preferences of the middle class (albeit in a 'watered down' way). But I will argue in this essay that the mass-market systems on which consumer culture depends provide specific conditions of conflict between classes, that is, conditions under which class differences are re-articulated, rather than eroded or disguised. To do this, I will suggest that the popular version of the New Look in the photograph is a deliberately different appropriation of it, not a poor copy.

Rather than simply 'reading off' clothes as expressions of class identity as fashion history tends to do, as if the consumer was a passive victim of fashion as a 'reflection' of socio-economic distinctions, I will show how the consumer skills of working-class women proliferated around commodities in the 1950s, enabling them actively to use fashion and other goods as a means of articulating class identity in new ways. I will show how the development of a mass-market fashion system was not merely a mechanism for the expansion of capitalism, but also created the circumstances under which this accumulation of consumer skills took place, even if this was not the intention of the fashion and marketing industries.

Wedding photograph, 1951 (courtesy of Angela Partington)

POST-WAR HISTORIES

The working class has been perceived as divided, in the period after the Second World War, between those on 'the margins' (who are thought to reject commodities or 'subvert' their values) and the mainstream (thought to consume passively). For instance, (masculinised) subcultural 'style' is distinguished from (feminised) mass cultural 'fashion'. While working-class women's activities have been associated with devalued cultural practices, male working-class culture has enjoyed the status of 'subversion', on the grounds that the commodity is either refused or creatively 'appropriated' – as in 'bricolage'.[1]

There are a number of links which have been made, between class domination and consumerism, which imply that femininity is a kind of weakness in working-class culture as a culture of resistance. It has often been assumed that in their role as consumers working-class women have helped to erode or disguise class differences. The 1950s, when working-class women were first actively pursued as consumers for many commodities, is often seen as a period in which contradiction and class conflict was absent. It is associated with a national consensus culture brought about by affluence, which was only interrupted by the emergence/identification of marginal groups in the 1960s (despite the fact that the 1960s were considerably *more* affluent and consumerist than the 1950s). It is this evocation of the 1950s against which I want to reconsider post-war femininity as a source of contradiction and conflict, by considering working-class women's adoption of New Look fashion.

The mechanism by which consumption is stimulated is often identified as 'fashion', or a similar conceptualisation such as 'built-in-obsolescence'. Definitions of post Second World War consumerism have emphasised the 'libidinisation' of consumption, the 'ideological manipulation' of the consumer, and the proliferation of 'needs'. But it can be argued that consumerism is an effect of the instability of capitalism as well as its expansion, and that fashion is a terrain on which new forms of class struggle have developed.[2] In the discussion of 1950s fashion which follows, I will show how the commodification of working-class culture involved contradictory attempts to regulate (i.e., discourage desires for certain kinds of commodities), as well as libidinise, consumption, in order to try and create 'good consumers' who were predictable in their choices. In trying to impose certain standards of taste on consumers, the design profession and the marketing industries created the opportunity for the roles of 'good consumption' to be broken, inadvertently allowing consumers to produce unexpected meanings around fashion goods, as was the case with the New Look.

Rather than expressing dominant ideological values of the 1950s, such as those upholding traditional femininity and domesticity, the New Look can be seen as a site of conflicting meanings. Analysis of the adoption of the style reveals that relations between classes were actually negotiated through the exercise of specific tastes and preferences. It can be shown that the merchandising of fashion goods in the 1950s involved appealing to class-specific consumer skills and preferences, encouraging the consumer's active use of an increasingly complex 'language' of clothes to express diffferences. For the fashion product to be historically and culturally placed, it must be read interdependently with other design and media products which, for the first time, presented certain commodities for the 'desiring gaze' of working-class women. For working-class women in the 1950s, fashion signified in terms of the skills it demanded and the pleasures it offered, and these were specific to that market. Their investments in the style, and the meanings they produced with it, cannot therefore be reduced to the emulation of another consumer group.

CLASS DISTINCTION AND FASHION

There have been many explanations of fashion which acknowledge its role in the *expression* of class difference in capitalist society, but they tend to perceive it as working automatically in the interests of dominant or privileged groups. Middle-class affluence, and 'conspicuous consumption', are seen as means of exclusion – disidentification with other groups; whereas working-class affluence is seen as a means of emulation – identification with other groups.[3] It is assumed that mass-production threatens to erode, to absorb or to make meaningless class differences, making the preservation of 'distinction' the prerogative of privileged and elite groups. The implication is that those in subordinate groups, rather than having their own means of exclusion, supposedly covet those of the higher status groups.

Such explanations appear to be drawn from two influential theories of fashion, namely Veblen's 'conspicuous consumption' theory from the late nineteenth century, and the 'trickle down' model used by Georg Simmel to describe fashion adoption in 1904.[4] Veblen explained fashion as evidence of struggle for status in 'a new society where old rules disintegrated and all were free to copy their betters'.[5] The 'trickle down' model has become an almost common-sense explanation for the 'fashion cycle'. Briefly, it describes changes in taste as innovations made by the dominant class, as necessary in order to preserve the 'unity and segregation' of the class, given that modern social codes allow the immediately subordinate group to emulate the tastes and preferences of the one above. According to this model, the high status groups are forced to adopt new styles in order to maintain their superiority/difference, as these tastes filter down the social scale. This happens periodically so a cyclical process is created, generating the otherwise mysterious mutations we know as fashion.

These theories have informed more recent approaches, such as the analysis of affluence as an ideology which appears to create a 'classless' society by disguising class differences or making them less visible. The phenomena of 'affluence' and 'privatisation' (the increased consumption of 'non-essential' goods within the domestic sphere) have been used as key concepts with which to analyse post-Second World War commodified leisure, but it has been thought that 'beneath them lurks the image of a classless society . . . Differences are mobilised in the leisure market as a means of producing consumer identification – and produce what appear to be different groups of consumers . . . real divisions . . . are represented . . . as differences in taste'.[6]

Within all these frameworks, women's identification with the commodity is equated with the fetishism and spectacularisation which create the 'illusion' of changed conditions of existence. Women's acquisition of tastes and interests in fashion are identified as the means of social betterment, and the modern woman is understood as spectacle used for the display of wealth and distinction. But at the same time these are not recognised as indicators of 'real' social change, but only as the means by which socio-economic differences are disguised or denied, as in the use of the term 'embourgeoisification' in relation to working-class affluence.

In these frameworks conspicuous consumption, trickle-down, and affluence-as-ideology, are all notions which are based on an understanding of culture as a mere expression of socio-economic relations, rather than as a site of the active production of class-specific values and meanings by consumers. As a description of post-Second World War culture, the notion of affluence as ideology makes too many assumptions about, and disregards the historical specificity of, working-class markets for fashion goods. In such theorisations, it is simply assumed that working-class affluence is the *effect* of the *diffusion* of cultural practices, rather than the *condition* of *struggles* between classes. These established theories of fashion are incapable of explaining how class-specific consumer skills enable the reproduction of differences. They support the practice of 'reading off' goods instead of enabling a consideration of the relations between consumer groups and practices on which the meaning-fulness of any commodity depends.

The developments to which the terms 'affluence' and 'privatisation' refer could more accurately be described as 'mass-markets' and 'gendered consumption', since they were objectives of the economic strategies which were deployed by the leisure industries, in the pursuit of profit, rather than the result of a philanthropic democratisation. The development of a mass-market fashion system enabled class-specific groups to be targeted as consumers, and relied increasingly on gender-specific consumer skills.

Consumerism did not create the illusion of a classless society then, but neither did it simply reinforce already established class relations. Rather it transformed the material relations between classes, and altered the conditions, means and processes through which, and the resources for which, class struggles were to be conducted. The introduction of mass-market systems for the production and distribution of goods (affluence), and the gendering of consumption (privatisation), while being necessary for capitalism's expansion of consumption, nevertheless enabled the production of new class-specific meanings for commodities by contributing to the development of a more complex 'language' of clothes which could be used by consumers in the articulation of class identity. My analysis of the marketing of 1950s fashion, and the popular adoption of the New Look, will exemplify this.

MASS-MARKET FASHION

In the post-Second World War period, it has been necessary for working-class markets to be found for commodities, in order for capitalism to expand or even survive. As with the marketing of other goods, it has been found necessary to develop a system for the production and distribution of fashion commodities, in which there is virtually no 'trickle down' in the ways in which styles are innovated or adopted by specific class groups. A 'trickle across' or 'mass-market' theory of fashion has been developed to describe this new system, which is based on several broad arguments about mass-market fashion. Firstly, that the fashion industry has reinvented the fashion 'season', and within this its manufacturing and merchandising strategies almost guarantee adoption by consumers across socio-economic groups simultaneously. Secondly, that there is always enough 'choice' between a range of equally fashionable styles to meet the demands of different tastes. Third, that discrete market segments within all social strata (not just privileged groups) are represented by 'innovators' who influence fashion adoption. And finally, that the mass media is also targeted at market segments, so the flow of information and influence is primarily within, rather than across, class groups.[7]

Within this system, the people who determine what becomes fashionable are professionals such as fashion editors in publishing, and fashion buyers in retailing. But these professionals act as agents of specific sections of the fashion-consuming public whose tastes and preferences it is their task to anticipate.[8] Styles in dress are either adopted and disseminated simultaneously by different class groups or remain contained within specific ones. So the roots of change in fashion design, manufacturing, and marketing 'are in response to the desire on the part of the large majority of consumers to innovate and to be fashionable in their styles of life.'[9] In a mass-market system, adoption of new styles is a process which depends on the flow of information *within* social strata rather than between them. Innovators are to be found amongst all classes and groups, not just amongst the privileged or elite, so there is no 'emulation' of privileged groups by subordinate groups in such a system. Difference exists in the *ways* in which fashions are adopted, rather than in any time lag, and many fashions receive wide acceptance within some class groups while being unsuccessful in others. Privileged groups can wear the same 'classic' styles and ignore the latest fashions in 'a concern for birth distinction and English heredity as against the distinction of occupational achievement'.[10] The upper-middle classes want clothes 'related to wealth and high living rather than to family connection'. Amongst the lower-middle classes 'there is a distaste for "high style", for what is "daring" or "unusual"'.[11] Women on very limited clothes budgets are keen to adopt the latest fashions, but often by making their own versions which are customised and individualised.

The traditional 'customer', who has an informal contract with the trader based on mutual expectations, is replaced by a 'consumer', whose 'expectations are altogether more specific: the maximisation of immediate satisfaction. If goods or services are not provided in the manner or at the price required, the consumer will go elsewhere'.[12] Exclusivity is not something confined to privileged groups, since all market segments can shop in retail outlets intended specifically for them. In a mass-market system women of all classes are responsible for the diffusion of fashion (preferences for innovative or restyled products), but class differences do not disappear in this system, on the contrary more complex and multiple differences are made possible through increasingly elaborate and complex manufacturing, media and retailing strategies.

For example, in the 1950s artificial fibres were being developed, especially in mass-produced and cheap clothing, but there was also a campaign to uphold the prestige of natural fibres, so they became associated with more expensive and exclusive ranges. Consequently the class connotations of fabrics changed, with cotton (previously associated with the labouring classes) and wool (the middle classes) both becoming more acceptable materials for high fashion products. Meanwhile the new synthetics became a sign of working-classness, because to working-class women quantity, disposability, colour, and 'easycare' became a priority while craftsmanship and 'naturalness' did not.

Christian Dior has been called the 'moderniser of the Haute Couture',[13] because he pioneered the system through which manufacturers and retailers could sell an 'Original-Christian-Dior-Copy' and clothes made from paper patterns licensed by Dior, and through which exact drawings and reproductions were allowed to appear only a month after the fashion show. In 1957 an estimated 30 per cent of Paris haute couture volume was accounted for by manufacturers and retail syndicates, and store buyers. The Fashion House Group of London, founded in 1958, produced 'the cream of British ready-to-wear'[14] for an upper-middle-class market. These goods were more expensive than chain store clothing but much cheaper than designer originals, and signalled the increased complexity of the system through which consumers could identify themselves according to much finer criteria. '"Ready-mades", far from being the shoddily made confections that in pre-war days were regarded as beneath contempt, now began to compete with couture . . . Brand names started to appear on garments as a guarantee of quality.'[15] The higher levels of turnover in fashion retailing achieved by the multiples, and the emergence of self-service supermarket chains in food retailing, had an important influence on forms of garment display and shop interiors, making the goods much more accessible to the customer. Design had to become a substitute for the personal attention of a sales assistant, and retailers had to develop a 'house style' or corporate image which would enable the consumer to identify the companies whose products they preferred. This new relationship depended on a much greater level of consumer skills, and indicates one of the ways in which consumer choices became an integral part of identity-formation.

Alongside these developments in retailing, the new disciplines of market research grew:

> Investigations into consumer behaviour required a massive apparatus for the gathering and processing of data on consumer habits, preferences, tastes and whims . . . The unifying principle of diverse market research techniques was the regulation of information flows, which were to proceed in one direction only: from the consumer upwards to the institutions of the image production industries . . . In the first instance, it is capital which dictates the forms which commodity consumption takes; yet the market remains dependent on the development by the female consumer of specific sets of social competences and skills.[16]

All these developments are evidence of market segmentation rather than the diffusion, or democratisation, of leisure. The developments in the textiles and clothing industries, and the expansion of the retailing trades, have all been interpreted as the eradication of the differences between the classes, on the assumption that mass-production made fashion goods available to the working class and that it also brought an end to the elite ends of the market. Perhaps the first fashion to benefit from these changes was the New Look, and it has been said that therefore the real significance of the 'New Look' was 'that it ushered in a period when fashion was to be more important – and more available – to everyone'.[17] But these developments actually allowed differences to multiply, because they created finer distinctions and a more complex vocabulary in 'the language of clothes' for the articulation of class relations. These included 'make', retail 'brand', and fabric, as well as style and quality. Simultaneous adoption, therefore, does not mean identical adoption. Although the fashion industry may determine the range of styles from which choices have to be made, certain styles or 'looks' may become much more popular amongst some consumer-groups than others, and certain styles completely fail to be adopted by some, or even all groups. Many styles, including the New Look, become adopted in different ways, through a process of customisation in which certain elements become more important than others, and which the consumer controls.

THE ATTEMPT TO 'TRAIN' WORKING-CLASS AFFLUENCE

In its self-promotion during the 1950s, the design profession assumed that the role of the designer was to 'open the eyes' of the consumer, claiming to open up new kinds of knowledge and relationships, because 'Untrained affluence was a threat to the attainment of standards and stability in taste'.[18] Modernist design was clearly an expression of a commitment to rationalisation, and a belief in goods as measurable solutions to simple needs, rather than as bearers of meanings and unpredictable emotional values. The promotion of simplicity, functionalism, and the attempt to outlaw decoration and 'clutter' was a logical translation of this. The idea of the end of style, and the establishment of permanent design values, was echoed in the belief in a classless utopia. British fashion, as in other design fields, tended towards the encouragement of *in*conspicuous consumption, by promoting rather restrained and tasteful styles of dress, and tried to counter the threat of untrained affluence by imposing strict distinctions between glamour and utility, in the attempt to educate consumers in the rules of proper consumption. The British fashion industry, incredibly, attempted to eliminate seasonal fluctuations in fashion, for example by setting up a central information and design centre from which manufacturers could be instructed.[19]

This programme of regulation was managed by institutions such as the Council for Industrial Design, and involved campaigning to change the attitudes of both manufacturers and the consumer, and the production of propaganda 'aimed at familiarizing the public with that new concept "design"'.[20] Looking at fashions in women's clothes in the 1950s however, it is apparent that this programme became limited and strained, since its prime target (working-class women) was fast acquiring consumer skills which ultimately enabled them to relate to goods in increasingly complex ways, which could not be reduced to simple needs or practical utility. As mass-market systems developed, working-class women were able to engage in forms of consumption to satisfy needs not anticipated or recognised by the professionals, and therefore 'improper'.

The New Look could only be tolerated within the perspective of the design establishment, if it was seen as a decorative but complementary contrast to utilitarian clothing. The utilitarian definition of the housewife (as an efficient machine for the reproduction of labour) co-existed with a notion of femininity drawn from the bourgeois ideal of womanhood as 'decorative'. Commentators have often noted the duality of 1950s femininity, in terms of the contrasting, but equally acceptable, images of womanhood which prevailed. Fashion historians have made two categories to accommodate these different identities:

> The ambiguities of the period's dress invested women with two very different personae: dutiful homemaker and tempting siren. The former wore the shirtwaist dress, apron and demure necklines – all proper symbols of domesticity. Yet at the same time an exaggerated image of sexuality prevailed. Woman-turned-temptress titillated her man with plunging necklines, veiled eyes and a come-hither walk. Fashion encouraged women to become chameleon-like characters, shifting effortlessly from wholesome homemaker to wanton lover with a change of clothes.[21]

Christian Dior's 'New Look', with its soft, rounded shoulders, nipped-in waist, and full, long skirts, contrasted sharply with the Utility styles of wartime, with their square shoulders and short, straight skirts. Previously, 'the silhouette was unadorned, a plain rectangle of clothing consisting of box-shaped jacket with padded shoulders and a narrow skirt. Even summer dresses and blouses had shoulder pads and conformed to the severity of outline demanded by wartime deprivation. Cecil Beaton said at the time that women's fashions were going through the Beau Brummel stage and were learning the restraint of men's taste.'[22] But a few years later: 'Paris clothes were conspicuously impractical for working women. Boned and strapless "self-supporting" bodices made it difficult to bend and corsets pinched the waist'.[23] However, fashion manufacturers were opposed to this change; on 17 March 1948, a delegation representing three hundred dress firms went to Harold Wilson (then head of the Board of Trade) and asked for a ban on long hemlines.[24] The new style was not in their interests because it meant less product for their investment of materials and labour.

Utility styles not only survived, but were translated and developed into the basis of a whole range of practical styles. The wartime shirtwaister, for example, flourished in the form of 1950s dresses which became almost symbolic of the housewife, and were invariably used to dress her in advertisements for household goods. Another example is the ubiquitous multi-purpose suit, often worn with sturdy shoes for women on their feet all day. Clothing, accessories and dress fabrics compatible with this aesthetic had been included in the Britain Can Make It exhibition in 1946, and due to the interest shown in the womenswear, a separate catalogue was produced to itemise the garments on display. Included in this was a 'typically British' sports outfit consisting of a beaver corduroy jacket and herringbone tweed skirt – the 'country look'. The hard-wearing materials and sensible accessories conveniently lent themselves to shopping as well as to rural walks. Variations on the Utility suit represented to the design establishment an image of 'modern' femininity, that is, the sensible and restrained attributes of the housewife. The look *signifies* restraint, rather than being necessarily functional (wartime clothing which *was* much more practical than the Utility suit, such as the siren suit and the turban, became fashion statements and were later translated into evening wear), but the utility image continued to represent an ideal to those professionals whose task it was to regulate and socialise consumption.

Fashion experts tended to preach the same virtues of rationality and aestheticism which were endorsed by the design establishment. The designs of couturiers such as Hardy Amies (known for reworking English classics rather than for the frivolous or ephemeral) were featured in women's weeklies, usually in the form of special patterns adapted from or inspired by them. These patterns were supplemented by articles on how to use line and colour in developing 'fashion sense'. In *Woman*, 9 September 1953, Amies draws parallels between dressing and cooking. So the promotions of the latest fashions were accompanied by advice and instruction which stressed the rules and regulations of 'good taste'. A certain amount of glamour was acceptable in its place, but only as a pleasing contrast to the rule of restraint.

As the consumers of fashion goods then, working-class women were being educated in the skills of 'good taste' (restraint, practicality, etc.) in much the same way as they were being trained as home-managers in order to consume domestic goods. But at the same time, feminine glamour was being promoted as a feature of high fashion. This glamour was not condemned unequivocally by all constituencies of the design profession (although the New Look was reviled by many as unpatriotic and irresponsible) but rather it was accepted as a separate but complementary look, which could exist alongside Utility styles as long as it was not adopted for 'inappropriate' situations. However, this attempt to construct clear distinctions between the utilitarian/practical and the decorative/glamorous and to impose codes of dress as a consequence, inadvertently encouraged consumers to acquire knowledges and competences which enabled them to be 'chameleon-like' in the production of these different femininities. I would argue that these competences make their 'improper' appropriation of fashion goods inevitable, and resulted in the sampling and mixing of different styles which ultimately characterised popular fashion of the 1950s.

ANGELA PARTINGTON

GENDERED CONSUMPTION

Since it was working-class women who were the target of the consumption-regulation programme, it is necessary to consider how a specifically feminine relationship with goods may have enabled them to continue to use clothing in symbolic/emotional (rather than utilitarian/rational) ways, despite the best efforts of the design profession. Since designers discouraged identification with and emotional investment in objects, and encouraged 'objective' or 'disinterested' relationships with goods instead, traditionally 'feminine' ways of relating to goods were considered 'vulgar' or 'improper'. It can be argued, however, that the 'female gaze' enabled women to respond enthusiastically to modern design, without surrendering this ability to identify with objects.

I have argued elsewhere that to identify narcissistically with objects does not preclude the ability to fetishise or objectify them from a voyeuristic position.[25] Rather than seeing narcissism and exhibitionism as inevitably feminine, and fetishism and voyeurism as inevitably masculine, as many theorists have tended to do, it has to be recognised that these tendencies are interdependent, albeit differently for women and men. In order for women to become skilled in inviting the gaze, they have had to acquire knowledges and competences which enable them to discriminate between other objects, with which to adorn themselves and their surroundings. In order to express preferences, women have had to become subjects of the (female) gaze, while at the same time identifying with the objects of that gaze (goods), in order to fulfil a role as object of the male gaze.

What has been referred to as 'masquerade' evokes very well this feminine fusion of voyeurism and exhibitionism. 'Masquerade' implies an acting out of the images of femininity, for which is required an active gaze to decode, utilise and identify with those images, while at the same time constructing a self-image which is dependent on the gaze of the other. In this sense, womanliness, or femininity, is a 'simulation', a demonstration of the representations of women – a 'masquerade', acted out by the female viewer. Although the design profession encouraged a pure and detached relationship with goods, the female gaze enabled objectification without sacrificing identification, therefore women were able to consume designed goods 'improperly', i.e. in ways not anticipated or understood by designers. The collective production of meanings takes place *within* consumer groups at specific moments; indeed, this is enabled and encouraged by a mass-market system. For example, 'masquerade' is a simulation of femininity, and as such confirms the

Mass-produced copy of the New Look (from Fashion in the Forties and Fifties *by Jane Dorner, courtesy of Catriona Tomalin)*

existence of a feminine cultural code, or shared meanings for women as markets for fashion and beauty goods.

POPULAR FASHION

The consumer's investment in a style may or may not involve a transformation of the fashion commodity's appearance, but any reworkings of the object are not simply a manipulation of a visual language. They are social acts in which the object only has meaning in relation to the circumstances surrounding them. A 'reproductive transformation' takes place, regardless of how much or how little the consumer alters the appearance of the object. The consumer determines the meaning of the fashion commodity through a redefinition of use-values which brings it within the circumstances of a particular mode of life, and of a cultural code which is specific to a target market (e.g. working-class women).

I began this article by commenting on how popular fashions are often regarded as 'watered down versions' of design 'originals'. But if we approach fashion as a discursive articulation of class differences, a practice through which class relations, and therefore economic conditions, are actually (re)produced, we can approach both the similarities and differences between high fashion and popular fashion quite differently. Both the changes and non-changes which take place in the series of mediations between production and consumption involve a number of investments in the style. The mass-market fashion system enables the consumer to appropriate fashionable styles by altering and transforming them, in the process of 'copying' them. It is in the mixing together of copied elements with other 'incompatible' elements that the distinctions and oppositions, which the designers hold sacred, are broken down. In the consumption of fashion goods, working-class women collectively simulate class differences.

1950s fashions were 'improperly' consumed by working-class women, in the sense that they were used to satisfy needs other than those which had been assumed by the fashion industry and the design profession. For example, the two complementary styles – 'Utility' and the 'New Look' – which 'express' the post-war ideologies of femininity so well, but which were clearly distinguished by designers as the 'functional' and the 'decorative', were sampled and mixed together by the consumer to create fashions which depended on class-specific consumer skills for their meaning.

A mass-market fashion system ensures that the diffusion of styles takes place *within* groups (rather than across class distinctions), so styles need not be adopted in the same way by different consumer groups. Indeed, the system itself encourages different forms of adoption. As I have already argued, differences in price, make, and retailer ensures this. But this does not mean that popular versions are merely cheaper or lower-quality copies of design-originals. If this were the case, popular fashion would resemble couture much more closely than it does. In the late 1940s and early 1950s, there were mass-produced copies of the New Look which were fairly 'accurate' (see p. 156), but it seems (from looking at my family album photographs) that these 'faithful' copies did not become widely popular among working-class women, while more 'hybrid' versions did. Working-class women did not keep away from the frivolous or the impractical, even at work; instead it was sampled and re-mixed with the comfortable and the serviceable, rather than kept separate and used on 'decorative' occasions only, as advised by fashion experts.

There were many professional designers who were outraged by the 'New Look', and who condemned it either as an antithesis to modernism and therefore regressive, or as a shameful indulgence in the face of economic restrictions. To an extent then, its popularity amongst middle-class women, or amongst women generally, can be read as a 'rebellious' or 'subversive' use of fashion, not dissimilar to that usually ascribed to youth subcultures. But there were those factions of the design profession who regarded it as a distinct but complementary aspect of modern femininity, which could exist alongside, and enhance, the dutiful housewife look. If women used fashion to resist the dominant ideologies of femininity then, it was through the 'improper' consumption, or appropriation, of the New Look. I will try to show that working-class women did do this, not in an act of rebellion, but in an investment of class-specific consumer skills.

If we take the cotton shirtwaist and the all-purpose suit as examples of 1950s Utility (since these were routinely identified with the practical housewife image), and the New Look cocktail dress (near right) as an example of its complementary glamorous opposite, we can see that working-class women did not keep these styles distinct and separate. They combined the practical and the glamorous in a range of hybrid styles, completely 'ruining' the achievements of designers in their creation of 'complementary' looks. Popular notions of the New Look, such as depicted in the wedding photograph, were quite different from both couture and 'accurate' (department store) mass-produced versions. The jacket of the suit is much looser and the fabric less stiff than the Dior equivalent. The neckline of the dress is much less revealing than the mass-produced copy, and the bodice is not boned or corseted, so the waist is not 'nipped in'. The length and/or fullness of the skirts are retained from Dior's original design, but these are combined with the button-through bodice and collar derived from the shirtwaist, and with the boxier shape and serviceable fabric of the all-purpose suit. The photograph taken at the Festival of Britain the same year (far right) shows a similar combination of shirtwaist bodies and New-Look skirt in the same dress. My mother insists that the wide-brimmed hat was not part of the New Look style (but only bought as a souvenir), and that the style was 'free' and comfortable rather than restrictive and ornamental, allowing it to be worn in an 'everyday' way rather than for evenings or special occasions. This contradicts the assumption made by fashion historians that the New Look was inappropriate for work or active pursuits.

Popular fashion mixed the glamorous and the practical, fused function and meaning (objectification and identification), by incorporating elements from styles which designers assumed would take their meaning from the clear distinctions between them. This can be read as a challenge to the dichotomy separating 'housewife' (functional woman) and sex object (decorative woman). But it can also be seen as a complete redefinition of the values of the clothes,

*Utility and New
Look combined,
Festival of Britain
(courtesy of Angela
Partington)*

*The New Look
cocktail dress,
February 1947,
designed by Dior,
photograph by Cecil
Beaton (courtesy of
Sotheby's, London)*

an insistence on the prerogative to use clothes in meaning-making practices which are dependent on class-specific skills. Through fashion, as with home-making, women invited the gaze of the other, in that they identified with commodities, that is, that were not 'disinterested', but conspicuously narcissistic, using goods to signify their economic and social position rather than to fulfil needs presumed by designers.

'GOOD TASTE' VERSUS DESIGN-LED MARKETING

The tensions between attempts to 'train' affluence and regulate consumption (in which the meaningfulness of goods is disavowed), and mass-marketing (which relies precisely on the meaningfulness of commodities), creates an insoluble conflict between design establishment and manufacturing/marketing industries. The attempt to construct markets, through the use of design, provides consumers with skills with which to counter the purism of the design establishment. The contradiction between design-led marketing and 'good taste' has been particularly marked in Britain, where an aristocratic distaste for industrial culture has a long history.[26] Attempts to renegotiate the relationships between designers, manufacturers, advertisers, and retailers, in the pursuit of a rational system of production and consumption, far from determining the meanings of goods, has actually ensured that the struggles over meanings, and the constant reappropriation of goods by consumers, has persisted.

As consumers, working-class women were able to articulate their own specific tastes and preferences, by using the cultural codes of the mass-market fashion system.

Notes and References

1 Dick Hebdige, *Subculture: The Meaning of Style*, London, 1979.
2 Mica Nava, 'Consumerism and its Contradictions', *Cultural Studies* vol. I, no. 2, 1987.
3 Georg Simmel, 'Fashion', (originally published in 1904) in Gordon Wills and David Midgley (eds), *Fashion Marketing*, London, 1973.
4 Charles King, 'A Rebuttal of the Trickle Down Theory', in Wills and Midgley, op. cit., p. 216.
5 Thorstein Veblen, 'The Theory of Conspicuous Consumption', quoted in Elizabeth Wilson, *Adorned in Dreams*, London, 1985.
6 J. Clarke and C. Critcher, *The Devil Makes Work* – Leisure in Capitalist Britain, London, 1985, pp. 82, 189.
7 King, in Wills and Midgley, op. cit.
8 Herbert Blumer, 'Fashion: From Class Differentiation to Collective Selection', in Wills and Midgley, op. cit.
9 James Carman, 'The Fate of Fashion Cycles in our Modern Society', in Wills and Midgley, op. cit., p. 135.
10 Bernard Barber and Lyle Lobel, 'Fashion in Women's Clothes and the American Social System', in Wills and Midgley, op. cit., p. 362.

11 Ibid., p. 363.

12 Clarke and Critcher, op. cit., p. 96.

13 Ingrid Brenninkmeyer, 'The Diffusion of Fashion', in Wills and Midgley, op. cit., p. 271.

14 Prudence Glynn, *In Fashion*, London, 1978, p. 186.

15 Jane Dorner, *Fashion in the Forties and Fifties*, London, 1975, p. 53.

16 Erica Carter, 'Alice in Consumer Wonderland', in Angela McRobbie and Mica Nava (eds), *Gender and Generation*, London, 1984, pp. 200, 207.

17 Elizabeth Wilson and Lou Taylor, *Through the Looking Glass*, London, 1989.

18 Barry Curtis, 'One Long Continuous Story', *Block*, no. 11, Winter 1985/6, p. 51.

19 Glynn, op. cit., p. 187.

20 Penny Sparke, *An Introduction to Design and Culture*, London, 1986, p. 65.

21 Barbara Schreier, *Mystique and Identity: Women's Fashions of the 1950s*, Chrysler Museum, New York, 1984, p. 13.

22 Dorner, op. cit., p. 7.

23 Nicholas Drake, *The Fifties in Vogue*, London, 1987, p. 13.

24 Pearson Phillips, 'The New Look', in Sissons and French (eds), *The Age of Austerity*, Oxford, 1963.

25 Angela Partington, 'The Gendered Gaze', in Nancy Honey (ed.), *Woman To Woman*, 1990.

26 Dick Hebdige, 'Towards a Cartography of Taste', *Block*, no. 4, 1981.

JUDY RUMBOLD

An A–Z of Sportswear

A

ANORAK Once the frequenter of Enid Blyton plots and 'wanted' posters outside local police stations, this quilted scourge of childhood wardrobes sprouted drawstrings, hoods and one hundred varieties of pocket and was reborn into fashionable, civilised society as a parka.
ATTITUDE Mysterious, intangible quality that couldn't be bought, borrowed or stolen. Generally speaking, American kids had it and we didn't. It became the hard-to-obtain prerequisite for a plausible, urban sportswear look.

B

BUMBAG A glorified money purse with a silly new name. Natural habitat: Swedish students' rucksacks and special offer small-ads in the backs of tabloids. It was essential that the bumbag was lashed to the waist with nonchalant aplomb, otherwise it ended up looking like an ill-fitting colostomy accessory. Just spacious enough to accommodate a small stash of youthful ephemera, while freeing the arms to perform flailing acid moves on the dancefloor.

C

COMFORT With the popularity of sportswear, the fashion industry superpowers for once gazed benevolently upon a clothes-buying public made extremely nervous by the cling-and-fit obsession of the late eighties. Because the sport ethic's practicality and user-friendliness couldn't be faulted, the let up in designer-tyranny went into injury time: it made the business of looking fashionable a good deal less stressful for the timorously trendy.

D

DAYGLO Against a backdrop of pasty British complexions and a sky the colour of tripe, fluro pink, orange and green made eerily glowing beacons of many, but flattered few.

DUNGAREES These have spent much of their lives mooching around on the peripheries of fashion, recruiting all those people who looked ridiculous in hotpants and minis. In the eighties they offered a capacious, sporty sanctuary away from unforgiving stretch knits and prohibitively short skirts.

E

ENORMOUS influence on everybody, not least impressionable fashion designers, who make their anoraks in gold lamé (Versace), their Reeboks in rhinestone-studded velvet (Ozbek), and their bumbags in expensively quilted leather (Chanel).

F

FUR TRIM When domestic pets you hardly knew began to graze at the hem of your garment, you knew you were truly fashionable. The height of hirsute trendiness was a parka hood edged in coarse, white hairy acrylic masquerading as fur.

G

GO-FASTER stripes sped down the outside of trousers and streamlined hard shoulders. They outlined and circumnavigated everything from knickers and bras to tights and shoes. Designed to flatter, they often achieved the opposite, making less than sylph-like figures look like violently undulating road maps that had buckled in the rain.

H

HOODS Pivotal to the eighties' sportswear look, although there were certain rules to observe; it had to flop in a flaccid, redundant heap at the nape of the neck and was rarely worn pulled up over the head. Even though it teasingly betrayed signs of functionalism and practicality, the hood remained one of the most superfluous fashion cults ever.

I

IRRITATINGLY HUMOURLESS Although sportswear gave the impression it might be good for a few laughs, sportswear devotees were about as relaxed as a holiday in Kuwait after the Gulf war. They disliked having their carefully arranged bits and pieces tampered with. They didn't appreciate having their hoods filled with popcorn at the cinema, nor did they enjoy being compared to trainspotters, or halfwit characters from *Crossroads* and *One Man and his Dog*.

J

JEWELLERY Conspicuous by the fact that it just wasn't there. You would no more mix dangly earrings and ostentatious brooches with sportswear than wear flares when there wasn't an 'R' in the month.

K

KNICKER LINE Visible. It became something of a badge of courage in the late eighties, when Lycra-made tight skirts, dresses and unforgivingly clingy catsuits performed the function of a second skin. But where, we ask ourselves, is the line-less knicker? Why hasn't it been designed yet? We must all pray to St Michael and hope he hears.

L

LOGO'S Promotional claptrap about hamburgers, fizzy drinks and in-house chainstore insignia was to be avoided at all costs. Logo's to covet were almost exclusively American and reminiscent of the football pitch, the campus and the football stadium.

M

MANCHESTER Just another accent until a group of neo-bedsit bands like the Happy Mondays and Inspiral Carpets made such aberrations as flares and pudding-basin haircuts popular. You tried to tell them that seventies' style was ugly, unflattering, that it was the era that style forgot, but they wouldn't listen. You realised then that you were getting old and were beginning to sound like your mother.

N

NEW AGE New age became old age before you could say white sweatshirt with rhinestone trim. I think it was about crystals, self-discovery, ephemeral plinky-plonky music and user-unfriendly white clothes, but I could be wrong. Dry cleaners enjoyed a boom.

O

ORDINARY LOOKING Never was a street uniform so easy to wear. Everyone looked the same, and for once it didn't matter.

P

PONCHO Fell into the wrong hands in the sixties and never quite recovered. Epitomised everything abhorrent about seventies' style, but nevertheless clawed back some credibility as a post-acid hippy statement. A bestselling version of the poncho was one with Magnificent Seven Navaho stripes, plummeting a magnificent 7 feet to the floor.

S

SWEATPANTS No credibility points were awarded for pristine, new-looking pants with shop-smart creases and efficient elastic. They had to look raddled and worn, as though they'd survived about twenty rounds with the 'Whites, Heavy Soil' programme.

T

TRAINERS Sprawling, three-piece suite of a shoe with showy cladding, one hundred superfluous details and the tread of a small tractor. The tongue had to loll out at the front, as if exhausted by its own fast, furious trendiness.

V

VELOUR TRACKSUITS Let's spare a thought for those lurid yellow and pink things from suburbia. They were, after all, unwitting forerunners of eighties' sportswear. They *were* there first, albeit with white stilettos, gold chains and a pushchair for accessories.

W

WORLD CUP Everyone became football junkies a year before the event. The World Cup inspired a pitch-invasionful of designer soccer clothes, although Union Jack boxer shorts and flags worn as capes remained the preserve of oikish away-crowds at Euston station.

X

XTRA LARGE Everyone looked like urchins in enormous hood T-shirts that hung off skinny teenage frames. And if you weren't skinny, here was blissful camouflage. The fact that big was also fashionable was a rare bonus in the tyrannical, undemocratic empire that is the fashion industry.

Y

YOUNG Sportswear appealed to youngsters because it was a cheap and easy look to put together. Mothers approved too, which is why its days are numbered.

Z

ZIPS Sportswear didn't have time to waste on buttons and fiddly fastenings, so zips were employed to facilitate the getting in and out of clothes in double-quick time.
ZITS Could languish unnoticed on foreheads and cheeks, because most fashion-conscious faces were hidden most of the time by baseball caps with enormous peaks.

JULIET ASH

Philosophy on the Catwalk

The Making & Wearing of Vivienne Westwood's Clothes

A man lives by his head
His head will not suffice. [1]

There is a dialectician hidden in every master of an art. [2]

AUGUST 1980 KING'S ROAD

A decade ago it was in Sex – the shop – that we met, the 'Queen of Punk' and I. All had been leather, zips, tears and masks, the authentic S/M; now all that is analysed for the uninitiated on the *Late Show* by the erotic intelligentsia. Vivienne Westwood had been in curlers; the shop had been packed with young buyers and Jordan served them in high heels, suspender belt and shirt.

AUGUST 1990 CAMDEN TOWN

Ten years later I'm waiting in Vivienne Westwood's workplace in Camden Town. 'Cut 'N Slash has just come back from Pitti Palace. Have a look'.

The words connect the inconspicuous production room in Camden Town with the Renaissance splendour of Florence. But not just with words and not just geographically. The collection transports us too: in fabric, colour, texture and ideals.

Cloth is not only better than flesh, more purely beautiful, but it can also seem more holy and thus more appropriate to the figuring forth of paradise. It is not subject, after all, to sin. [3]

But clothes can be accessories to the fact of sin. The racks of sumptuous garments stand like idle courtiers lining the corridors. Pink, blue and bluer, pale green, white, red and yellow satin men's frock coats with printed, eighteenth-century furnishing fabric as lapels, and photographic roses; rafia

JULIET ASH

Catwalk performance of Vivienne Westwood's 'Cut N Slash' Collection, shown at the Pitti Palace, Florence, July 1990, photographs by Robyn Beach (courtesy of the photographer)

jackets, bolero tops and denim slashed – small machine cuts – in ritualistic patterns; large frayed slashes across the leg; to feel the slash, the fray, is to feel the exposed skin beneath. The satin is smooth. Pyjama suits in stripes hang loose and move their silky texture in the slight breeze. Immaculately tailored suits in cotton-cool white, yellow-gold, blue and rust hang limp with diagonally cut flies, waiting to be filled; rounded Dickensian bowler hats, neckties, and kipper-printed portrait ties lie in a period piece.

For, this is menswear, and amongst it, slashed swimming trunks and a balloon dress – a huge circle of fabric hoisted around a woman's waist – and undercuts in knickers. It matters that there was one woman model in this collection of men; a woman to cut carefully with her razor blade the foamy stubble of a man (below). It matters that the details in menswear have changed but that the ideas are androgynous. 'The polarities of dress and undress' may take a different form for the two genders but they contain a similar effect.

Here, in this corridor, is colour and light, a feeling sensation of texture and cut, and as one moves down the rack, pinching, the colours resemble a cacophony of sounds: 'Ah', 'Oo', 'Oh' – pleasure, like Rimbaud's poem 'Voyelles' (Vowels):

> A noir, E blanc, I rouge, U vert, O bleu: voyelles
> Je dirais quelque jour vos naissances latentes:
> A, noir corset velu des mouches éclatantes[4]

The mysterious origins of these clothes, the method by which they are conceived, then made, and performed on a catwalk demand inquiry. The juxtaposition of imagery in Rimbaud's phrase 'A, black velvet jacket of brilliant flies' resembles Vivienne Westwood's method of making clothes – a sort of surmontage of dissimilarities (cultural and technical) from which comes a new form and from which emerges a new idea, whether concerning sexuality, dress, cut, history, painting, music, dance, catwalk performance, philosophy, age, youth, time. Rimbaud based notions of colour on mysteries connected with colour and alchemy: black is the depression which precedes gold (the colour), and the 'brilliant flies' contrast visually with the black of the velvet jacket. Similarly, Vivienne Westwood looks at paintings, such as Watteau's *Voyage to Cythera*, and contemporises them through a rearrangement of folds, cut and innovative technique, watching the new 'synthesis' formulate a new idea. Often the shock for the audience results from this new combination, derived from the normal becoming abnormal in a changed context.

Vivienne Westwood's Making of Clothes

Vivienne returns and lays out a black mac from her Witches Collection of 1983. She explains that the cut of the mac was on the square, the sleeve square, gusseted to a point at the elbow; the waist gathered from the side of the square to the middle. Most of the Pirate Collection shirts and shifts had been cut like this. She explains that all her early collections (apart from the fitted bondage) had been characterised by looseness – a dynamic of fabric with the body from a square. More recently, tailoring and the fitting of fabric round the body 'like a shell' has become interesting to her as puzzles of cut, yet the square cut is still used to 'untidy clothes for elegance' – big shirts hanging out under tightly cut jackets.

A garment of Vivienne Westwood's, or indeed a whole collection, may produce diverse reactions, of entrancement, revelation, confusion, fragmentation, dislike or shock, depending on the person perceiving, wearing or watching her clothes in performance. She is acutely aware of the potential reaction of her audience and is never more delighted than when the complex process of making arouses distaste or shock.

AUGUST 1980

'I've always said that in order to make people think, you do have to emotionally hurt them in some way. For example, the word Seditionaries, which I used to rename the shop, has always meant to me the necessity to *seduce* people into revolt. The main thing is always to confront the culture and find out where the culture lies, because that's the only thing which keeps you alive – to receive culture – that's what gives you vitality.'

I had wandered out of Sex in 1980 wondering *what* culture she was referring to. Not until a decade later did I start to understand the labyrinth of cultures she alluded to in her collections, her shops, and how important it was to her in the 1980s to communicate visually and technically 'an accumulated process of acquiring knowledge'. And how unimportant for her was the accumulation of money.

How does she know that she *is* communicating ideas?

AUGUST 1990

'And I came out with the fig-leaf tights on (at the end of Cut 'N Slash) and with a shirt on over. I like to put the cat among the pigeons, so I just came out with those flesh coloured tights. And Michael Clarke and his boyfriend, Steven (who'd danced a mock-sabre embrace in slashed denim on the catwalk) – they carried me on, and I had my legs going all over the place, and it was really funny. Some people from *Vogue* were saying how it would have looked vulgar if it wasn't for Vivienne being able to carry it off on the catwalk. And others said, "My wife's her age, and if she ever contemplated such a costume, I'd turn her out of the house." So I liked that.'

Reactions overheard amongst fashion specialists and buyers at the womenswear collection (Britain Must Go Pagan, autumn 1989) where these tights first appeared included, 'just stupid', 'unwearable', 'uncommercial', 'vulgar'. Words were used which reflected the fashion world's entrenchment in the commercial norm of the 1980s high street, and married men's terrors about their wives' moral (fleshy) exposure.

A year later the fig-leaf tight could still succeed in disconcerting respectability, despite Gombrich's warning that 'at the end of the eighties we are all anaesthetised against shock'.[5]

Vivienne Westwood insists on the orthodox as 'unorthodox' – the subversion of visual assumptions, 'I just thought them funny . . .'

This insouciant remark conceals the process, the search behind the making of this deceptively simple pair of tights. To look at this process with Vivienne Westwood is to reveal, partly, her method of making, which she describes as common to her diverse fashion collections of the 1980s and early 1990s.

'. . . a technical thing, all the collections have a dynamic and rapport with the body . . . It's a question of judging and assessing – this is what technique is: it's all your experience brought to bear on what you're making. And that experience is practical . . . You build up a working formula which is elastic and it can be turned around and inside out . . . There are certain polarities operating in whatever I do, very strong ones – between masculine and feminine (how much femininity goes into men's clothes, how much masculinity can go into women's clothes) . . . There's dress and undress (whether it's nun-like to the neck, or it's lace-up boots, or fig-leaf tights) . . . There's the way the specific hem and seams of a garment balance the cut for the required proportion . . . The form and the idea are the same thing. When you finish a garment, what has made the result is the way you've done it; and whatever ideas you started off with, it's the way you carry them out or change them . . . or build them up and consider everything in a three-dimensional way with what I call 'spatial intelligence', with reference to cultural charges and triggers. The garment will then be imbued with all these decisions for all time – and it is this final synthesis of the polarities in the garment itself which will be suggestive to people of the idea.'

Making the Figleaf Tights

[The Greeks] went out on a voyage of discovery to add more and more features from observation to the traditional images of the world. But their works never look like mirrors in which any odd corner of the world is reflected. They always bear the stamp of the intellect which made them.[6]

Vivienne Westwood's techniques are essential to her craft but more important to her is the endless discovery of ideas which emerge through the creative process. She observes the past in the context of her own vision of the future. In the making of clothes her knowledge of the traditions of the past inspires a new knowledge for her, achieved through elucidating the complexity of history in the new simplicity a garment represents.

'First of all I showed the tailoring and you didn't see any cuts in it; then I wanted to bring the cuts on and mix them in with it. So before I did I had Suzi come on with just a little pair of knickers with all these cuts in them and a plain white shirt over the top and some red satin high-heeled shoes, and a cut-throat razor [see p. 168]. And then this bloke comes on with cuts in a vest and a pair of trousers all covered in cuts, and his face covered in shaving lather, and she started to shave him – just to let people know that we were going to start bringing in the cuts and slashes.'

The action on the catwalk, the garments on the catwalk are the spectacle, but the simplicity of the individual garment and/or action belies the complexity of references. The shaving breaks up the 'cut' of the tailoring and the 'slash' to come but also enacts the process of pattern cutting or fabric cutting. In the action of shaving, the deliberate cut with the razor (scissors) of hair (fabric) is done to avoid the skin (table) surface, which is not intended to be cut.

The activity of making is as important for the ideas engendered in the garments and on the catwalk as the original idea was to the making process. Vivienne Westwood is fully aware both of the traditions with which she works and her own reference points:

'Art is parody: it uses what went before; it simplifies, but it also synthesises something else with it, that's what makes it interesting.'

But to parody there must be knowledge of the item being parodied.

In the Cut 'N Slash Collection there is a train of thought which affects the technique, which in turn modifies the original idea embodied in the final garment. Talking about how *Voyage to Cythera* inspired some of the collection, Vivienne Westwood mentions the 'cuirass', which appears in doublet form in the menswear Cut 'N Slash (July 1990), but she herself reappears with the fig-leaf tights (of autumn 1989), accompanied by a slashed, voluminous men's shirt. To follow the process from idea to catwalk is to journey through fashion and painting history. Knowledge, acknowledged as uncertain, is reinterpreted to become certain inspiration. We continue to create dualities of meaning in our reinterpretation. Not eclecticism, not pluralism for lack of something to say; what Vivienne Westwood presents us with is dualities of possible meanings.

The Cuirass

This garment was 'a Roman soldier's skirty tabs which went out like a ballet skirt'.

Trajan wears a cuirass formed of two metal plates, protecting his torso, completed by leather tabs trimmed with metal.[7] (See right.)

'In Watteau's *Voyage to Cythera*, I liked the idea that a Roman soldier was looking like something that had been devised at the Court of Louis XIV. It then became a baroque theatrical convention and it lasted for some 100 years. And I like the idea that theatrical convention is always delayed like that.'

Vivienne Westwood's reinterpretation of the early eighteenth-century (Watteau's) softer tabs flowing from the red velvety doublet of the man on the right of the painting (see below) kissing a woman's shoulder, becomes almost a high-waisted ballet skirt in slashed denim in the Cut 'N Slash Collection. Michael Clarke swirls around the stage in a sword dance with a male rival/lover, with slashed, loose, denim breeches and reinterpreted cuirass. The hard leather/metal tabs have been metamorphosed by Watteau in nature's moving erotic feast on the way to the land of Venus, and likewise by Vivienne Westwood in the fabric-folds of the erotic dance. The sexuality is explicit in the clothes (their slashes of dress and undress) and in the fervent kiss of the two male dancers. The hardness of the Roman Empire – '"authoritarian, organisational,

*The Emperor Trajan,
2nd century,* AD
*(The Ancient Art
and Architecture
Collection)*

*Jean Antoine
Watteau,* Pilgrimage
to the Island of
Cythera, *1717
(courtesy of Musée du
Louvre)*

grandiose, rhetorical"'[8] – has been historically recontextualised to create clothes which represent the Greeks, who were '"life-loving, crafty, hedonistic–spiritual"'[9] (in the categories invented by the art critic, David Sylvester). It is the Greeks with whom Vivienne Westwood has cultural sympathy. What Karl Miller says about Melville is equally true of Westwood's outlook, which is so different to routine rag-trade philosophy:

> This is a sceptical view of human nature which severely restricts the amount that can be held to be known about it . . . In its subversion of literature the novel nevertheless leaves the spectator with a novelist. It leaves us with a novelist who wants to displease and deceive, and to undeceive: to convert – to a doctrine of uncertain scope which is made to seem very forbidding –
> the reader he senses he has lost.[10]

Vivienne Westwood says: 'It's a question of cultivating doubt.'

And so the fig-leaf tights, worn by Vivienne Westwood herself, round off a menswear collection. The fig-leaf conceals the genitals under a man's shirt. Is this person male or female? The red satin platform high-heels elongate the legs. Traditional male attire at the top of the body; traditional feminine footwear at the end of the body, and between – the androgynous tights. The Westwood dialectic communicates to the observer the duality of the ancient world, of Aristotle's 'in-betweens', 'anomolies'; a fitting, doubting culmination to a menswear collection.

Not a 'practice comparable to a child "investigating" adult garments, rummaging through the historical wardrobe,'[11] but more the Proustian woman:

> I think what he's talking about is that memory is the creative key . . . the key, when people go into ecstasy.[12]

The inspiration for the fig-leaf tights came originally from seeing a representation of a Greek statue:

> The Greeks wore drapery and that was sensual, and we lack that experience with clothes now. The Greeks pointed out that the Barbarians were very unsensual and bad lovers. They didn't have enough contact with their naked bodies and they wore trousers. The piece of drapery above the nudity is ennobling, it's like passion coming out. It suddenly clicked, seeing that statue, that, just before 1800, the women were trying to copy what they thought Greek statues looked like – the clinging Empire-line drapes, which they wetted. The men at that time were swathed on top in quantities of fabric. But the men's breeches, in pale colours, were tight and high-waisted and the focus was on the genitals. So the women, in a different way, were trying to do that too.[13]

The Apollo Belvedere (overleaf) exemplifies this and shows the ideal model of a Greek man's body. Gombrich says of the statue:

These statues are, in fact, beings from a different world, not because the Greeks were healthier or more beautiful than other men – but because art at that moment had reached a point at which the typical and the individual were poised in a new and delicate balance.[14]

The delicate balance seems almost like a tense elegance, on the brink of something else. Vivienne Westwood, in the fig-leaf tights, precariously balanced on platform heels, is suggesting that the typical (the nostalgia for the 1950s through to the 1970s, identifiable in most fashion designers' collections of the late 1980s and early 1990s) is perilously balanced against an individual vision – a cultural coherence enhanced by technique overleaf. The technique here lies in the idea that

'[the Greek statue motif] would be the most brilliant look for a woman, and I just wanted my outfit to look like a girl dressed like a man with no trousers on'.

A version of this was represented in one of the 'Britain Must Go Pagan' collections (autumn 1989) as a woman wearing pink knickers with a penis graffiti'd on the front, and a man's large shirt with a loose collar and dishevelled tie: the half-dressed city gent as woman. Another, more classic version, became the androgynous fig-leaf tights, hiding the genitals, worn by a woman wearing a man's shirt and skewy tie. The simplicity of the make of the knickers and the fig-leaf tights (the latter in pink stockinette – like surgical tights but much softer – with a green-glass fig-leaf appliquéd on the front) belied a complexity of allusions. The technique is surmontage – the layering of idea upon make upon idea – realised in the making and wearing of the garment.

Vivienne Westwood's collections are made up of historical dialogues merged with contemporaneous references to fabrics and appearance. She talks and works with her team of six or so people – two pattern cutters, two designers, a head of production, and her son, Jo, the director – as she talks to me, as she talks with students on placement and as she talks to her audience.

She is a sophisticated ironist, who exposes our contemporary misapprehensions and our 'philistinism': our preoccupations with the 'right' answer so unswervingly fragmented in the vacuity of a so-called 'postmodernist' world; our preoccupations with finance, money, status (in Vivienne Westwood's vocabulary, 'elites' and 'aristocracies' – the duplicity existing in so-called democracies); our preoccupations, thus, with *fashions*, which are rarely commercially viable; our academic concerns with desire as a commodity to

Apollo Belvedere,
350-320 BC
(The Ancient Art
and Architecture
Collection)

The fig-leaf tights,
here not worn by
Vivienne Westwood
but by a model on
the catwalk of
Vivienne Westwood's
autumn 1989
collection,
photograph by Robyn
Beach (courtesy of
the photographer)

be analysed rather than expressed. All these are turned on their head by the catwalk spectacle; the masquerade where normality becomes abnormality in the context of transformation through technique (in this case innovative 'cut' and contemporised references to historicism).

A Westwood collection transports me back to adolescent identification with Shakespearian characters to the medieval pilgrimages of Chaucer, the mysteries of Greek iconography on jars in the British Museum, the writings of de Sade, the devil's hoof under the antediluvian habit of the rural minister in James Hogg's *Confessions of a Justified Sinner*, the Situationists' vision ('Under the Paving Stones the Beach') of Paris 1968, and to a visual tradition spanning the precisions of Greek sculpture, the intrigues of Renaissance painting and the romantic irony of Watteau.

Where we part company is in her dismissal of twentieth century art and modernism. But 'the calculated riddle'[15] of Vivienne Westwood's collections and thought requires a positing of thoughts and references in relation to *pre-twentieth century art and culture*.

Westwood's work eludes the journalist (attempting synopsoid descriptions of this season's predictions); the fashion historian (extracting linear references to costume developments); the postmodernist critic (delving into all meanings as a reductionist form based on fragmentation, and consciously rejecting the desirability of knowing the world as a whole); the fashion business 'rep' and the buyer (relying on the commercial viability of the 'Sell').

Vivienne Westwood's success lies in her acknowledgement of the process by which she works, thinks and articulates her ideas. It is simple, and one wonders at the clarity with which, after being booed by Terry Wogan's audience, she could declare, 'I think that went down very well'.[16] Taboos had been broken; communication had taken place; the receivers had reacted. Better any reaction than passivity.

Bertolt Brecht's notion of Epic Theatre illuminates Vivienne Westwood's method and similarly explains the advent of her success – not financial success, but the fact that her name as a British designer has become an international household word in a decade in which she has been systematically considered 'eccentric', 'uncommercial', but 'unstoppable'.

Not the purging of emotions through identification with the hero's turbulent destiny (the Aristotelian notion of cathartic dramas) but Epic Theatre, by contrast, advances by fits and starts, like the images on a film strip. Its basic form is that of the forceful impact on one another of separate, distinct situations in the play . . . Thus distances are created everywhere which are, on the whole, detrimental to illusion among the audience. These distances are meant to make the audience adopt a critical attitude, to make it think.[17]

Vivienne Westwood connects with the world of manufacturing and creating for an audience. Her making depends on industrial products, her parodies are of Western cultures and her creating combines autobiographical historicism with contemporary inspiration.

Lack of informed dialogue keeps people fragmented. She is only too aware that the material conditions of people ('the pittance' earned by textile and garment workers) is a precondition for cultural decline (traditional fabrics of which she is so fond will increasingly disappear in a de-industrialised Britain). But what also connects her to a vision of a better future is her acceptance of 'pluralities' as fundamental to her work, a form of primitive dialectics: 'I would prefer to see the world a better place. I do care'.

For the artist as for the mescalin taker, draperies are living hyroglyphs that stand in some peculiarly expressive way for the unfathomable mystery of pure being.[18]

Wearing Vivienne Westwood's Clothes

'This is why it's still vital and valid [fashion]; it has to be because it's defined by the fact it's got to be worn.'

AUTUMN 1981

World's End in the King's Road on a hot umber day – slashed T-shirts, leather jackets, tartan mini-sirts over tight black leggings; mohicans. Olympia had been full of fashion victims (the glitterati still fox-furred before the greening of the fashion industry) observing the Pirate Collection of Vivienne Westwood and Malcolm McClaren. Adam Ant's 'Stand and Deliver' was number one and could be heard tinnily emanating from early personal stereos at the tops of still-red London buses. Four-year-olds slashed at each other with toy swords which had replaced the previously ubiquitous gun. The models had pranced up the catwalk, men and women in billowing reds and blue/reds and white/reds and yellow, large-print shirt-dresses, loose waistcoats, the pirate trousers cut with fabric pulled through the crotch, tied sashes, pirate hats plundered from the past, leggings in swirled prints and large belted boots. Couture's swashbuckling fun was to be overtaken by reality's war of bombs and guns, not personal stereos and colourful panache. I wore the red and blue pirate shirt-dress, hoisted high with red boots, and gloated over eyebrows raised at a bourgeois wedding in the Sussex countryside. Single-parenthood in anxious London streets was transformed to revels in the shocking of rural complacency.

AUGUST 1982

The Falklands War, the jingoism of a bloodthirsty nation ruled by a woman determined to entrench herself at the helm for a decade by the rule of 'philistine' force:

> 'We don't care about value, we just care about money . . . the price of everything and the value of nothing . . . That's Oscar Wilde's definition of an auctioneer; somebody who knows the price of everything and the value of nothing.'

AUGUST 1990

Vivienne Westwood's pirate costume stands sublime in the costume section of the Victoria & Albert Museum, marking a decade of creative couture-carousing by the ideas, making and wearing of '200 m.p.h.' clothes:

> 'What are my politics? I believe the only subversion lies in ideas; I think that is the only form of subversion that really changes people. I'll just tell a little story. When I went to Italy, a long time ago, I found an agent – I no longer have him – called Carlo D'Amario. He could see where I was coming from – my head in punk rock ideas still – and he said: 'Look, imagine the establishment is like a car. The car is going at 100 m.p.h. and you want to try and stop it – well, you can't. You might throw some rocks at it, you might even slow it down for a second or two, but it will go faster with your energy. What you have to do is go at 200 m.p.h.' It was the changing point, from my attitude when I was in punk rock. I try to live my life fast because it's the key which stops me getting depressed. Because you're miles down the road before anybody can catch up with you.'

Museums, which should be attempting, 'to push back the frontiers of knowledge',[19] reflect precisely Britain's narrow perspective with museum-goers being treated as 'customers' rather than 'visitors'. 'Shortage of money should *not* be a matter of policy.'[20]

The pirate costume stands in the V & A, a reminder of a decade of Britain's cultural contradictions and decline into a state of uneducated 'barbarism', where people are forced to pay to look at their heritage. The experience of looking has become a financial exchange. No wonder only 2 per cent of the population[21] look any more, but with the sacking of experts and scientists throughout the museum and gallery network, the quality of what is seen is also diminished. The cultural importance and knowledge of traditions and ideas become reduced to a minimum. Vivienne Westwood's garment becomes as much a part of an elitist experience of looking as it is part of a fashion industry which has costed its possessions out of the reach of ordinary people.

> It's legitimate that museums and galleries should make money where they can, but this should be over and above sufficient funds allocated by the state . . . Without the experts to communicate the value of the object, the museums will lose their prestige, attract less custom, until they get to the point where, to balance the books, they have to sell off the objects. In my opinion the self-help being brought in by museum management is a sort of cancer or virus from which our sick museums may never recover. Our reaction to this crisis is crucial as to whether we want civilisation or not. [22]

When in summer 1990 one hundred people were to lose their jobs at the Natural History Museum and sixty scientists faced the sack, Vivienne Westwood's reaction was to 'put on my fig-leaf tights – Greek, you see, to make the point about civilisation – and I went to give my support to the scientists who had come out on strike and were picketing the Natural History Museum.' [23]

The human process of the making and wearing of the pirate garment has become fossilised in the experience of the few in the V & A, denied to the curious gaze of the collective majority through the loss of free access to their history.

AUGUST 1982

Not yet aware of the extent of Britain's decline into Thatcherite Barbarism I embark on an ill-fated reproduction of the future generation. The pregnancy is larger than average and the baby is sick. Her father gives me a World's End white dress – the label says 'Born in England' – with McClaren and Westwood imprinted alongside an arm raised with a pirate's sword in turquoise. There is a passion for these clothes, a passion that lasts a decade. The cumbersome belly is swathed in beautiful white folds of cotton from an open shirt-neck, ending in shirt-flaps to the knee; the sleeves billowing from gathered armhole to tight cuff. It is loose, comfortable, and transforms the anxious weight into airy waiting.

This is not maternity-wear: dowdy and long, restrictive to udder-like breasts, marking you off from 'normal' men and women who are shaped. This is a beautifully made garment for a different beauty which is more shapely in its largness, folded in fabric; a beauty not confined to the 'norm' of the average.

The fat and the pregnant would be deified in the wearing of such garments. The whiteness of the garment and the joy in its wearing, an optimistic yearning for birth and life is remembered at the moment of holding the 8-week-old body at death, all in white with a white carnation in her hands. The sword – a premonition of her hastily cut from the womb in fear for her life.

AUGUST 1986

I wear a Top Shop version of Vivienne Westwood's mini-crini.

> Vivienne Westwood had shown her mini-crini collection in Paris in 1985 and made a huge impact on other designers but not on the general public. As always she was ahead of her time. [24]

Maybe the American buyers hadn't taken up the mini-crini, but it was on the streets within nine months. It was flattering, flexible, 'easy' to wear and 'when you sit down it just collapses around you, so you don't even notice it'. [25]

But the Top Shop version does not have 'lightweight plastic hoops', nor is it cut on the bias, so it doesn't 'bell out'. [26] The Top Shop version is just another skirt which is short, reveals legs, and is worn because it is a fashion. The mass market could have made the authentic garment cheaply, but by cutting out attention to manufacturing detail, the effect of the end product is diminished. Only the young made it work. The 12-year-old girls who wear it are slender stalks, looking as if their skirts are pulled up around their knees to paddle in the sea. For this effect, Lewis Carroll pinned up Alice Liddell's skirts and was considered perverted for looking. And on 'a day of dappled sea-born clouds' James Joyce similarly observed:

> A girl stood before him in midstream, alone and still, gazing out to sea. She seemed like one whom magic had changed into the likeness of a strange and beautiful sea-bird. Her long slender legs were delicate as a crane's and pure save where an emerald trail had fashioned itself as a sign upon the flesh . . . her slate-blue skirts were kilted boldly about her waist and dove-tailed behind her. [27]

This was no ordinary image but one which enabled Steven Daedalus, the onlooker, to exult in life as opposed to contemplating arid religion: 'to live, to err, to fall, to triumph, to re-create life out of life', and thus to write. [28]

To be aware of the recognition of a reality transformed as an observer, is as important an experience as to be transformed by the wearing oneself. As a young street fashion the mini-crini flourished – a popular, 1980s assertion of youth over age; although Vivienne Westwood's original idea of the garment had altered in mass production, it had worked on another level. So had the experience of the lived image become the realisation of an alternative life for Steven Daedalus.

JULY 1990

Cut 'N Slash Menswear Collection, Pitti Palace

'These fig-leaf tights – I wore them in the Finale at the show I did in Florence and I wore them because I loved the show so much.'

In Westwood's fig-leaf tights and a man's shirt one feels different. Nude but not nude, the material sexually soft. I yearned to wear them with rocking platform shoes, to feel the whole effect of the woman looking like a man. One is returned to a Garden of Eden, to a quasi-natural genderless state. Transformed from working woman to active Eve, still with the potential to sin in retrospective wisdom. A simple pair of fig-leaf tights.

SEPTEMBER 1990

The street is full of young women in leggings and big shirts. Not fig-leaf leggings but black leggings, matched with men's shirts, dishevelled collars and sometimes an askew tie. The half-dressed female city gent emerges on the street, although the original pale pink tights are rarely to be seen. Pink flesh is not beautiful but there lies the contradiction. The soft pink tights are. The feel of the fabric, the irony of the fig-leaf, retains attention. Androgyny and multi-culturalism stalk the streets, not because of Vivienne Westwood's collections, but perhaps stimulated by their appearance a year earlier on her catwalk.

OCTOBER 1990

Vivienne Westwood saunters elegantly on to the stage at the Royal Albert Hall – with kisses in turn from Rifat Ozbek, Anthony Price and Joseph Tricot – to receive the Designer of the Year Award at the British Fashion Awards. The Duchess of Kent's white arms flab against her sleeveless white dress as she approaches Vivienne Westwood, who is in black and gold to the floor. Westwood is regal and announces that she has 'much to say', unlike Mary Quant

*Sarah Stockbridge
wearing the 'Half-
dressed City Gent'
outfit designed by
Vivienne Westwood
for her spring 1990
collection, photograph
by Robyn Beach
(courtesy of the
photographer)*

who is brief in her thanks for the Hall of Fame Award. Two great dames of the British fashion industry, 1950–1990, with the difference that Vivienne Westwood has numerous ideas as well as clothes to her name.

Two days later I stop a girl in a street in East London with long frayed slashes symmetrically and carefully cut all over her jeans. I ask her whether they were inspired by Vivienne Westwood. 'Yes, I did them at the weekend. They're safe.' From couture to DIY in two days is perhaps even more of a recognition than the receiving of the British Designer of the Year Award.

We like to call our governments democracies but they are plutocracies, i.e. ruled by money . . . Cultivation of art, intellectual speculation and pure science (the sum total of knowledge) have become devalued.[29]

But in what way and in what forms will works of poetry, of drama, of novels, of music, painting, of fashion, of language be born? What is to be done? What remains to be done? Nothing else but to destroy the present form of civilisation . . . spiritual hierarchies, prejudices, idols, rigid traditions . . . Destroy means not to be afraid of novelty and audaciousness.[30]

I wear my Vivienne Westwood (half-dressed city gent) knickers, with a penis graffiti'd on the front (previous page). No one knows. I am aware, going into a Board meeting, of a hidden gender transformation, and am all the more confident of its significance in the ignorance of others. As the transvestite acknowledges to himself the feel of silk cami-knickers under the grey suit, so I, female, relish my secret metamorphosis – the potential for audaciousness – in a world of drab conventions.

Notes and References

I would like to thank Vivienne Westwood for her vivacity, Nick Knightley for his inspiration, and fashion students at Ravensbourne College of Design and Communication for their comments. I would also like to thank David Widgery, Jesse and Annie. Most of all thanks goes to Ravensbourne Library staff for their tolerance and help.

Unless indicated otherwise all the Vivienne Westwood quotations are from two interviews I had with her: the first in August 1980, at her World's End shop, which was published in *Zeitgeist*, issue no. 2, and the other in August 1990 at her Camden Town workshop.

1 Bertolt Brecht, 'Song of the Inadequacy of Man's Higher Nature', in *Selected Poems*, New York, 1947, p. 71.

2 Walter Benjamin, *Understanding Brecht*, London, 1973, p. 38.

3 Ann Hollander, *Seeing Through Clothes*, London, 1980, p. 16.

4 Arthur Rimbaud, 'Voyelles' in Oliver Bernard (ed.), *Rimbaud Collected Poems in 'Penguin Poets'*, Harmondsworth, 1962, p. 171.
   A black, E white, I red, U green, O blue: vowels
   One day I will see your gentle birth:
   A, black velvet jacket of brilliant flies.

5 E.H. Gombrich, *Start the Week*, BBC Radio Four, 25 September 1989.

6 E.H. Gombrich, 'Of the Greeks', in *The Story of Art*, Oxford, 1967, p. 78.

7 François Boucher, *A History of Costume in the West*, London, 1967, p. 127.

8 David Sylvester joke, quoted by Colin MacInnes, quoted by Tony Gould, in *'Inside Outsider* – The Life and Times of Colin MacInnes*, London, 1983, p. 81.

9 Ibid.

10 Karl Miller, *Doubles*, Oxford, 1985, p. 103.

11 Caroline Evans and Minna Thornton, *Women and Fashion*, London, 1989, p. 152.

12 Vivienne Westwood on 'Remembrance of Time Past', interview with Juliet Ash, 1990.

13 Ibid.

14 Gombrich, op. cit., 1967, p. 70.

15 Edgar Wind, *Pagan Mysteries in the Renaissance*, Harmondsworth, 1967, p. 242.

16 Quoted orally by Nick Knightly when he was working with Vivienne Westwood.

17 Benjamin, op. cit., p. 38.

18 Aldous Huxley, *The Doors of Perception and Heaven and Hell*, London, 1970, p.73.

19 Vivienne Westwood, *Dodos and Dinosaurs*, BBC Radio Four, September 1990.

20 Ibid.

21 Paul Willis, *Moving Culture*, Gulbenkian Foundation, 1990.

22 Vivienne Westwood, *Dodos and Dinosaurs*, September 1990.

23 Ibid.

24 Lynn Barber, interview with Vivienne Westwood, the *Independent on Sunday*, 18 February 1990, p. 10.

25 Vivienne Westwood as quoted in Caroline Evans and Minna Thornton, op. cit., p. 150.

26 Catharine McDermot, *Street Style in British Design in the 1980s*, London, 1987, p. 37.

27 James Joyce, *Portrait of the Artist as a Young Man*, London, 1971, p. 172.

28 Ibid.

29 Vivienne Westwood, unpublished piece on 'Why Britain Should Go Pagan', p. 1.

30 Antonio Gramsci, from *The Prison Notebooks*, quoted in 'An Introduction to His Thought', A. Pozzolini, London, 1970, p. 110.

Utopias and Alternative Dress

SHEILA ROWBOTHAM

A New Vision of Society

Women Clothing Workers & the Revolution of 1848 in France

Working-class women usually enter history as victims of oppression, or they appear momentarily in apparently spontaneous actions. It is quite rare to find records not only of their complaints and protests but of their ideas about alternatives.

During the French revolution of 1848, working-class women put their demands, created alternative forms of co-operative production which spanned work and home, and envisaged the transformation of daily life.

Two clothing workers, Desirée Gay (née Veret) and Jeanne Deroin, also wrote about the condition of women and workers, and developed economic and social theories which they believed could guide strategies for changing relationships within capitalist society and lay the basis for a co-operative world.

In 1848 a combination of workers and the radical middle class overthrew the government of King Louis-Philippe. They formed a provisional government, declared a Second Republic and introduced adult male suffrage. Sovereignty was with the people, but 'the people' were all men.

Women, influenced by the utopian socialism of Saint-Simon and Fourier, were quick to argue that they too were 'the people' and should have a part in shaping a new political and social order.

For four months there was a sustained struggle to get the provisional government to respond to workers' desperate economic needs. The slogan was 'the right to work'. In response to the agitation, the provisional government set up National Workshops which provided employment and kept the jobless off the streets. To the hopeful, like the socialist Louis Blanc, who tried within the provisional government to defend workers' interests, they seemed like a new social form for the future organisation of labour. They became sites for battles over workers' democracy and in this context working women began to assert themselves too.

In June the workers were suppressed violently. From this point workers could expect little state help, but the struggle to change conditions of work and society persisted until Louis Napoleon seized power in December 1851.

In France in 1848 the capitalist economy was in a process of dramatic transformation, and it is perhaps because everything seemed in flux that working-class women emerged with new concepts of co-operative forms of economic development which were at once conscious of class and of the specific needs and problems of women.

The clothing trades in this period were in the process of transition from custom-made tailoring and dressmaking to ready-made clothing. Leaders of the skilled male tailors were asserting the importance of their craft skills and demanding that home-work, which they argued lowered the rates of pay, should be abolished. The women responded rather differently, insisting on their right to work and saying decent pay was necessary for them to fulfil their responsibilities as wives and mothers. Though they were prepared to criticise the excessive tyranny of men in families, they accepted the existing division of labour. Indeed their position in the family was asserted as a means of legitimising their claims as workers.

This led the women to make different demands of Louis Blanc for the reorganisation of work which were connected to various forms of social provision. One seamstress suggested that married women should be allowed to take work home instead of having to go to the National Workshops; home-work should be paid at the same rate as shop work. Others said that the state should open crèches and national restaurants so that families would be provided for when women worked; a variation was shorter hours, so that women could be with their families for the evening meal. Women also called for training centres for seamstresses so that skills would be preserved. Two seamstresses, 'Rosalie C' and Julia Hémal, argued that job sharing would be preferable to sweated work or unemployment.[1] These ideas were presented in deputations, having been worked out in the co-operative associations formed by women workers, in women's clubs and in journals like the socialist women's paper *La Voix des Femmes*.

Most women clothing workers were illiterate but a few had gained an education in the political milieu of the left. Desirée Veret was active in the utopian socialist movement in Paris in the 1830s and in 1832 had helped to produce a journal called *La Femme Libre*, which was committed to 'Liberty for Women, liberty for the people, by a new organisation of household and industry'. For her and for Jeanne Deroin, who contributed to the journal along with Suzanne Voilquin (a seamstress who became a midwife), these were to be continuing preoccupations.

Desirée Veret went to London, where she moved in Owenite circles, becoming enthusiastic about their ideas of co-operative production. She worked as a milliner and married a follower of Robert Owen, Jules Gay. In 1837 she returned to France, and in 1841 contributed an article about 'Workers' Association' to the journal of the utopian socialist Fourier, *Le Nouveau*

Monde. She argued that association would be preferable to a system based on competition because ideally it would unite capital's enterprise and labour's skills.

By 1848 Desirée Gay was working as a dressmaker and organising seamstresses into a club. The revolution was to make her more aware of the interests of workers and specifically of the needs of working-class women. She gravitated to *La Voix des Femmes*, and when it collapsed formed *La Politique des Femmes* as a political and editorial group.

Desirée Gay had initially agitated for National Workshops for women and was elected by *La Voix des Femmes* to represent the Second Arondissement. However, as a delegate she criticised unequal rates of pay and differentials. She argued that women needed separate assemblies to build up their strength and confidence. The formal democracy of electing workers' delegates was inadequate and left women underrepresented. But her ideas of how a politics of gender would alter concepts of workers' control were cut short by her dismissal. *La Voix des Femmes* protested indignantly but to no avail. Louis Blanc remained silent. He was powerless when women were shot in the National Workshops because they rebelled.[2]

It was after the workers' defeat in June that Desirée Gay formed another women's journal, *La Politique des Femmes*. But when Louis Napoleon came to power she was forced into exile in Switzerland and eventually went to live in Belgium.

A self-educated dressmaker who was also associated with *La Voix des Femmes*, Jeanne Deroin argued that women's emancipation required the combined transformation of individual, family and social existence. She rejected the idealisation of the existing circumstances of motherhood by socialist thinkers like Proudhon. Maternity could not be regarded under an oppressive social structure to be women's noblest attribute since motherhood could not be freely chosen by women. Choice was necessary if mothering was to be a consciously accepted responsibility.[3]

For Jeanne Deroin, democratisation of maternity was directly linked to the transformation of social existence and not simply a personal right. In her book *Cours de droit social pour les femmes* (1848) she maintained that women's experience as mothers was necessary for the transformation of society. This experience is not culturally static. As it moves from the confinement of the domestic sphere and combines with men's social experience, a new synthesis of values will be possible.

'Man only knows how to establish order through despotism; the woman only knows how to organise by the power of her love as a mother; the two united would know how to reconcile order and liberty.'[4] Jeanne Deroin thus argued that women's participation was necessary to the project of 1848.

La Voix des Femmes takes up the same theme. Men can no longer claim to constitute 'humanity'. The end of servitude in production will mark the end of women's slavery.[5] The links are simply presumed. In the revolutionary ethos of 1848, women associated with *La Voix des Femmes* imagine that the public world of politics and work will change along with personal relations. There is, though, an apparent wariness around sexuality; the free unions of the 1830s had caused scandal and discredited socialism. Jeanne Deroin saw freedom in love as the right to chastity. As she had three children with her husband Desroches, things evidently did not go according to plan.

La Voix des Femmes places, however, considerable stress on self-emancipation through action and education. Changing oneself is inseparably bound up with changing society. This political and personal dynamism affects the meaning Jeanne Deroin brings to mothering. It is partially an idealised state, cut off from capitalist relations. But it is not the fixed moral nature which features in later and more conservative versions of feminism. It is an active force for change which is itself being created by women and changed as it acquires a wider social sphere. The context for its transformatory potential is the opening created by political and economic revolution. In *La Politique des Femmes* in 1848, a working woman observes. 'As the people are sovereign now, it is only just that we are also someone.'[6]

However, in practical terms, even before the June defeat women were not allowed to participate in many clubs. They lacked the vote and their pay was not equal to men's. Moreover, the reorganisation of labour and the demand for a redistribution of wealth, to enable the creation of public social services to meet working-class women's needs, went far beyond the boundaries of the middle classes' revolution.

On the workers' side there was an enormous gap between what they could imagine and what they could make practicable. For example in Lyon, in the first few months of 1848, workers met in the great hall of the municipal library and tried to work out solutions to economic problems. The role of women workers was fiercely debated, for although women silk workers had entered the new factories they were still excluded from the men's associations and the men opposed their right to equal pay. A group of women workers who made contact with *La Voix des Femmes* decided that they would act on their own behalf rather than continue to argue with the men. They created a workshop to provide women workers with jobs and their scheme also ensured housing and food. However, they then encountered problems in the wider economy. There were few orders for silk fabric in March and April, and by the end of April they were still unable to set up a single shop.

By June the basic principles of social need which the workers' power had secured from the state, in the form of the dole of bread and meat organised by the city since March to feed 30,000 impoverished people, were abandoned amidst crisis. Instead of planning alternative schemes to reorganise production, men and women alike in the working-class movement had to concentrate on survival.

In Lyon, the Association of Women Workers was set up in September 1848. The problem of obtaining sufficient capital was solved by the backing of bourgeois women, who provided capital which the manufacturers accepted as security. They were consequently willing to buy the 'canutes' (women silk workers) thread to reel or weave in the workshops which the women ran co-operatively. Women who worked at home were also members of the association, which thus linked the co-operative changes in the form of workshop production to home-work. Each workshop had a maximum of one hundred women and elected a forewoman and a woman director who was responsible for organising the flow of work and finding a market for their produce. They thus eliminated the sexual power wielded by male supervisors. Also, because these posts were democratically elected, the supervisory and managerial staff were not likely to cheat or overwork the other women. The benefits of the co-operative, however, provided an incentive to contribute one's labour. For through the association women secured regular wages, a share in profits, medical benefits and sick pay. All these were much better than in the ordinary workshops. The women wanted to develop the social aspects of associated production by starting a crèche, a school and a training workshop. But the arrival of Napoleon III put an end to their schemes.

Financial backing was an important factor in a co-op's success. Another Lyon workshop failed because it had no capital behind it and economically was too vulnerable. A group of seamstresses set up a store, a workshop and a laundry on the right bank of the Saône. They found there were real social advantages in association, for they could live much more cheaply as a co-operative group than as individuals. But they were not economically viable. [7]

There were some interesting tensions in the co-ops. The fierce spirit of class independence which emerged in the course of 1848 had to make a compromise if capital was to be obtained, because after June the state was no longer a source of capital. It was not easy to balance the women's social needs with the development of production. Moreover, it became apparent that concentration on the reorganisation of production was not sufficient – thought had to be given to the circumstances of the wider economy.

In August 1848 Desirée Gay's *La Politique des Femmes* published an interesting discussion between a group of women about the economy, class and women's capacity to act. 'The Lady' tells them, 'If the workers kept peace, business would recover and all would be better off.' 'A Woman Worker' retorts, 'Yes, particularly the bosses. They would get the workers for half the price and they would pay the interest for the revolution.'

'The Lady' maintains that the workers *are* better off. Hours have been reduced and wages are higher. 'The Woman Worker' says this is true only on the posters; in reality women's wages are lower. According to 'the Lady', the man is the main breadwinner so the women's wages do not matter. But the working women will not let this pass. They ask, 'And if the man is ill or a bad fellow? And when the women are widows? And if she does not find anyone who marries her?'

The women workers debate among themselves how to get change. Revolt seems futile. They put their faith in education and organisation. They believe a social revolution is necessary but they accept the need to make some immediate changes. 'The Socialist Woman' maintains, 'Women should not neglect the concrete things which are possible while they strive for an ideal.'

Though there is a strong emphasis on the need for a new kind of education for adults and for children, there is also an affirmation of their tacit knowledge as working-class women. 'The Socialist Woman' asks for their help and opinion. But the women ask, 'What opinion? We know nothing.' To this 'the Socialist Woman' replies, 'How come? You don't know how you feed your children, care for your husbands, how you work, think, observe and you don't have enough common sense to distinguish between what is right and wrong?' 'The Women': 'Oh, yes, this we know.' 'The Socialist Woman': 'All right then, that is all that is needed. We shall find ways and means to look after our household and family collectively, so that we are able to form an association, to build up shops and workshops. We shall be so persevering that they finally will have to respect our wishes and demands.'[8]

When Karl Marx came to reflect upon the tragedy of the workers' defeat in France in the revolution of 1848, he stressed the hopelessness of the attempts to change the economy and society once power in the state had been wrested from them. However, with hindsight, the problem which troubled politically conscious working-class women like Desirée Gay – how to move from society as it is to society as it might be – is still of great political relevance. The process of transition to a co-operative, equal society has proved much harder than Marx envisaged. Part of the difficulty has been how a socialist economy, which serves needs democratically and effectively, can be established. Another aspect of the complex transition is how to change values and redefine needs. Our wants and aspirations are shaped by the society we know.

'The Socialist Woman' acknowledges that her theories are not always the same as women workers' aspirations and seeks a meeting place. 'I am too democratic not to respect the freedom of all. The women have habits with which they cannot break immediately in order to live a communal life. These are the shackles which hinder them doing so. But we could form provisional associations for this or that work.'[9]

Jeanne Deroin also turns her attention to the overall economic context of producer co-operatives and searches for a means of transition from a capitalist organisation of production to a co-operative society. She is still insisting that mothering is a source of alternative values and that the predicament of women as mothers necessarily gives women an interest in a co-operative rather than a competitive society. She decided that there was a need for new kinds of financial institutions. Working-class women who set up producer co-operatives lacked capital and found it difficult to obtain credit. So they needed banks geared to their situation. Interestingly, this is exactly the problem faced by poor, Third World women who create small enterprises; there is now a growing awareness in development agencies of the importance of alternative structures for loans to poor women. However, reshaping financial institutions in the interests of clothing homeworkers was not high on the agenda of the European socialist movement and Jeanne Deroin's arguments appear to have been completely ignored. Her appeal to rich, middle-class, Parisian women also yielded little response.

The other economic aspect of association which troubled Jeanne Deroin was how to ensure that the producers' associations linked in with consumers' needs. She consequently suggested a means of democratic intervention to establish equilibrium between production and consumer needs. The element of flexible adjustment was quite simply democracy. She put forward the idea of a federation of workers' associations. There were seamstresses and makers of linen underwear and novelty goods actually forming new associations. Also, the seamstresses' fraternal association had been set up with financial help from richer workers, tailors and saddlers. She proposed linking associations like these together. Delegates from each of the associations would form a central commission. This could monitor producers' and consumers' needs and secure a balance. A General Assembly would meet and make decisions to change the number of workers in each trade to avoid unemployment and ensure harmony between production and consumption. Although Jeanne Deroin had a strong awareness of women's specific subordination in the working class, she also saw the need for workers to combine.

By August 1849, forty-three delegates from different areas had met to discuss this plan. Four hundred associations did in fact affiliate. The organisation was open and legally registered. Jeanne Deroin believed in peaceful and legal means of change. However, the extent of the organisation made it appear to the authorities as subversion.[10] In 1850 the police raided one of the local meetings. They found seditious leaflets, socialist songs and bullet casts. The federation was declared to be a plot against society. Jeanne Deroin was arrested along with other women and men, including a member of the laundresses' association called Femme Nicaud, who was accused of hiding material for making weapons. Interestingly, the prosecution found equally subversive the fact that another woman, called Lavanture, protested against marriage 'by a triple maternity'.[11] Similarly, the militant teacher Pauline Roland was cast as sexually as well as politically dubious.

For many years she has held communist–socialist opinions. A mother without being married, she is opposed to marriage which, subjecting the woman's obedience to the husband's authority, consecrates inequality. Needless to say, according to her, no one has the right to possess another.[12]

The response indicates the seriousness of the rebellion against male sexual authority, which was an undercurrent in the socialism and feminism of the women in the association.

The prosecution seems to have been at a loss how to smear the Christian Jeanne Deroin, settling rather unsatisfactorily for: 'She regards socialism as a religion and has placed a fatal organisational intelligence at the service of her political principles.'[13] Though the police file noted her use of her maiden name.

As the implication of dubious morals would have been patently ludicrous, they suggested fanaticism. However, when she was tried in November, *La Gazette des Tribunaux* reported that she gave her evidence calmly and with evident 'socialist erudition'.[14]

The judge cross-questioned her about her economic theories. What was all this about free loans and a system of friendly societies? Jeanne Deroin explained that workers would contribute to a social fund which others could use to establish their associations and that goods and services would be exchanged between the workers. 'The hairdressers will do the hair of the shoemakers who will supply their footwear.'[15]

The judge, pursuing a conspiracy against society, was perplexed. But how would the value of the products be determined? he asked her. How could the delegates of laundresses, of spectacle-makers be competent to decide the value of shoes, for example?[16]

Jeanne Deroin patiently explained that the Committee of Consumption and Production would monitor the value of goods and services in each association. The federation of associations would enable workers to get tools, equipment, raw materials, and research into consumer needs and production methods, as well as exchanging produce.

In her Project for the Union of Associations she had envisaged the means of production becoming gradually the collective property of the entire society. She believed goods should be exchanged at the cost it took to produce them. Profit and private capital would no longer be necessary.

On 15 November there was a fuss because she insisted on being called by her own name, not her husband's. Firstly, because she did not want to involve him. She also said, 'I protest against marriage. It is a condition of bondage for woman. As for myself, I want absolute equality between the two sexes.'[17] She was careful to explain that she did not agree with promiscuity. Her desire for democracy and equality in relations between men and women elevated their union.

All this proved too much for the judge, who shut her up at this point. She was attacking one of the most respectable institutions in society and the terms of the Civil Code.

Jeanne Deroin persisted in arguing against women's subordination as a sex, not only with her political opponents but with her allies in the socialist movement who said there was no conflict except for the struggle against the despotism of capital in the workshop.

However, in prison Jeanne Deroin faced a painful dilemma between her commitment to socialism and her feminism. She was visited in prison by the lawyer of some of her male colleagues in the association who were embarrassed by her prominent role in the organisation. 'I was urgently begged in the name of the masculine associations not to let it be acknowledged that I was the originator of the project and of the act of forming the Union. Prejudice still dominated in the Association and people were offended by the prominent part played in its formation by a woman devoted to the cause of women's rights.'[18]

Alone and in prison for her socialism, Jeanne Deroin was being asked to contribute to the prejudiced assumption that women were incapable of theory or leadership. But the alternative was to provoke a split in the unity of the accused in front of a court intent upon their mutual destruction. She consequently decided to remain silent about her initiatory conceptual and organisational role in the Association. She explained in a letter to a friend that she did not want 'to stir up a dispute between socialists in the presence of our adversaries.'[19]

After she was let out of prison, she found her family had been badly affected by the trial. Her husband was in a state of nervous depression. Ever resourceful, she took her family to England where she started a school and established yet another journal.

That it was not easy for Jeanne Deroin to enter the public sphere, even in the revolutionary moment of 1848, is evident in her reflections, in exile in Britain, aged seventy.

When in 1848 I wrote and spoke in public, it was not because I believed myself to have talent, but I was pulled outwards by a powerful impulse which made me overcome my natural timidity.'[20]

Her power and forcefulness was not 'to attract attention to myself, but for the cause to which I was dedicated'.[21]

She reveals that she put herself forward as a candidate to the National Assembly in 1849 after having begged both George Sand and Pauline Roland to stand and they had refused. 'It was because I had the conviction that it was necessary to strike at every closed door that I did it.'[22]

Jeanne Deroin died in Britain in 1894, an obscure figure to the world at large, though British socialists followed her to her grave and William Morris paid tribute to her.[23] Like many of her political companions, her memory has been eclipsed by the fragmentation of the causes she sought to combine.

There is, however, a fascinating echo. The Leeds socialist and feminist Isabella Ford, who had been deeply involved in the organisation of the tailoresses in the militant new unionism of the 1890s, and who later worked to create an alliance between the suffrage movement and labour, published a letter in *The Labour Leader* in 1906, which had been originally written by Jeanne Deroine [sic] and Pauline Roland from their prison cell in Paris in 1851 when 'the darkness of reaction' had 'obscured the sun in 1848'.[24] They greeted the American Women's Suffrage Convention and regretted the silence in the French Assembly about women's rights. Liberty, Equality and Fraternity were evidently insufficient. They believed 'only by the power of association based on solidarity – by the union of the working classes of both sexes to organise labour – can be acquired . . . the civil and political equality of women and the social right for all'.[25]

The ideas of working women long ago about the reorganisation of the economy and society, and their remarkable efforts to both enter and transform the political sphere of sovereignty and citizenship challenge assumptions about class consciousness which have disregarded gender or an exclusive focus on gender relations which implicitly ignores the shared experiences of class. The interconnecting vision of political, economic, social and personal emancipation was to be fractured many times in the years following the defeat of 1848. Our contemporary dilemma is how it can be redefined as a means of moving from society as it is to society as it might be.

Notes and References

I am grateful to the United Nations World Institute for Development Economics Research (Helsinki) for its financial support while this paper was being written, and to Northern College for providing me with an impetus to work on the economic and social ideas of the women of 1848.

1 See Joan Wallach Scott, 'Work Identities for Men and Women: The Politics of Work and the Family in the Parisian Garment Trades in 1848', in Joan Wallach Scott (ed.), *Gender and Politics in History*, New York, 1988, pp. 96-108. For the demands of working women in 1848, see *La Voix des Femmes*, Journal Socialiste et Politique, Organe des Intérêts de Toutes, Paris, 1848. On the utopian socialist background and feminism, see Jane Rendall, *The Origins of Modern Feminism, Women in Britain, France and United States 1780–1860*, London, 1985, pp. 220-2 and pp. 291-6; and Sheila Rowbotham, *Women, Resistance and Revolution*, London, 1972, pp. 50-6.

2 See Edith Thomas, *Les Femmes de 1848*, Paris, 1948, pp. 53-4 and p. 71; and Maria Mies, 'Utopian Socialism and Women's Emancipation', in Maria Mies and Kumari Jayawardena (eds), *Feminism in Europe, Liberal and Socialist Strategies 1789-1919*, Institute of Social Studies, The Hague, Netherlands, 1981, pp. 53-9.

3 See Michèle Riot-Sarcy, 'Une vie publique privée d'histoire: Jeanne Deroin ou l'oubli de soi', in Michelle Perot (ed.), *Silence émancipation des femmes entre privé et public*, in Les Cahiers du CEDREF, *La Revue des Études Féministes a l'Université*, Paris VII, pp. 81-93.

4 Jeanne Deroin, *Cours de droit social pour les femmes*, Paris, 1848, p. 7.

5 *La Voix des Femmes*, 19 March 1848.

6 See Appendix: A Worker Woman, 'La Politique des Femmes, August 1848', in Mies, op. cit., p. 78.

7 See Laura S. Strumingher, *Women and the Making of the Working Class, Lyon, 1830–1890*, Vermont, USA, 1979, pp. 105-6; and in *La Voix des Femmes*, 29 March 1848.

8 'La Politique des Femmes, August 1848', in Mies, op. cit., pp. 71-9.

9 Ibid., pp. 75-6.

10 Thomas, op. cit., pp. 71-4.

11 Ibid., p. 75.

12 Ibid.

13 Ibid.

14 Ibid.

15 Ibid.

16 Ibid.

17 Ibid.

18 Evelyne Sullerot, *Histoire et Sociologie du Travail Féminin*, Paris, 1968, p. 114.

19 Ibid., p. 115.

20 Evelyne Sullerot, 'Journaux Féminin et Lutte Ouvrière, 1848-1849', in Jacques Godechot (ed.), *La Presse Ouvrière*, Paris, 1968, p. 97.

21 Ibid.

22 Ibid.

23 See Riot-Sarcy, op. cit., p. 88.

24 Quoted in June Hannam, *Isabella Ford*, Oxford, 1989, p. 121.

25 Ibid.

KATE LUCK

Trouble in Eden, Trouble with Eve

Women, Trousers & Utopian Socialism in Nineteenth-Century America

In 1851 American newspapers began to document a new and startling phenomenon; on the streets of New England, and then farther afield, women began to appear in trousers, hitherto an item of clothing exclusively identified with men. Worn beneath short skirts, and popularly known as 'the bloomer', this novel costume was claimed by its wearers to be a rational and healthful alternative to contemporary fashions. Nevertheless, there was a strong suspicion that trousers represented a usurpation of men's rights and prerogatives, and, as such, were an instrument of the newly organised Women's Rights movement.

This was not a surprising conclusion, since the origin of this trousered dress for women could be easily traced to Amelia Bloomer, a progressive Women's Rights activist, and to her editorial comments in *The Lily*, probably the first newspaper to be devoted to feminist issues. Inspired by the personal example of Elizabeth Smith Miller, the daughter of a radical congressman, and spurred

The bloomer dress as a Women's Rights costume, hand-painted print by John Leech (courtesy of Kate Luck)

into action by the adverse comments of a rival editor, Bloomer had introduced the dress to the women of Seneca Falls only two years after the first Women's Rights Convention had been held there. Over the next few years, trousers were given a high visibility by the principal speakers on the Women's Rights circuit, including Bloomer, Elizabeth Cady Stanton, Susan B. Anthony, Lucy Stone, and Sarah and Angelina Grimké.

However, it would be inaccurate to describe any of the principals of the Women's Rights movement as the 'inventor' of women's trousers. Bloomer herself was quick to point out that the costume was not of her own design:

> The first we heard of it, it was worn as an exercise dress at the 'Water Cure', the first article we saw advocating it was an editorial in the *Seneca County Courier* . . . The first person we saw wearing such a dress was Mrs CHARLES D. MILLER of Peterboro, daughter of GERRIT SMITH, who has worn it for the last five or six months . . . and we recently received a letter from a lady in Wisconsin, in which she states that herself and others have worn them for the last nine or ten months . . . We wish for no more credit than belongs to us, and while we should be proud to admit that we were the leaders of the great reform, justice demands that we render to others what is justly their due.[1]

Another influential voice, Horace Greeley's *New York Daily Tribune*, held that to identify the dress as a 'spawn' of the Women's Rights conventions was to impede its progress; many of the women who already wore the dress were opposed to the women's movement, just as many supporters of women's politics detested the dress.[2]

In fact, the history of women's trouser-wearing went back much further than even Amelia Bloomer imagined, and belonged to a more complex framework of radicalisms than Women's Rights alone. Before its introduction at Seneca Falls, trousered dress had been worn by American women for over two decades, and had been championed by members of a number of different, but overlapping, reforming constituencies, most vigorously by socialist communalists and practitioners of water-cure medicine. Among these groups, women's trouser-wearing had provided a focus for discourses around woman's physiological development, professional capacities, the nature of her sexuality, and place in nationalist politics, and, as such, had anticipated most, if not all, of the questions which were to occupy the supporters and adversaries of bloomerism.

American women, in all probability, first wore trousers in the context of utopian communal socialism, a movement inaugurated by Robert Owen,

Charles Fourier and Henri Saint-Simon. These men, mistrustful of industrial capitalism, and the inequalities it fostered in the name of private property and a free-market economy, believed that social progress lay in co-operation, rather than in competition. They envisaged the settlement of ideal communities, where improved systems of economics, labour, and education would provide a 'heaven on earth' for their followers and a blueprint for a new and better world. Under their influence, over fifty utopian socialist communities were established in America between 1820 and 1860, forming an important tributary of a wider communal movement which embraced a wide spectrum of beliefs and reforms.

In the discrete spaces which these co-operative ventures occupied, the designing of objects and physical environments marked the transition between utopian theory and practice. Generally speaking, the most successful (long-lived) communities were those which originated distinctive forms of architecture, furniture and dress, and in which the members had had a large say in the planning and construction of their surroundings. [3]

Many nineteenth-century utopian communities, 'socialist' and otherwise, devised a 'uniform', potentially changeless dress, which gave the members a 'family likeness' and marked their difference from outsiders, thus acting as a powerful indicator of shared values and community boundaries. Moreover, dress was usually regulated in a way which emphasised comfort and use, rather than 'fashion' and 'taste', leading to the assumption that its wearers, freed from the codes and conventions which contextualised conventional costume, would invest their time and energy in self-improvement, rather than in the 'useless consumption' of fashion goods.

Though some works of utopian literature described an elegant, often fanciful costume as the communal ideal, practical experiments in communal living led to a simpler, more austere model for clothing, privileging utility above decoration, and dress for work above dress for leisure. These were very real priorities for those struggling to maintain a viable, self-sufficient economic base, often in harsh and unfriendly surroundings. Most communal dress styles evolved informally, and, most typically, were the result of a process of 'fossilization'. [4] Here, the style of dress prevalent at the time the community first came into being, often the 'plain' dress worn by rural and working women from the seventeenth up to the early nineteenth century, was adhered to by successive generations of communalists, and thus became an unchanged norm. As fashions in the world outside of the community evolved, this 'fossilized' dress appeared increasingly distinctive and unique. In this sense, it could be said to be symptomatic of those communities who sought to preserve their shared values, often of a religious or ethnic nature, in the face of a changing world.

In comparison, the evolution of women's trousered dress within utopian socialist communalism followed a less typical pattern, the result of a more formal decision-making process, and representing a more wholesale reform of existing dress codes. It is not surprising that trousers, which were a revolutionary departure in women's dress, should have first appeared in the context of utopian socialism, since it was here that the most radical social revisions were being projected.

In this context, trousers were first introduced for women at Robert Owen's ill-fated New Harmony community, established in Indiana in 1824. They were a feature of a more general dress reform for both sexes:

> The female dress is a pair of trousers tied round the ankles over which is an exceedingly full slip reaching to the knees, though some have been extravagant enough to make them longer, and also to have the sleeves long. I do not know whether I can describe the men's apparel, but I will try. The pantaloons are extremely full, and also tied round the ankle; the top garment is also very full, bound round the waist with a very broad belt, which gives it the appearance of being all in one. A fat person dressed in this elegant costume I have heard very appropriately compared to a feather bed tied in the middle. They are not tied round the neck like the girl's slips, and as many wear them with no collars visible, it is rather difficult to distinguish the gentlemen from the ladies.[5]

Any account of the derivation of the trousered aspect of the New Harmony women's dress can only be speculative. Trousers held obvious practical advantages for women involved in manual labour. Beyond this, the dress of childhood, with its 'pantalettes', may have provided a model, suggesting a 'fresh start', and an innocence which befitted the utopian vision of a 'New Eden'. It may also be the case that the trousers, which were gathered at the ankle in the 'Turkish' style, were a reference to the Greek war of independence against the Turks (1821–1829), thus mobilising ideas of revolutionary struggle.

The costume had been introduced by the 'literati' of the community, a group of teachers and scientists who were Owen's staunchest supporters. Their intention, first and foremost, was to 'equalise' the members, who were drawn from different social strata and backgrounds, and who tended to fall into factions. Ironically, only the intellectual elite of the community took to the new dress, and, though they were staunch champions of the idea of equality, its practical application, when it came to doing their share of manual labour, and mixing socially with others, was less of an enthusiasm, making a mockery of the costume's equalising intention.

Whatever the origins of women's trousered dress might have been, the significance it held for its 'inventors' was only imperfectly communicated to the rank and file of the community's membership, many of whom refused to put it on. Significantly, amongst the community's ordinary members, the greatest resistance to the new dress came from women, many of whom thought it improper to indicate the shape or even the existence of their legs. That the dress held no positive values for them is perhaps symptomatic of their uneasy status as female communalists, and their generally unsatisfactory experience of community life. Owen had given little thought to specific issues of gender, and had less understanding of the problems of flesh-and-blood women. Though he had, prior to New Harmony, formulated plans to communalise housework, and to grant women full and equal rights, there was a significant shortfall between his utopian dream and its realisation.[6]

Domestic work, still women's province at New Harmony, was not counted as a form of 'productive' labour (i.e. could not be 'exchanged' for other goods and services), leading to the perception that women were contributing less than men to community life. Owen seems to have endorsed this view, issuing the directive that 'no anger should be felt against the female members upon their aversion to the work of the co-operative, or when they brawl, quarrel, or indulge in loud talk'.[7] Oblivious to the anomaly in his system of 'labour exchange', he attributed the problem of women's apparent low productivity to flaws in their character, brought about by their general oppression under industrial capitalism, and particularly by their exclusion from property rights.

However, despite the fact that Owen believed that the abolition of private property within the community would transform women, he never clearly articulated a view of what they could become, once 'perfected'. Given the absence of a positive ideological framework for women's experience, and an 'agenda' for their development, and in the light of their unresolved problems as 'unpaid' domestic labourers, it is not surprising that they could see little 'value' in the dress which was supposed to symbolise their 'New Moral World'. We are told that when Owen, who had instituted a new marriage ceremony which recognised the partners as equals, persuaded the first bride to lay off her 'bridal white' in favour of the striped trousered dress which symbolised his new order, 'the change cost her many tears'.[8]

By the time that New Harmony collapsed as a communal venture, sections of the press, no doubt spurred on by Owen's attacks on conventional marriage, were referring to it as 'one great brothel'.[9] In this light, trousered dress was seen to be a sign of sexual laxity, allowing its wearers to 'show all'. This signification was strengthened by the appearance of Frances Wright, an early exponent of feminism, in the New Harmony costume. Wright, who had lived at New Harmony for a time, and was a close associate of Robert Dale Owen, held opinions on marriage similar to those of Robert Owen. She had established her own community at Nashoba, including in her membership a number of black slaves, who were to work towards purchasing their freedom. Once it became rumoured that miscegenation (sexual relations between blacks and whites) had taken place there, Wright became an object of opprobrium to 'respectable' Americans, and was widely believed to be a woman of the loosest, most vicious, morals.

Later within utopian socialist communalism, as a more coherent position on gender relations (than at New Harmony) was formulated, women's trouser-wearing came to suggest a defeminised, 'manly' ideal, to which community women could aspire. From 1840, a number of Fourierist communities were established in America, and these more consciously addressed Fourier's precept that the position of Woman was the true barometer of social progress. Generally speaking, the women who joined these groups had the same membership rights as men, and, in comparison with New Harmony, a greater role in the organisation of community life.

The positive signification which attached to trousered dress in the Fourier-inspired communities where it was worn can be indicated by an examination of the Oneida community, established by John Humphrey Noyes in New York

A contemporary view of Robert Owen's ideal of womanhood, Pictorial Times, *1841 (courtesy of the Mary Evans Picture Library)*

state in 1848. Noyes, who had trained in theology, sought to practise a Christian Socialism, or 'Bible Communism', linking Fourier's ideas on labour and gender with his own belief that mankind could, within a nurturing environment, enter into the state of grace and freedom from sin which had been promised him in heaven. The most radical outcome of this was the introduction of a system of 'Complex Marriage', whereby exclusive marriage, as in heaven, was abolished, and was replaced by the spiritual union of the entire communal group. The widest selection of sexual partners was insisted upon and, in the first decades of the community, birth control was practised by all, lest the presence of children should deflect the attention of the members from the community and back to the family unit. Women were freed from the demands of motherhood, and could take part in all community activities, and all kinds of community labour, manual and professional.

According to Oneidan beliefs, in the main formulated by Noyes and passed down to the members, there was an intimate connection between the form or style of dress, and the social freedom of its wearers. Consequently, women could only attain that liberty which men enjoyed by giving up heavy and encumbering clothing and time consuming coiffures. Noyes had hinted at a reform in his First Annual Report of 1848:

> Woman's dress is a standing lie. It proclaims that she is not a two-legged animal, but something like a churn standing on castors! When the distinction of the sexes is reduced to the bounds of nature and decency, a dress will be adopted that will be the same, or nearly the same, for both sexes. The dress of children – frock and pantalettes – is in good taste, not perverted by the dictates of shame, and it is well adapted to the free motion of both sexes. This, or something like it, will be the uniform of a vital society. [10]

Shortly after this, Harriet Noyes (Noyes's wife), Harriet Skinner (his sister), and Mary Cragin (the first woman he had drawn into Complex Marriage), shortened their dresses and used the discarded fabric to make trousers. By January 1849, Noyes was claiming for these women the 'invention' of the dress, and reporting its general adoption throughout the community. Pierpont Noyes, his son, wrote that the few women who had not put on the new dress, and who wore lace caps, long dresses and hooped skirts, and prefixed their names with the epithet 'Lady', represented 'a female dignity that I recognised but could not understand', highlighting the demarcation he perceived between the proper dress of the community, and the false gentility conveyed by fashionable garments. [11]

To many members, the new dress was a sign of the new order of Complex Marriage, and of the freedom which women were said to enjoy under it. An idea of the ideological significance of trouser-wearing at Oneida is given in George Noyes Miller's *Strike of a Sex*, a fictionalised account of the institution of Complex Marriage. Here, the women appear in procession, grouped as old maids, courtesans, those who have married unsuitable husbands, or borne unwanted children, girls about to be married, their bloom soon to wither and in gilded chains, the 'happily' married. Their resolve to change their position, and to adopt Complex Marriage and birth control, is synonymous with the adoption of a new dress, 'their comely outlines invested with a new sense of freedom of motion such as one might have who had been suddenly released from a weary dragging ball and chain'. [12]

At the same time, trousered dress belied the 'dangerous sexuality' of Oneidan women, who were, in conventional terms, profligate, since their sexuality was divorced from its 'proper' maternal function. Noyes pointed out that Oneidan dress was more modest than conventional costume, since it covered the wearer from head to foot, and did not 'telegraph' the physical difference between the sexes. [13] Moreover, the dress shielded women from unwanted sexual advances, and saved her from the 'counterfeit' of fashion and the behaviour that this implied. It was no longer considered necessary or desirable for women to manipulate their dress in order to increase their 'feminine allure'.

Femininity, seen to be a learnt behaviour which acted powerfully in the serious work of getting husbands, could, in this ideal world, be jettisoned, and women's natures be differently prioritised, in favour of physical and mental improvement and useful work. In this respect, the reform of dress was central to the work of co-operative communalism. Noyes wrote that in the long discord he had had with them over 'the spirit of dress and ornament', women had 'had to bear the brunt of the battle for Communism'. [14]

Despite the fact that trousered dress was worn by Oneidan women for many decades, it has been suggested that trouser-wearing operated as a mechanism of male control, rendering female communitarians unattractive to outsiders, and locking them into communal sexual practices. It is significant that no similar radical change was proposed for male dress. Indeed, women's trousered dress generally conformed to the outlines of the masculine frock coat and pants, suggesting that masculinity, here as elsewhere, was taken as the norm. As a repudiation of the feminine, women's trousered dress expressed Noyes's belief that the perfected woman was 'a female man, like the son in the Godhead'. Noyes's son wrote, in a criticism of the fashionable shoes worn by community women prior to the invention of a 'perfect' shoe,

Your trouble is that you are a woman, while you ought to be a man . . . You think you are a 'weaker vessel', but there is no 'weaker vessel' in Christ. All are one; there is no male nor female; all are strong; all are soldiers. So long as you count yourself a woman bound to follow the fashions, tripping about in your high heeled boots to prove yourself distinct from men, as the 'weaker vessel' you will be weaker according to your faith . . . Women must come up into unity with men . . . Paul says 'put off the *old* man with his deeds'. I say 'Put off the old woman, with her deeds, which are a great deal worse'.[15]

Problems of dress occupied the community throughout its existence. The 'official' Oneidan attitude to fashionable dress, that it was a temptation and a snare for women, impacted upon women's trousered dress, even though trouser-wearing constituted an extreme reaction to feminised fashion. Oneidan women were subject to strict surveillance, lest they should succumb to the disruptive 'feminine vices' of vanity and 'adornment', seen to be the legacy of Old World selfishness, and a violation of the anti-consumption ethos of community economics. Though their per capita expenditure on dress was low, women were periodically asked to curb their 'dress spirit', and to refrain from wearing the small amount of jewellery normally allowed them.[16]

Oneidan women may well have hankered after fashionable dress, not least because it held the heightened attractiveness of forbidden fruit. It is debatable how far their experience of community dress, defined in terms of morality rather than aesthetics, could have afforded them any pleasure. That their consumption of dress remained a problem at Oneida suggests that they did not entirely embrace the repudiation of gender difference. It has been observed that for some women, at least, the positive experience of motherhood[17] did not accord with community doctrine; which construed maternity and family life as burdens to be avoided, and it may be that dress was one area where women could retreat to a separate feminine sphere in which, in the face of official opposition, they found a positive value. However, such speculations are of recent origin, and certainly never emerged in any of the writings of, or about, Oneida communalists. In the community newspapers, and other official publications, dress was construed in only the most positive light; critics of the Oneidan way of life, while not approving of the dress, saw it not as a mechanism of restraint, but, on the contrary, as a vehicle of the most unrestrained sexual licence.

Despite the fact that practical experiments in utopian socialism were meant to inspire a more wholesale social reform, there was no widespread interest in the dress of these communal groups until some time after the instigation of bloomerism at Seneca Falls. The immediate precursor of Bloomer's attempt to popularise trousers as the everyday dress of 'ordinary' women, came from a reforming constituency considered less radical than utopian socialism, and less 'dangerous' in terms of its gender politics. By 1849, two years earlier than Bloomer's articles on trousers in *The Lily*, *The Water-Cure Journal* had started to promote bifurcation in dress as a principle of health reform. Fowlers & Wells, the publishers of this periodical, were aware of utopian socialist precedent, but chose to introduce the question of trousers afresh, giving the impression that they were responding to reader demand. Over the next few years, they identified trousered dress as a 'natural', healthful and functional costume, as well as a proper 'republican' dress, by wearing which women could decently assist in the great reforms of the age, assuring America of world leadership. A number of readers of *The Water-Cure Journal* including some who had first worn trousers when taking a bathing cure, began to sport them openly, as everyday wear, and to report on their progress, in print. After some debate as to whether trousers with or without skirts offered the best model, readers finally threw their weight behind a skirted alternative, significantly at the point where such a costume, as 'the bloomer', was becoming identified with Women's Rights.

The characterisation of trousers as a moral, hygenic, and patriotic dress no doubt made them attractive to Bloomer, and other early feminists, anxious to establish the most respectable credentials for their movement. At the point where they put them on, they, the general public, seem to have been largely unaware that trousers had an earlier, more dangerous provenance; had they known of utopian socialist precedent, it is unlikely that trousers would have enjoyed any significant patronage within Women's Rights.

However, the presence of Mary Gove Nichols (a leading light of *The Water-Cure Journal*, a strong advocate of the bloomer dress, and a supporter of Women's Rights) at the 'anarchist' commune of Modern Times, Long Island, meant that, by 1852, trousers were becoming more publically associated with extreme radical thought. Though Modern Times catered for every species of progressive opinion, and allowed for the widest variation in appearance, from peasant costume to nudity, it was widely believed that its members were free lovers, and that its women members were wearers of 'the breeches'. It was rumoured that Nichols had recruited, as students of hydropathy and holistic living, a number of young girls, who were being introduced to trouser-wearing and pre-marital sex. Though unfounded, this was a serious accusation, and one not easily shaken off.

From this point, attempts to present the bloomer dress in a wholesome light became increasingly futile, particularly once the conservative press had taken up the issue in such a negative way. In 1852 *The Ladies Wreath* published a fictional conversation between a young lady and her professor on the subject of dress. When the girl expressed her opinion that the bloomer dress was healthful, practical, and attractive, and that she intended to wear it, the professor explained that women's trousers were 'one of the manifestations of that wild spirit of socialism and agrarian radicalism which is at present so rife in our land'. Upon hearing this, the young lady exclaimed, 'If this dress has any connexion [*sic*] with Fourierism or Socialism, or fanaticism in any shape,

I have no disposition to wear it . . . no true woman would so far compromise her delicacy as to espouse, however unwittingly, such a cause.'[18]

The identification of trousers with Free Love remained strong for many years. In 1861 Artemus Ward, a comic writer with a large following, contributed an article to the popular *Vanity Fair*, which made this connection manifest. He described a visit he had supposedly made, some years previously, to the trouser-wearing community at Berlin Heights. Characterising the Heighters as Free Lovers, Spiritualists, and 'high presher reformers on gineral principles', Ward described the community women as, 'wus than the men. They wore trowsis, short gownds, straw hats with green ribbins, and all carried bloo cotton umbrellers'. When Ward is accosted by a 'perfeckly orful lookin female', wearing a 'skanderlusly short' dress and trousers 'shameful to behold', and is claimed by her as her 'Spiritual Affinity' (popularly believed to be a euphemism for 'free lover'), he is outraged, and advises the females present to return to their husbands, to 'take orf them skanderlous gownds and trowsis, and dress respectful like other wimin'.[19]

It does seem to be the case that, once 'free lovism', which was seen to be an outcome of utopian doctrine, became the focus of a 'moral panic', trousered dress became a much less attractive proposition. This sheds some light upon the fate of the bloomer as a Women's Rights' costume. It is certainly apposite that, in 1853, members of the Women's Rights 'inner circle' decided to lay

Arrival of a male recruit at the Oneida Community, from Free Love and Its Votaries *by John Ellis, 1871 (Courtesy of Kate Luck)*

the dress aside. Cady Stanton, one of the organisers of the first American Women's Rights Convention, took off her bloomers in that year, believing that they had lost her the presidency of the ultra respectful Women's Temperance Association, where she had hoped to make recruits for feminism. She wrote, 'As some of those who advocated the right to suffrage wore the dress, and had been identified with unpopular reforms, in the reports of our convention, the press rung the changes of "strong-minded", "Bloomer", "free love", "easy divorce", "amalgamation".'[20]

From the mid 1850s, critics of Women's Rights could easily cash in on the identification of trousers with communal socialism and sexual unorthodoxy, hinting at a common philosophical platform. In 1857 Currier & Ives, the foremost manufacturers of popular prints in America, published an image entitled 'The Great Republican Reform Party', which showed a Women's Righter, dressed in bloomers, in the company of other supporters of John C. Fremont, the first Republican presidential candidate. These included Fourierists and Free Lovers, who are described as 'Freemounters', a pun on the candidate's name, and hinting at gross sexual irregularity.[21] Some years later, John Ellis, an opponent of socialist communalism and feminism, was still harping on this theme, lumping together advocates of women's suffrage and other trouser wearers, including 'Oneida Communalists, Individual Sovereigns, Berlin Heights, Free Lovers', concluding that they were equally desirous of the abolition of marriage, the dissolution of the American family, and the destruction of religion and purity.[22]

However, public speculation that feminism, and bloomerism, had an undisclosed, anti-social, and immoral agenda did not immediately signal the demise of bifurcation as a principle of dress reform. Instead, those health reformers who had been advocating trousered dress as a hygienic therapy continued to do so, whilst striving to distance themselves from the dangerous associations which trousers had acquired. The proprietors of *The Water-Cure Journal*, for example, continued to publish reports on the progress of trousers within dress reform, but refused any further articles by Mary Gove Nichols, once she had identified her interest in communalism and Free Love. Similarly, the originators of the 'Dress Reform Association' (founded in 1857), whilst trouser-wearers themselves, were circumspect in their advocacy, and dropped the name 'bloomer' from their reform vocabulary, attempting to sanitise their appeal by rechristening it as the 'American Costume'. However, their attempts to win American women over to bifurcation by shifting the signification of trousers into safer territory bore little fruit. Those who continued to argue the advantages of trousered dress for women were, by then, not simply up against public hilarity at the sight of an eccentric dress, as has sometimes been supposed; the real obstacles to their progress were the shibboleths of unrestrained female sexuality, and social liberty, and all that this implied.

Notes and References

1 *The Lily*, Seneca Falls, June 1851.

2 *New York Daily Tribune*, 16 June 1851, p. 4.

3 Rosabeth Moss Kanter, *Commitment and Community: Communes in Sociological Perspective*, Cambridge, Ma., 1972.

4 For 'fossilization' see Beverley Gordon, 'Dress in American Communal Societies', *Communal Societies*, vol. 5, 1985.

5 Mrs Pears to Mrs Bakewell, 8 April 1826, quoted in Thomas and Sarah Pears (eds), *New Harmony; An Adventure in Happiness; Papers of Thomas and Sarah Pears*, Indianapolis Historical Society Publications, vol. 11, no. 1, 1973. (Originally published 1933.)

6 Carol Kolmerton, *Women in Utopia: The Ideology of Gender in the American Owenite Communities*, Bloomington and Indianapolis, 1990.

7 George B. Lockwood, *The New Harmony Communities*, Marion, Indiana, 1902.

8 Pears to Bakewell, in Thomas and Sarah Pears, op. cit.

9 Arthur Bestor, *Backwoods Utopias, The Sectarian Origins and the Owenite Phase of Communitarian Socialism in America 1663–1829*, Philadelphia, 1970.

10 Oneida Association, 'First Annual Report of the Oneida Association, Exhibiting Its History, Principles and Transactions to Jan 1, 1849', Oneida: Oneida Reserve.

11 Pierpont Noyes, *My Father's House: An Oneida Boyhood*, New York, 1937.

12 George Noyes Miller, *The Strike of a Sex*, London, 1895. (Originally published 1891.)

13 Oneida Association, 'Bible Communism: A Compilation from the Annual Reports and Other Publications of the Oneida Association and Its Branches: Presenting, in Connection with Their History, A Summary View of Their Religious and Social Theories', Brooklyn, New York: Office of the Circular, 1853.

14 The Oneida Circular, 22 May 1865, quoted in Constance Robertson, *Oneida Community: An Autobiography 1851–1876*, Syracuse, 1981.

15 The Oneida Circular, New Series, vol. 77, quoted in Louis J. Kern 'Ideology and Reality: Sexuality and Women's Studies in the Oneida Community', *Radical History Review*, vol. 20, Spring/Summer, 1979.

16 Expenditure on dress varied from year to year. In 1856 it was $16.98 per individual, in 1865, $38.62, in 1875, $33. In the early days of the community, women submitted their requests for dress to a dress committee. Later a fixed sum was allocated.

17 Once the community had a firm economic base, Noyes relaxed the ruling on compulsory birth control. He introduced a eugenics programme, whereby the most 'perfected' men and women could pair to produce offspring.

18 Quoted in Barbara Welter, 'The Cult of True Womanhood 1820–1860', *American Quarterly*, vol. 18, 1966.

19 Reprinted in Artemus Ward, *Artemus Ward, His Book; Being the Confessions and Experiences of a Showman*, London, 1862.

20 Elizabeth Cady Stanton, Susan B. Anthony and Matilda Joslyn Gage (eds), *History of Woman Suffrage*, vol. II, New York, 1882, p. 470.

21 Loise R. Noun, *Strong-Minded Women; The Emergence of the Woman Suffrage Movement in Iowa*, Ames, Iowa, 1970.

22 John B. Ellis, *Free Love and Its Votaries; Or American Socialism Unmasked*, San Francisco, 1870.

LINDA COLEING

Ann Macbeth and the Glasgow School

Ann Macbeth was a radical teacher of embroidery at the Glasgow School of Art from 1901 until 1928. She had entered the school as a student in 1897, where she came under the influence of Jessie Newbery who had begun teaching on the embroidery course there in 1894. The school pioneered the teaching of embroidery as a design subject, including artistic dress. The school was considered avant-garde in the 1890s, at the forefront of modern design, and the work of its pupils became known as the 'Glasgow Style'.

The Glasgow School of Art acquired its reputation under the headship of Francis Newbery, Jessie Newbery's husband. Francis Newbery was only 32 years old when he was appointed Head c. 1885. Before his appointment he had taught at the Government School of Design in South Kensington; thus he took to Glasgow an awareness of the latest London designs. He sought out the best teachers he could for the decorative arts, and travelled abroad to investigate developments in design education on the Continent.[1] He appointed a French teacher of decorative arts, and in 1908 interviewed the architect designer C.F.A. Voysey, for the post, although it was eventually offered to W. Britten.[2]

Craft pursuits provided women in the 1890s with a much needed 'respectable' source of income, and the Glasgow School of Art gave women the opportunity to gain the necessary artistic skills. As well as drawing and painting they could learn embroidery, jewellery, woodwork, bookbinding, leatherwork and metalwork. Outlets for the sale of craft produce, such as the Arts and Crafts Exhibition Society (founded in 1888), were beginning to appear.[3] Patronage was available in Glasgow from manufacturers such as James Templeton and James Morton, who were external examiners at the school, and from individuals such as Miss Cranston, a member of the Temperance movement who established a number of tea-rooms decorated in the Glasgow Style. The Macdonald sisters, ex-pupils of the school, set up their own craft studio in 1894, from which they carried out commissions.

The work of the Glasgow School did not meet with universal approval or obtain mass support; the graphic work of the Macdonald sisters, for example was described as 'ghouls and gas pipes' in the Glasgow press in 1894;[4] patronage and support came from a few enlightened individuals. Francis Newbery consistently publicly defended his students' work and stressed the importance of individuality and originality in the school's output. The avant-garde work of Glasgow designers, however, was to find more support on the Continent, particularly in Austria, Hungary and Italy.

English Arts and Crafts designers, after having invited the participation of Glasgow designers at the 1896 Arts and Crafts exhibition, reacted to the work in a horrified fashion. They considered 'the distortions accorded the human figure in the Glasgow designers' work were beyond Beardsley, and could not conceivably be reconciled with a due respect for Nature'.[5] The Glasgow Four[6] were not invited to exhibit again, but work of the embroidery school, which showed less distortion of the human figure, was regularly exhibited.

Glasgow designers found rare support in England from Gleeson White, the editor of *Studio* magazine. Founded in 1893 the magazine had a forward-looking policy and an international circulation. It was one of the first magazines to feature the work of Ann Macbeth. It was Francis Newbery's policy to encourage students to gain a sound knowledge of the skills of drawing and painting before attempting to study the decorative arts. In an article published in *Studio* in 1902 he praised Ann Macbeth's adherence to this policy.

> Unlike so many art workers of the present day who start designing before they draw . . . Miss Macbeth kept her design aspirations in the background until she had made herself a competent draughtswoman, and had mastered the art of drawing, without which design is as lifeless as a body without a soul.[7]

This was to be the beginning of an extremely successful career for Ann Macbeth. Her embroidery was regularly featured in magazines, she participated in Arts and Crafts exhibitions, she designed a banner which was presented as a civic gift from the City of Glasgow to the City of Lyons,[8] and she published books on design.[9] She also became an extremely successful teacher and an inspiration for other women.

Ann Macbeth was radical in her approach and also deeply religious. She saw no conflict between making banners for the Women's Social and Political Union or designing hangings for a church. In terms of dress, she evolved an approach to the creation of individually designed, non-restrictive clothing which developed from her teacher Jessie Newbery's style of dress. In the early 1900s, when the fashionable image was of a tight-corseted, 'S' bend figure, Jessie Newbery, in common with other women in 'Aesthetic circles', rejected such restrictive dress in favour of loose-flowing garments with a natural waistline. Mrs H.R. Haweis, a spokeswoman for the Aesthetic Movement, advocated loose corseting rather than abandoning the corset altogether.[10] Margaret Swain suggests that Jessie Newbery went yet further in refusing to wear a corset at all.[11]

Illustrations of Jessie Newbery's clothing show loose-flowing garments fastened at the waist with embroidered belts (overleaf). Collars and cuff, often richly embroidered, were fastened separately to the dresses for practical reasons; detachable they made the dresses easier to wash. This also provided an economic means of dressing since a variety of looks could be achieved with a few dresses by swapping around accessories.

Ann Macbeth continued to develop this approach both in her dressing and in her teaching. She is shown at around 1900 wearing an embroidered collar with the Glasgow rose motif (overleaf). Her contemporaries Frances and Margaret Macdonald and Jessie King also wore artistic dress. A book by Anna Muthesius shows Frances and Margaret Macdonald wearing dresses of their own design.[12]

Radical alternatives to fashionable dressing were by no means new at the turn of the century.[13] In the 1850s fashion and feminism had been combined by Amelia Bloomer, who had promoted the wearing of bifurcated garments (see Kate Luck's article in this volume). In 1884 the Rational Dress Association was formed; backed by medical opinion it urged an end to the practice of tight lacing and tried to have the weight of clothing reduced. A more aesthetically appealing alternative to previous attempts at dress reform was offered in the 1890s by the Healthy and Artistic Dress Union. This venture was supported by Members of Arts and Crafts' circles and Walter Crane provided designs for its magazine, *Aglaia*. The practice of the Glasgow School was most in sympathy with this venture. Arts and Crafts ideology linked 'the useful' with 'the beautiful' and certainly from the 1880s many Arts and Crafts sympathisers supported the notion of universal good design.

In 1901 Ann Macbeth became an assistant in the embroidery class and in 1908 she took over from Jessie Newbery. Through her teaching and design publications she endeavoured to spread her radical approach to dress and domestic embroidery. The teaching of the Glasgow School put the ideas of the Arts and Crafts movement into practice by elevating the status of home dressmaking, encouraging every woman to create her own individualistic clothing. Ann Macbeth advocated the use of 'humble materials' such as cotton, linen and crash, with richer, more expensive materials such as velvet and silk confined to decorative details.[14] This brought 'designer dressing' within the reach of modest households. (Ann Macbeth was the eldest of nine children, a circumstance which may have influenced her practical approach.)

In the nineteenth century home dressmaking was despised as something to be undertaken only by those who could not afford the services of a couturier

Jessie Newbury,
c. 1900, wearing an
embroidered dress and
cape of her own
design (courtesy of
Glasgow Art Gallery
and Museum)

Ann Macbeth,
c. 1900, wearing a
collar embroidered
with the Glasgow
rose motif by herself,
Studio magazine,
1908

or dressmaker, or philanthropically, to provide clothing for the poor. Ann Macbeth elevated home dressmaking to the status of an artistic craft. She believed the designing of clothing was a subject worthy of being taught in schools, and advocated that boys as well as girls should learn embroidery. Mathematics could be taught through dress designing as it was necessary to understand mathematical principles to calculate proportions of the body.

The embroidery classes held at the Glasgow School of Art were open to the community as a whole. In addition classes were held on Saturday mornings for schoolteachers who were interested in the school's teaching methods. The Saturday course lasted for three years and led to a certificate presented by the Scottish Education Department which was recognised as a teaching qualification. From 1906 these classes became known as Article 55 classes.[15] In 1907 the school was empowered to grant its own certificate for Art Needlework and Embroidery, a qualification which was accepted by the Scottish Education Department as 'testimony of professional capability'.[16]

Thus the ideas and practice of Jessie Newbery and Ann Macbeth spread beyond the realms of an artistic elite, in keeping with Ann Macbeth's philosophy of good design for all and active involvement with the community. After Jessie Newbery's retirement Ann Macbeth was joined by Margaret Swanson, a former primary schoolteacher from Ayrshire who had followed the 'Article 55' classes for four years. Together they wrote a textbook, *Educational Needlecraft*, which was published in 1911. The book revolutionised the method by which embroidery was taught in schools, being based on the developmental capabilities of the growing child rather than advocating a rigid formula of tasks. Ann Macbeth and Margaret Swanson also ridiculed the practice of making samplers whereby for the sake of symmetry the last few letters of the alphabet were jettisoned. (In any case samplers were produced merely as a technical exercise; they did not result in a useful and beautiful end product and so were eventually abandoned altogether.) Ann Macbeth and Margaret Swanson also considered the current practice of whitework (embroidering with white thread on a white ground) to be as intelligible as 'drawing with white chalk on a white board'.[17]

The book is filled with examples of useful household articles and garments related to the age and manual dexterity of the child. But there are no patterns as such. Instead, the principles of design are taught and delicate line drawings of construction techniques and finished garments are shown (overleaf and p. 220). Ann Macbeth was dedicated to producing a new generation of designer–craftswomen, rather than creating more copyists and dressmakers.

The boy or girl who uses material and needle freely in independent design (shoe, cap, chemise, coverlet) ranks on a plane with the scientist who makes a hypothesis, with the artist who makes an experiment.[18]

The first steps towards becoming a designer of garments were taken at the age of six when schoolchildren learned how to cut out a neckband from paper. Through a gradual progression until the child was 9 or 10, measurements and paper patterns were cut for the neck, wrist, waist and armhole. At each stage the proportions of the body were compared; for example, the wrist being roughly half the neck. The children measured each other and created their own patterns. In this way they were encouraged and given the confidence to produce their own designs from the beginning. Margaret McMillan, in her preface to *Educational Needlecraft*, suggested that by using the book's methods schoolchildren could combat contemporary social ills by making clothing for themselves and others.

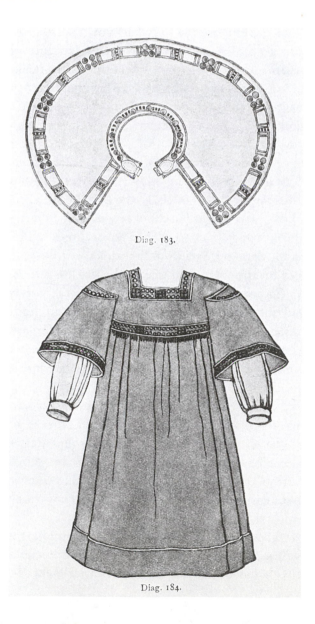

Diag. 183.

Diag. 184.

Designs for a pinafore dress and collar in Educational Needlecraft, *1911*

In every great capital there is great display in dress – splendid robes are described in the Press, and the rapid changes of fashion make it needful for thousands of women to appear constantly in splendid new clothes. Side by side with all this, in the poor quarters, thousands of people do not even know what it is to wear a dress specially made for them. Children go to school swathed in half a dozen wretched skirts and bodices or half naked even in winter. They wear old, cast-off clothes, which somehow hide even the grace of childhood. Yet all this is unnecessary. The elder children – of twelve years – might alter all this in the schools. They could make all their own clothes ... given strong and cheap materials they will clothe themselves and the little ones.[19]

To Ann Macbeth beauty, creativity and individual expression were equally as important as practicality in making clothing, which is evident throughout the teaching method in *Educational Needlecraft*. She continually advocated a less rigid curriculum, encouraging schools to provide a more holistic form of education. For example, in 1920 she wrote,

The geometry lessons in our schools should help greatly in making pattern to add to our craft work, but at present they are poles asunder.[20]

In *Educational Needlecraft*, principles based on design from natural form were given, but design advice encouraged flexibility and originality. For example,

One may make use of a four-petalled flower where there ought to be five petals, but it is not desirable that roses should grow on ivy stems.[21]

The Arts and Crafts principle of making decoration part of the construction of garments was followed throughout the scheme; decorative darning reinforced necks and armholes, hems were held up by running stitches in coloured threads. Ann Macbeth's own garments were often stitched together with decorative insertion stitches. After her retirement she pieced them together whilst travelling by bus to give lectures at Women's Institutes.[22]

The success of the scheme set out in *Educational Needlecraft* was phenomenal. By 1916 it had been 'adapted for school use in many districts of Great Britain and Ireland and also in New Zealand, Australia, South Africa, Canada, the United States, the West Indies, India and in many other foreign countries'.[23] By that time 1,600 students had undertaken the course at the School of Art.[24] Ann Macbeth and her new assistant, Miss Arthur, were kept busy giving lectures about the teaching method and offering short practical courses. They taught in all the cities and larger towns in Scotland, in London and in twenty towns in England. The demands upon them became so great that they set up a loan scheme whereby parcels of work illustrating the method were sent out all over Scotland and England. In the Isle of Man the interned Germans showed great interest in the work.[25] Examples of work were sent abroad to Holland, the Bermudas, South Africa, New Zealand, Tasmania and St Helena.

In the post-First World War period Ann Macbeth wrote of a 'New World' to be created and of the role of teaching in its construction.[26] In the introduction to *School and Fireside Crafts* (1920) she wrote that she advocated social reconstruction through development of a community spirit.

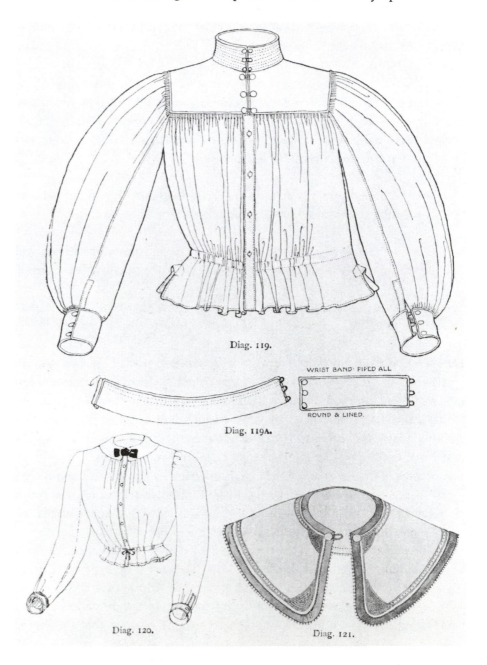

Diag. 119.

WRIST BAND: PIPED ALL ROUND & LINED.

Diag. 119A.

Designs for a blouse and an embroidered collar in Educational Needlecraft, *1911*

Diag. 120.

Diag. 121.

First of all it is important that our *teachers* should learn to think in new ways, and that there be put before each pupil some definite outlet for his work, so that it may, if possible, have some bearing upon the good of the community, as well as upon his own personal interests.[27]

She felt that it was important to provide workers with an outlet for their work in order to generate a native craft industry. Educational authorities could help the process by finding a market for the work produced in schools at a reasonable price 'without undercutting manufacturers or trade production'.[28] That was quite a revolutionary proposal for 1920. Ann Macbeth proved that a market existed by experimenting with the sale of regional crafts in tourist areas, finding that there was a great demand for British craft work.

Americans coming to Britain would prefer to take away with them British made products, however crude, rather than those made in Japan or elsewhere.[29]

In the introduction to *Embroidered and Laced Leatherwork* she commented on the familiar pattern of women producing crafts in their spare time and devaluing their work and spoiling the market by undercharging.

The many industrious workers in Women's Institutes are particularly guilty of want of thought . . . partly because they entirely forget that work done in leisure time ought to count as work done in working time, and they too often charge so low a price that it barely covers the cost of materials.[30]

Practicality runs through Ann Macbeth's philosophy both in design work and in its marketing. She was aiming after all to generate a means of livelihood for craftworkers in the community at large. Her books were always intended as a stimulus to original design rather than patterns to be copied. She urged embroiders to exploit the resources of their own particular district to create regional styles of work.

It is desirable that such work should, when firmly established show definite local characteristics and styles, or should be applied when possible to materials which are made, or are specially suited to the usage of the community in different districts.[31]

Her professional life as a designer brought her into contact with manufacturers, and reinforced her attitude to the marketing of design – one based on real-life knowledge of commercial manufacture. She designed carpets and embroidery for the Scottish manufacturing company, Alexander Morton & Co. Some of the carpet designs were illustrated in *Studio Yearbook of Decorative Art* (1914) but her scheme for producing appliqué embroidery was never commercially launched.[32] A more practical scheme was produced by Liberty & Co., who sold both finished embroideries and transfers adopted from Ann Macbeth's designs. These included designs for borders which could be used for both furnishings and dress, and a design for the yoke of a child's dress. The designs continued to feature in Liberty catalogues until c.1914.[33]

In 1920 Ann Macbeth went to live in the Lake District, but she remained as a visiting lecturer at the Glasgow School of Art until her retirement in 1928. She continued to design and practice, making embroidery, church hangings, and vestments for the local church in Patterdale, and decorating ceramics. Her friend, Miss Little, recalled occasions when she and other local women were led by Ann Macbeth on expeditions to collect rushes for the teaching of basket-weaving.[34] Ann Macbeth set up local classes in embroidery, encouraging every woman to create her own designs. If they protested that they could not draw she persuaded them to draw round leaves which could be cut out to make a pattern.[35] When local farmers could not sell their wool from Herdwick sheep she devised a simple method of rug-weaving from a beam suspended above the cottage door, the warp weighted with stones. A range of techniques for rug-weaving was published in her *Country Woman's Rug Book* in 1929.[36]

Although Ann Macbeth's ideas were rooted in Arts and Crafts principles, craft practice for her had to be a living tradition. She continually looked forward, despising advocates of a return to the past.

> We of the twentieth century ought to have a type of design and art native and proper to our own age, and it is this type we should nurse and develop. Instead of this we suffer from its loss and neglect, through the fact that those who are reckoned authorities in things artistic have limited their sympathies too much to things of olden times, till they are blinded to the beauty and romance of the present.[37]

Like C.R. Ashbee,[38] she came to recognise the importance of the machine in the democratisation of design and advocated its use.

> If the artist craftsman will realise that no machine can, of itself, be artistic or inartistic, and if he will look into it and understand its workings, and be diligent to learn its ways, the machine work will have as high an artistic quality as the work of medieval days.[39]

In the summer Ann Macbeth lived on a crag at Helvellyn in a house built to her own design with a large picture window through which she used to embroider the effects of light and weather on the hillside, working 'like a painter' directly in stitches with a huge range of coloured yarns.[40] She had dye pits sunk into the ground outside the house. She was still remembered in the Lake District in the 1970s for her colourful clothing and long, flowing cloaks. (She died in 1948.) An even more radical form of dress which she adopted for walking in the 1930s was a trouser suit which she made from heavy tweed and waterproofed herself.

Although she can be considered the equal of male Arts and Crafts designers and theorists such as C.F.A. Voysey[41] and C.R. Ashbee, Ann Macbeth's contribution has never become as well known as theirs. Some of the reasons for the neglect of women designers and theorists have been put forward elsewhere. Attitudes to embroidery have been examined in Roszika Parker's *The Subversive Stitch*,[42] and reasons for the lack of visibility of the many women designers of the Arts and Crafts movement have been discussed in Anthea Callen's *The Angel in the Studio*.[43] The exhibition and excellent supporting catalogue *The Glasgow Girls* (1990)[44] represents a long overdue assessment of the contribution of the women designers of the Glasgow School of Art.

Of significance in assessing Ann Macbeth's overall contribution was her constant encouragement of women as designers and her aim to generate a living craft tradition. In that aim she can be considered to have succeeded: following her encouragement and inspiration the craft of embroidery still lives on in the Lake District. Whereas other designers criticised the 'cult of the amateur' for devaluing design standards, she offered only enthusiasm and encouragement. She had a holistic approach to her work, operating from a firm spiritual basis for the good of the community. Her political contributions were to nurture and develop the design talents of the individual, and to give women the confidence to value their own design work, both in terms of personal achievement and in the wider commercial sphere.

Notes and References

1 Press cuttings, Glasgow School of Art.

2 C.F.A. Voysey's interview was discussed in the transcript of the meeting of the Subcommittee on Design, Glasgow School of Art, 22 May 1908.

3 Between the first Arts and Crafts Exhibition of 1888 and the Exhibition of 1910, the number of women designers exhibiting increased fivefold. Lynne Walker, 'The Arts and Crafts Alternative', in Judy Attfield and Pat Kirkham, (eds), *A View from the Interior*, London 1989, pp. 165-73; p. 172.

4 This episode is discussed in Elizabeth Bird, 'Ghouls and Gas Pipes: Public Reaction to the Early Work of "The Four"', *Scottish Art Review*, vol XIV, no. 4, 1975, pp. 13–16; 28.

5 Robert Macleod, *Charles Rennie Mackintosh*, Feltham, 1968, p. 44.

6 The Glasgow Four consisted of Frances and Margaret Macdonald, Charles Rennie Mackintosh and Herbert McNair.

LINDA COLEING

7 F.H. Newbery, 'An Appreciation of the Work of Ann Macbeth', *Studio*, 1902, pp. 40–9; 40–1.

8 J. Taylor, 'The Glasgow School of Embroidery', *Studio*, 1910, pp. 124–35; 133.

9 Ann Macbeth, *The Playwork Book*, London, 1918; *Embroidered and Laced Leatherwork*, London, 1924; *Needleweaving*, Kendal, 1926; *The Country Woman's Rug Book*, Leicester, 1929; and Ann Macbeth and May Spence, *School and Fireside Crafts*, London, 1920; Ann Macbeth and Margaret Swanson, *Educational Needlecraft*, London, 1911.

10 Mrs. H.R. Haweis, *The Art of Dress*, 1879, Garland reprint, New York and London, 1978, p. 35.

11 Margaret Swain, 'Mrs Newbery's Dress', *Costume*, vol. 12, 1978, pp. 64–73; 69.

12 Anna Muthesius, *Das Eigenkleid der Frau*, Krefeld, 1903.

13 See Stella M. Newton, *Health, Art and Reason: Dress Reformers of the 19th Century*, London, 1974.

14 This approach is explored in Macbeth and Swanson, op. cit., see also Taylor, op. cit., pp. 128, 131, and Newbery, op. cit., pp. 45, 46.

15 Liz Arthur, 'Jessie Newbery', in Jude Burkhauser (ed.), '*Glasgow Girls' Women in Art and Design 1880*–1920, Edinburgh, 1990, pp. 147–51, 147.

16 Prospectus, Glasgow School of Art, 1907–8.

17 Macbeth and Swanson, op. cit., p. 1.

18 Ibid.

19 Margaret McMillan, Preface to Macbeth and Swanson, op. cit., (1922 edition, London, New York, Bombay, Calcutta, Madras) p. vii.

20 Macbeth and Spence, op. cit., p. xii.

21 Macbeth and Swanson, op. cit., p. 112.

22 This information was provided by a friend and pupil of Ann Macbeth, Miss E. Little, in an interview in 1974.

23 Ann Macbeth, 'Modern Needlecraft and its Application', in *Exhibition of Ancient and Modern Embroidery and Needlecraft*, exhibition catalogue, Glasgow, 1916, pp. 10–11; 10.

24 Anne K. Arthur, and Francis Newbery, 'The Glasgow School of Art, Section of Needlecraft and Embroidery', ibid., pp. 11–12; 11.

25 Ibid.

26 Macbeth and Spence, op. cit., p. ix.

27 Ibid.

28 Ibid., p. x.

29 Ibid., p. xi.

30 Macbeth, op. cit., 1924, p. 10.

31 Macbeth, op. cit., 1916, p. 10.

32 Four designs are illustrated. *Studio Yearbook of Decorative Art*, 1914, p. 70.

33 Barbara Morris, *Liberty Designs 1874–1914*, London, 1989, p. 58.

34 Interview with Miss E. Little, 1974.

35 Ibid.

36 Macbeth, op. cit., 1929.

37 Macbeth and Spence, op. cit., p. xiii.

38 For a discussion of C.R. Ashbee's theories, see Alan Crawford, *C.R. Ashbee: Architect, Designer and Romantic Socialist*, New Haven and London, 1985.

39 Macbeth and Spence, op. cit., p. xiii.

40 Interview with Miss E. Little, 1974.

41 For a discussion of C.F.A. Voysey's ideas, see John Brandon-Jones *et al.*, *C.F.A. Voysey: Architect and Designer 1857–1941*, London, 1978.

42 Roszika Parker, *The Subversive Stitch*, London, 1984.

43 Anthea Callen, *The Angel in the Studio: Women in the Arts and Crafts Movement 1870–1914*, London and New York, 1979.

44 Burkhauser, op. cit.

AILEEN RIBEIRO

U topian Dress

One of humankind's enduring characteristics has been a striving after perfection, both spiritual and worldly. This can take the form of imagining a paradise or abode of the blessed – what the *Odyssey* describes as Elysium, 'the place beyond the world . . . where the lines of life run smoothest for mortal men'. On the other hand, many writers have been attracted to more specific blueprints for an ideal society, set either in the present or the future. One recent authority finds such utopias to be 'ideal imaginary societies described in their entirety as if functioning in the present.'[1] While utopias often involve criticism of existing societies, they contain a crucial element of fantasy, which is their distinguishing characteristic. They are more than a discourse of good government, such as we find in Plato's *Republic*, although to Plato they are indebted for the notion of the perfect city state free both from the corruption of extreme freedom and the dangers of tyranny, and from the pre-eminence of the state over the claims of the individual.

An interest in the fantastic (the pleasures and perils of a voyage into *terra incognita* figure prominently in many utopias) came with the expanding of mental and geographical horizons in the Renaissance. Almost certainly, it was the publication in 1507 of the Florentine Amerigo Vespucci's account of his voyage to the continent named after him, which helped to inspire Thomas More's *Utopia* (1516), a work which gave its name to a whole new genre of publications on the theme of the ideal state.[2]

Having laid down the lines on which an ideal society should be based, More, and those who followed him, had to turn their attention to what the inhabitants of their utopias should wear. More himself, noting the 'reckless extravagance' of those in contemporary society who spent a fortune on dress, and aware of fruitless attempts to curb this through largely ineffective sumptuary legislation, decided that rational and happy societies should have few, if any, distinctions in dress, and certainly nothing that could be called 'fashion'. Fashion, with its necessary expenditure and the elements of envy and competitiveness involved, was seen to be divisive and inimical to true equality.

Thus, distinctions in the real world, created by official dress, are to be despised along with idolatry of gold and jewellery; they are indications of a class-ridden and extravagant society which the Utopians have left behind. For this reason, in *Utopia* gold is used for humble items of domestic equipment like chamber pots, and those convicted of serious crimes are forced to wear gold jewellery. Pearls and precious stones are regarded as toys for children; why, ask the inhabitants of *Utopia*, should anyone 'be fascinated by the dull gleam of a tiny stone; when he has all the stars in the sky to look at'?[3]

It was a widely held belief in More's time that tailors and dressmakers were partly to blame for what were seen as rapidly changing fashions, and so in *Utopia*, these trades do not exist. Everyone wears roughly the same sort of clothes, which 'vary slightly according to sex and marital status', but we are not told what they look like, except that they are pleasant on the eye, and allow free movement of the limbs. For work, leather clothing is worn, but otherwise Utopians wear wool, esteemed for its cleanliness, and linen, valued for its whiteness; by implication, silks and lavish decoration are alien to the spirit of equality and practicality. Furthermore, in *Utopia*, clothing continues to be worn until worn-out, and can last almost a lifetime.[4]

With regard to dress, writers on the subject of utopias have a problem; either they conceive an ideal dress in terms of the dress of the past (sometimes misunderstood, and usually seen through rose-coloured spectacles), or they have to use their imagination to invent it. It is inevitable that writers find it difficult to stand outside the aesthetic of their own age and put into print what they cannot visualise. Sometimes they ignore dress altogether, and at all times they play down the role of clothing, as the very notion of fashion must be inimical to a perfect and 'timeless' society. In a sense true utopian dress is a contradiction in terms, particularly in the visual sense, for clothing is so personal, so entwined in the spirit of the time in which it exists, that it cannot be contemplated in terms of an unknown future. Perfection is impossible to record in terms of the mundane details of clothing, and many writers, like More, resort to deliberate vagueness about the dress in their ideal societies.

The impression created in many utopias is the desirability of the Spartan ideal of frugality and austerity, and the power of the state to pursue its political or social aims is enforced by clothing. Rules about dress are often implicit, usually a command; in some cases, equality of sex and status can be obviously enhanced by the uniformity of clothing. In Tommaso Campanella's *City of the Sun* (1602),[5] the utopian vision of a Dominican monk, written during a period of imprisonment, men and women are described as wearing virtually identical clothing, which consists of:

a white undergarment next to the body, and over this a garment which covers both trunk and legs, and has no wrinkles. This has openings on the sides extending from the navel, between the legs to the buttocks. The edges of these openings are fastened by passing the globular buttons on one side into buttonholes facing them on the other. The portion covering the legs extends down to the heels. They cover the feet with thick socks, half-buskins as it were, fastened with buckles, and over these they wear shoes.[6]

The main sartorial difference between the sexes is that men wear a cloak ('toga') to the knees, whereas that worn by women is longer. With the moral comment that is implicit in many utopias – in More's *Utopia* we are told that husbands preferred modesty to beauty in their wives – Campanella's ideal city state metes out severe punishment to women who use cosmetics, or other artificial aids like long trains to their gowns or high-heeled *chopines*.

Less seriously, Joseph Hall's Rabelaisian utopia, *Mundus Alter et Idem* (c.1605) satirises fashionable men and women who adopt elements of the clothing of the opposite sex. In a ship called *Phantasy*, his traveller visits Crapulia ('the Land of Inebriate Excess'), Yvronia (Drunkenness), Moronia ('the Land of Fools') and so on to Hermaphrodite Island, where men can wear 'bodies, rebatoes, and periwigges' along with their breeches and boots, and women choose 'doublets to the rumpe and skirts to the remainder'.[7] It was a widely held belief in the reign of James I that men were tending to effeminacy in their clothing, and women were assuming masculine airs.[8]

Where moralists and utopian dreamers often agreed was on the belief that in an ideal society luxury in dress – what Robert Burton in his *Anatomy of Melancholy* (1621) called 'prodigious riot in apparell' – should be discouraged, although this was sometimes difficult to square with a feeling that status should be distinguished through sumptuary regulation. Burton, for example, wants no 'Utopian parity' in his 'poeticall common-wealth', but a hierarchical society in which trades and professions are to be identified by their clothing.[9]

Even further removed from 'utopian' uniformity in dress is the sumptuous clothing described by Francis Bacon in his *New Atlantis*, an ideal Christian society set in the South Seas, and written in 1624, a few years after his fall from high office. During his eminent legal career, Bacon was an *habitué* of court and aristocratic circles, and a taste for luxury in textiles and dress manifests itself strongly in his utopia, Bensalem, which possesses 'papers, linen, silks, tissues, dainty works of feathers of wonderful lustre, excellent dyes', some of which are made by 'divers mechanical arts which you have not.'[10]

The clothing which he details is redolent of masque imagery, an entertainment familiar to Bacon. Men wear wide-sleeved gowns 'of a kind of water-camlet, of an excellent azure colour', and 'daintily made' turbans; the costume is obviously derived from that of masquerade orientals. The ruler of the kingdom wears a white linen gown, a robe of black cloth, jewelled gloves and shoes of peach-coloured velvet; on state occasions he travels in a jewel-encrusted chariot, attended by fifty young men in 'white satin loose coats up to the mid leg', white silk stockings, blue velvet shoes, and hats 'with fine plumes of divers colours'.[11]

A similar sense of luxury and fantasy interpreted through the imagery of theatrical costume can be seen in the elaborate pageantry which accompanies religious and civic ceremonies in Samuel Gott's *Nova Solyma* (1648). While purporting to be a description of utopia in the new Jerusalem (where the Jews, converted to Christianity, have resettled), it is more a work of missionary Puritan propaganda.[12] While we are not told much about the everyday dress of men in this ideal society except that long gowns are equated with rank and dignity, and short tunics are worn for work, the author becomes much more detailed in his descriptions of the dress of ceremony. When Jacob is elected Father of the Senate, and is driven through the streets dressed in purple with a chain of office which 'glittered with precious jewels', he is attended by trumpeters in 'blue jackets with silver stripes', civic guards in blue cloaks stamped with silver angels, heralds in long robes 'severally embroidered with the ensigns of the twelve tribes [of Israel]', and companies of noble boys, some of whose tunics are 'elaborately adorned with leaves and flowers in fine needlework'.[13] Even a Puritan author, writing in anti-monarchial times, has to fall back on regal and civic pageantry to epitomise luxury and splendour. Furthermore, the pageant includes the Daughter of Zion, carried in a bower of vines, and wearing a costume inspired by the masque, a girdled robe over which is a veil 'of sky-blue byssus interwoven with the finest threads of silver, and sprinkled all over with little jewel stars of various hues, even as they are on the spangled veil of Night'.[14]

If by a utopia, we mean a serious discussion of an ideal political and social system, relatively little of importance was published during the next hundred or so years; the word itself virtually disappears from the intellectual vocabulary. We can only speculate on the reasons for this, and perhaps conclude that in an age of enlightenment, the ideal society might be more realistically achieved, via the works of the *philosophes*, by a gradual process of secular and political freedoms. The last real utopia, in the sense of being a discussion of society and politics within a framework of a voyage into the fantastic, is Swift's *Gulliver's Travels* (1726), where the nearest approach to a perfect society ruled by reason is the land of the Houyhnhnms, the noble horses which, of course, wear no clothes at all.

Any discussion of clothing in the ideal societies imagined by writers in the eighteenth century tends to revolve around the question of freedom both from the corruptions of luxury and the constrictions imposed by fashion. The opening out of the furthest corners of the earth led to the idealisation of 'primitive' tribes, the noble savage admired by Rousseau. Rousseau's recipe for a perfect society, *The Social Contract* (1762), makes no mention of dress, except to say that men and women should dress more for utility than for show; it seems likely that his ideal would be (as in *Émile*) unconstricted clothing which was both frugal and healthy.[15] It was an admirer of Rousseau, Louis-Sébastien Mercier, who published in 1770 a work entitled *L'An Deux Mille Quatre Cent Quarante, Rêve s'il en Fut Jamais* (The Year 2440, a Dream of What Will Never Be).[16] As the title implies, this is a somewhat despairing account of how – given the impossibility of reforming the political system – a perfect society could exist only well into the future. The time-traveller wakes up in 2440, to find a society no longer 'Gothic and capricious', but inspired, as in Mozart's *The Magic Flute*, by Nature, Reason and Wisdom. The inhabitants of the new, enlightened Paris are amazed at the absurdity of the dress of the late 1760s, and soon the traveller adopts the dress of the future:

> His arms enjoyed their full liberty in sleeves moderately large; and his body neatly enclosed in a sort of vest, was covered with a cloak in form of a gown, salutary in the cold and rainy seasons. Round his waist he wore a long sash that had a graceful look, and preserved an equal warmth . . . He wore a long stocking that reached from the foot to the waist; and an easy shoe, in form of a buskin, inclosed his foot.[17]

This combination of a tunic or vest, with what sounds like fairly tight-fitting pantaloons, anticipates the 'republican' dress designed by J.L. David during the French Revolution;[18] this would be entirely appropriate, for Mercier was a Republican and sat as a Girondist deputy in the 1790s. David's costumes were actually worn, although only by a few men who shared the artist's fiercely idealistic republican views, and thus they should be more accurately described as 'reformed' rather than utopian dress. Although the ideals behind dress reform and dress in utopia are often similar, the former is usually more practical, related to and deriving from existing garments, and sometimes actually worn, albeit by relatively small numbers of people. Dress reform, to be successful (not all was) has to be linked to some utilitarian considerations; it cannot indulge in the wild flights of fantasy and theatricality which inform much utopian dress – dress that will *never* have to pass the test of being made-up and worn.

Aesthetics, far more than reason or utility, dominate considerations of dress in utopia in the late nineteenth century. Even when, as with some of the many dress-reformers of the period, the idea of practical and useful dress is proposed, it is usually described within the framework of contemporary aesthetic perceptions, notably favouring the dress of the past. Alfred Robida's *Le Vingtième Siècle* (1883), for example, set in the year 1952, has emancipated women wearing a uniform of knee-breeches, over which are draped dresses (tightly corseted) inspired by styles of the time of Louis XIII and Louis XVI.[19] Strictly speaking, this work, illustrated with the author's amusing drawings, is a novelettish work of prophecy and fantasy rather than a true utopia; politics is subordinated to a science-fiction view of the future which, paradoxically, is set very firmly in the early 1880s.

By this time, however, the idea of utopia (as expressed in the work of More and those who followed him), was seen as a kind of precursor of the ideal socialist state. The American Edward Bellamy's *Looking Backward* (1888) has his hero Julian West (who has been put to sleep by 'a remarkable mesmerist') wake up in the Boston of 2000, to find a transformed society run on military lines (men and women work in the 'industrial army' from the ages of 21 to 45) and with everything made easy by machines. A vast centralised state bureaucracy enables women to shop with ease and pay by credit card, although we are not told what garments they buy; with late nineteenth-century coyness, Bellamy describes their clothing as 'lovely demonstrations of the effect of appropriate drapery in accentuating feminine graces'.[20]

Bellamy probably had in mind a vaguely classical costume of the sort that was favoured by those who resented the excesses – the tight-lacing, the frills, flounces and multifarious accessories – of high fashion. F.H. Pettycoste in his *Towards Utopia* (1894) declared that the woman of the future will wear 'a dress of purely artistic make – both in shape, colour and combination'; it will be 'graceful and flowing' and quite unlike 'the incredible and hideous absurdities that some crack-brained milliner in Paris dictates as the next fashion'.[21]

The Angel in 'The House' or, The Result of Female Suffrage, *engraving by Linley Sambourne for* Punch, *14 June 1884 (courtesy of* Punch)

While the more practical dress-reformers advocated variants on masculine dress for the emancipated woman of the present and the future,[22] those of a more visionary bent who were, like William Morris, as he described himself in *The Aims of Art* (1887), 'impelled towards the Socialist or Optimistic side of things', were often inclined towards the dress of the past as a feature of their utopias. In Morris's *News from Nowhere* of 1890 (subtitled 'Being some chapters from a Utopian Romance'), the writer finds himself projected into the London of the future, a rural craft-centred society where men wear 'medieval' tunic, surcoat and hose, and women's dress is 'somewhat between that of the ancient classical costume and the simpler forms of the fourteenth-century garments'.[23] When the Fabian H.G. Wells envisaged a peaceful world state in his *A Modern Utopia* (1905), he conceived the costume of its inhabitants as being a mixture of the classical and the medieval/Renaissance past. The male 'Samurai' (these are the noble rulers of this utopia who can be of either sex) wear a white tunic with a purple band, and leggings – the general effect, according to Wells, being rather reminiscent 'of the Knights Templars'. Female 'Samurai' can either wear a similar costume, 'or they may have a high-waisted dress of very fine, soft woollen material'; women generally are to be seen in 'loose coloured robes . . . amber and crimson' in styles which echo those of fifteenth-century Italy.[24] It all sounds as though Wells had been looking at contemporary Liberty catalogues.

Modes Parisiennes en Septembre 1952, *illustration by Gillot and Robida from Alfred Robida's book* Le Vingtième Siècle, *Paris, 1883*

AILEEN RIBEIRO

Illustrations by
'C.H.' to an article
entitled Future
Dictates of Fashion
by W. Cade Gall in
Strand, *June 1893*[25]

Much more imaginative are the science-fiction utopias such as Lord Lytton's *The Coming Race* (1871) which is set in a vast underground country ruled by the Vril-ya, the most striking part of whose costume is a pair of large wings made 'from the feathers of a gigantic bird' which fold over the breast and reach to the knees; they fasten round the shoulders with steel springs.[26] Lytton may have read Francis Godwin's *The Man in the Moone* (1638), a description of a lunar utopia where – aided by lack of gravity – the inhabitants fly through the air with 'Fans of Feathers'.[27] Lytton's men wear tunics and leggings 'of some thin, fibrous material', and his women wear robes of different colours denoting their marital state,[28] a kind of colour coding which is one of the features of Aldous Huxley's *Brave New World* of 1932, the first 'anti-utopia' or pessimist vision of a future society.

In Huxley's chilling description of the kind of utopia which might arise in a totalitarian society, reproduction is planned by the state to produce people of different intelligence who are then clothed in the colour laid down for their group. Huxley concentrates on what the women wear, imagining that in the future synthetic materials will have taken over from natural fabrics, but the styles he envisages would not have looked out of place in *Vogue* of the period – zipped (zips, just entering the world of high fashion in the early 1930s, are seen as the most futuristic fastener) acetate jackets with optional viscose fur collars and cuffs, acetate silk shirts, bell-bottomed trousers or shorts 'of adorable viscose velveteen'; underneath the women wear 'zipp-camiknickers' and in bed, 'one-piece zippypyjamas'.[29]

The variety of clothing available in Huxley's utopia is vast compared to the blue overalls which are the uniform of Party members in George Orwell's *Nineteen Eighty-Four* (1949). The overall, with its connotations of the masses at work in factories and its ability to suppress individuality, was the most depressing garment Orwell could think of; paradoxically, the real masses, the proles, wear cheap synthetic clothes which, however crude, admit of distinction between the sexes. Orwell's disturbing political parable, also, of course, an anti-utopia, is the other side of the coin to the belief expressed by the psychologist J.C. Flügel at the end of the 1920s that:

The most advanced countries, so far as political and social conditions are concerned, exhibit, on the whole, the greatest uniformity and consistency; in these countries there are the smallest sartorial distinctions between class and class, and such as they are, these distinctions seem about to disappear'.[30]

With the virtue of hindsight, we might think it dogmatic to equate 'progress' with uniformity in dress, and when in 1962 Huxley published his last novel *Island*, an exploration of the possibility that intelligent men and women *could* create a perfect utopia, there are no rules about dress. Set on an island in South-East Asia, cut off from the rest of the world, a ship-wrecked journalist finds an open, free society where – because there is no shame about sex – a minimum of clothing is worn; it is a society free from the materialist cravings of the West, but in the end it succumbs to conquest by oil-hungry, American-backed politicians from a neighbouring country.

Perhaps the moral is that Utopia can only be achieved in the mind; the word itself, after all, taken from the Greek, means nowhere. It might thus seem a fruitless exercise to look at imaginary clothing in non-existent societies. But the history of dress is more than the mere sum of fabric and style; it is image, wish-fulfilment and fantasy, all of which can be found in a discussion of dress in utopia. Those who write on this subject reveal as much about the sartorial tastes and aspirations of their own time as they do about their visions of the future.

Notes and References

I am grateful to the editor of *Costume* (where this article first appeared in 1987) for permission to reprint it here; I have made a few slight alterations and additions to the original text. Due to limitations of space, this article has no claims to be anything but an introduction to an aspect of a vast and complex topic, about which there is a considerable literature mainly concentrating on the politics of utopias, ignoring their clothing. When I wrote this article, there was, so far as I know, nothing in print on the subject of dress in ideal societies. Since then, the American fashion historian Richard Martin has published a useful, brief critique, entitled *Dress and Dream: the Utopian Idealism of Clothing*, in *Arts Magazine*, New York, October 1987. Further thoughts on this theme can be read in the same author's *Brave New Wardrobe, or James Laver's Speculations on the Prospects for Fashion in a letter to a girl on the future of clothes*, *Arts Magazine*, November 1987. I am grateful to Professor Martin for sending me these articles both in typescript, and as published.

The subject of dress in utopia remains wide open to historians, and I would like to think that the publication here of *Utopian Dress* might encourage further research.

1 M. Eliav-Feldon, *Realistic Utopias. The Ideal Imaginary Societies of the Renaissance 1516*–1630, Oxford, 1982, p. 4.
2 More's *Utopia* was originally published in Latin. The first English translation, by Ralph Robinson, was published in 1551; it was not published in England while Henry VIII lived, as the implicit criticism of the corruption of English society and government was thought to be too dangerous.
3 Sir Thomas More, *Utopia*, trans. and ed. P. Turner, London, 1965, p. 89.
4 Ibid., pp. 75–8. There is some confusion as to the exact nature of the clothes in *Utopia*. Over the working costume of leather (or skins) is worn what Robinson translates as 'a cloke whyche hydeth the other homely apparrell'; the Latin text uses the Greek '*chlamys*', a cloak fastening on the shoulder and open down the side. As to the ordinary dress worn by the Utopians, More apparently had in

mind the capacious cloak of the Grey
Friars, or Franciscans; see a letter to
Erasmus, December 1516, quoted in
J.C. Davis, *Utopia and the ideal society.
A study of English utopian writing
1516-1700*, Cambridge, 1981, p. 59.

With regard to the longevity of
clothing in Utopia, we are told that
the leather working clothes last seven
years; the general Utopian dress is
described as lasting for a lifetime,
although we are also told that 'the
Utopian is content with a single piece
of clothing every two years'.

5 Tommaso Campanella (1568-1639) was
a defender of empirical and open-
minded scientific research, a fervent
believer in the doctrine of papal
world supremacy, and suspected of
subversive political activity; for the
latter he was imprisoned and during
his captivity he wrote *La Città del Sole*,
first written in Italian and then in
Latin.

6 Tommaso Campanella, *The City of the
Sun*, trans. W.J. Gilstrap, in G. Negley
and J.M. Patrick (eds), *The Quest for
Utopia: An Anthology of Imaginary
Societies*, Maryland, 1971, p. 328.

7 Joseph Hall, *The Discovery of a New
World*, trans. from the Latin by J.
Healey, London, 1609, p. 111. In later
life, Joseph Hall was Bishop of Exeter
and Bishop of Norwich. He fell into
controversy with Milton, who found
the *Mundus Alter et Idem* 'a mere
tankard drollery' and a burlesque of
serious ideal Commonwealths. Hall's
satirical utopia is in direct line of
descent from the fourteenth-century
poem *The Land of Cockayne* (an attack
on monastic gluttony), which describes
a land of magical abundance including
rivers of honey, oil and wine, and
roasted geese which fly to a great
abbey made of cakes and puddings.

8 For further details on the controversy
over the supposed encroachment by
men and women into the costume of

the opposite sex, see my book *Dress
and Morality*, London, 1986.

9 Robert Burton, *The Anatomy of
Melancholy*, 2nd edition, Oxford, 1624,
pp. 49-56. Burton's somewhat tongue-
in-cheek 'Utopia of mine owne' is set
in 'Terra Australis Incognita'.

10 Francis Bacon, *New Atlantis*, ed. H.
Osborne, London, 1937, p. 38.

11 Ibid., p. 3, and pp. 51-2.

12 *Nova Solyma* was published
anonymously and until the twentieth
century it was attributed to Milton,
no doubt due partly to its messianic
Puritan zeal. The early seventeenth
century – a period of intense religious
controversies – produced a number of
utopias which are specifically
Christian. One example is
Christianopolis (1619), by Johann
Andreae, the son of a Lutheran cleric
and himself ordained in the Lutheran
ministry. Andreae visited Geneva, a
Calvinist society which impressed him
with its discipline and order (as it
later helped to form the character of
Rousseau), and Christianopolis is a
Christian republic where virtue is the
true nobility. Austerity of living is
carried into the clothing of the
inhabitants, a uniform costume (one
suit for work, the other for holidays)
'made of linen or wool, respectively
for summer or winter, and the colour
for all is white or ashen gray; none
have fancy, tailored goods'. (Johann
Andreae, *Christianopolis*, trans. and ed.
F.E. Held, New York, 1916, p. 157).
The costume is based on that of
More's *Utopia*.

13 Samuel Gott, *Nova Solyma*, ed. W.
Begley, 2 vols, London, 1902, vol. II,
pp. 222-7.

14 Ibid., vol. I, p. 80. This is close to the
figure of Night in Cesare Ripa's
illustrated *Iconologia* (1603), one of the
most important source books for
masque costume in the seventeenth
century.

15 Rousseau believed the austere and military city state of Sparta to be the perfect model for utopia. In this he followed Plutarch's life of Lycurgus (written towards the end of the first century AD) in which the celebrated ruler of Sparta ordained that children, the property of the state, should be brought up wearing very few clothes in order to become hardy and healthy.

16 In 1772 William Hooper prepared an English translation, adding, presumably in the cause of symmetry, another sixty years to the title. In addition, he makes his own comments on Mercier's work in the form of footnotes.

17 William Hooper (trans. after Louis-Sébastien Mercier), *Memoirs of the Year Two Thousand Five Hundred*, 2 vols, London, 1772, pp. 21–2. Although Mercier dispensed with the fashionable three-cornered hat in the clothing of the future, he still envisaged hair with 'a slight tinge of powder', so much was this the custom in the 1760s.

18 On the subject of David's costume designs, and the political and social considerations behind dress reform during the revolutionary period, see my *Fashion in the French Revolution*, 1988.

19 Alfred Robida, *Le Vingtième Siècle*, Paris, 1882, p. 42. As nearly all transport is by air – airships, aerocabs and 'omnibus-aéroflèche' – women find it more convenient to adopt 'le costume semi-masculin'. Robida's drawings show women with the elaborate frizzed hairstyles of the early 1880s, tight-waisted dresses kilted up to show knickerbocker breeches, and high-heeled boots or shoes. Men also wear the same kind of breeches, with the jackets or coats of the early 1880s.

20 Edward Bellamy, *Looking Backward 2000–1887*, Boston, 1888, p. 17.

21 F.H. Pettycoste, *Towards Utopia*, London, 1894, pp. 159–60.

22 In a series of lectures delivered in Boston in 1874 (and published as *Dress Reform* in the same year), a number of speakers urged the adoption of masculine dress which, although not beautiful, had the virtue of relative stability. The editor of this volume sighed for 'the far future wherein women shall move ... clothed simply and serviceably as men are clothed'. (A. Goold Woolson, *Dress Reform*, Boston, 1874, p. 231). The Rational Dress Association exhibited in 1883 the 'Dress of the Future' (made by Worth of Hanover Street, London), which consisted of a loose, pleated tunic and black satin knickerbockers slashed with red satin and trimmed with lace. It was declared to be 'too fanciful for present taste, but extremely picturesque and convenient'. For nineteenth-century dress reform, see S.M. Newton, *Health, Art and Reason*, London, 1974.

23 William Morris, *News from Nowhere; or, An Epoch of Rest*, Boston, 1890, p. 23.

24 H.G. Wells, *A Modern Utopia*, London, 1905, pp. 295 and 225. Slender women can also wear the costume of children, i.e. close-fitting trousers and 'beltless jacket fitting very well, or a belted jacket' (p. 227).

25 In the late nineteenth century the distinctions between true utopian dress (what it *ought* to be) and that in science-fiction/works of prophecy (what dress *will* be) often overlap. As the text of the article explains, the ideal can never be visualized in dress, which can only be described in terms of the present and the past.

This understandable poverty of the imagination is revealed in a number of ways. *Punch* cartoons, for example (see p. 230) show a fear of the emancipated woman in their depiction of the female MP of the future as an unattractive middle-aged Bloomerite. Alfred Robida's notions of what dress would be like in 1952, written from the perspective of 1883, show both men and women (see p. 231) in whimsical mixtures of the fashions of the early 1880s (somewhat exaggerated and with occasional 'historical' touches) worn with knickerbockers. In spite of its novelettish approach *Le Vingtième Siècle* is a fairly serious and imaginative work with some startling predictions of the reversal of the traditional sex roles.

Comments on the future of clothing are often a convenient excuse for attacks on current fashion, which is described in *Future Dictates of Fashion* (*Strand* Magazine, 1893) as 'a whim, a sort of shuttlecock for the weak-minded of both sexes'. This article, a jocular commentary on the fashions of the future, purports to be a review of a book called *Past Dictates of Fashion*, published in 1993 by a 'Vestamentorum Doctor'. Covering the period 1893 to 1993, the illustrations (see p. 232) show a bizarre medley of historical styles which owe more, perhaps, to the late nineteenth century fondness for fancy dress than to a serious consideration of what the clothing of the future might really be. Plus ça change, plus c'est la même chose? (Thanks to Michael Dillon for bringing this article to my attention.)

26 E. Bulwer-Lytton, 1st Baron Lytton, *The Coming Race*, intr. F.J. Harvey Darton, Oxford, 1928, pp. 9 and 114.

27 Francis Godwin, *The Man in the Moone: or A Discourse of a Voyage thither*, London, 1638, p. 80. The book is enlivened with drawings showing the traveller 'Domingo Gonsales' flying to the moon with the help of specially trained large swans, but there are no illustrations of the clothing of the inhabitants of the moon – a place of peace and plenty; the author knows no word for 'stuffe to resemble the matter of that whereof their Clothes were made', nor can he describe 'a colour never seen in our earthly world'.

28 Lytton, op. cit., pp. 9 and 145. If women prefer to be single, they wear red; if grey, they are looking for a husband; if dark purple, they have to make a choice; orange is worn by those betrothed or married, and women who wear light blue are divorced/widowed and wish to marry again.

29 Aldous Huxley, *Brave New World*, London, 1932, p. 139. It is interesting to note that while some dress reformers welcomed the appearance of synthetic fibres as an aid to the production of lightweight, easy-to-care-for clothes, many writers disliked what they considered to be evidence of a move towards a more artificial society. E.M. Forster's short story *The Machine Stops* (written c.1912 but published 1928) describes a world state where everyone has gone underground, lives in a cell-like room, and whose needs – such as synthetic food and synthetic clothing – are provided by the 'Machine' at the touch of a button.

30 J.C. Flügel, *The Psychology of Clothes*, London, 1930, p. 113.

Notes on Contributors

Rosetta Brookes is a freelance writer and art critic, currently living in New York. She has been the editor of *ZG* magazine for the last ten years. She contributes to art catalogues and has written articles for magazines and books published in both the United States and in Britain.

Linda Coleing is Senior Lecturer in History of Design at Staffordshire Polytechnic, specialising in the history of fashion and textiles. After graduating, she participated in numerous exhibitions and worked to commission, producing one-off pieces with a fine art emphasis. This was followed by a qualification in museum studies and a period working in the textile department at the Whitworth Art Gallery, Manchester. She has lectured at Birmingham, Manchester and Huddersfield Polytechnics. At Staffordshire Polytechnic she was instrumental in setting up a fashion archive for teaching and research purposes. Currently she is joint editor of the Textile Society magazine which is produced twice yearly. She has lectured at the Victoria & Albert Museum on 'The Work of Ann Macbeth', 'The Textiles of C.F.A. Voysey', and 'C.F.A. Voysey's Pattern Designs for the Interior'.

Naseem Khan is a writer and freelance journalist. She has been extensively involved with multi-cultural arts in Britain. Her report, 'The Arts Britain Ignores' – commissioned by the Arts Council, Gulbenkian Foundation and Community Relations Commission –- opened the debate on black Arts. She set up and ran the Minorities' Arts Advisory Service (MAAS), and was Co-ordinator of the Alternative Festival of India.

Ellen Leopold graduated in Economics from Birkbeck College, London, and has written extensively on economic consumption and the history of fashion. She is at present living in Boston, where she is working on a construction project which will release land in the centre of the city.

Kate Luck is an art history graduate of Nottingham University, where she also undertook postgraduate research on the work of Vanessa Bell, and nineteenth-century social-realist graphics. She has taught at West Bridgehead College, Central, St Martins, and Bath Academy of Art, and is currently teaching undergraduate and postgraduate students of art and design/visual culture at Bath College of Higher Education.

Hilary O'Kelly lectured in Art and Design History at the National College of Art and Design in Dublin and The Crawford College of Art and Design in Cork for the last four years. She is now working at University College, Cork as Visual Arts Co-ordinator.

Angela Partington lectures in Cultural Studies on Art and Design degree courses. She has published a number of articles concerning the relationships between women and visual objects, and recently has completed her Ph.D.

Aileen Ribeiro read history at King's College, London, followed by postgraduate studies in history of art and dress at the Courtauld Institute of Art. Since 1976 she has been Head of the History of Dress Department at the Courtauld Institute of Art. She is the author of a number of articles and books on the history of dress. Among her books are *Dress in Eighteenth-Century Europe 1715–1789* (1984), *Dress and Morality* (1986), and *Fashion in the French Revolution* (1988). She has acted as costume consultant to a number of exhibitions, including 'Masquerade' (Museum of London, 1983), 'Reynolds' (Grand Palais, Paris and the Royal Academy, London, 1985–6), 'Winterhalter and the Courts of Europe' (National Portrait Gallery, London, and Petit Palais, Paris, 1987–8), and 'The Earl and Countess Howe by Gainsborough' (Kenwood House, London 1988). She is currently working on a book on dress in art in France and England, 1750–1820, to be published by Yale University Press.

Katrina Rolley is a dress historian whose particular interest is in the links between identity and self-presentation. She lectures in fashion history and has taught at polytechnics and colleges throughout Britain. She is the author of an article on 'Fashion, Femininity and the Fight for the Vote', *Art History*, March 1990, and of two pieces on lesbian dress and identity: 'Cutting a Dash: the Dress of Radclyffe Hall and Una Troubridge', *Feminist Review*, summer 1990, and 'The Lesbian Sixth Sense: Dress as an Expression and Communication of Lesbian Identity', *Feminist Art News*, summer 1990. She has also been an occasional contributor to the independent arts magazine *Square Peg*, and is the joint author of a forthcoming book on fashion from 1900 to 1920 as represented in photographs from the National Portrait Gallery Archive.

Sheila Rowbotham is a freelance writer who has written extensively on women's history. Her books include *Hidden from History* (1972), and *Dreams and Dilemmas* (1983). Her most recent work, *The Past Is Before Us* (1990), is published by Pandora and Penguin, and is about the contemporary women's movement in Britain.

Judy Rumbold started as a fashion journalist for the *Guardian*, and is currently a full-time journalist for the *Guardian*.

Neil Spencer is a journalist and has worked for *Arena* magazine. He is currently the editor of *20/20*.

Valerie Steele received her Ph.D. from Yale University, and teaches in the graduate division of the Fashion Institute of Technology (State University of New York). She is the author of *Paris Fashion: A Cultural History* (1988), and *Fashion and Eroticism* (1985). Valerie Steele is also the co-editor and principal author of *Men and Women: Dressing the Part* (Smithsonian Institution Press, 1989), a study of clothing and gender roles. In fall, 1991, Rizzoli Books International will publish her newest book, *Women of Fashion*, a study of women in the fashion industry.

Lou Taylor is the author of *Mourning Dress: A Costume and Social History*, (1983). She was Consultant to the BBC TV series, *Through the Looking Glass*, and co-author (with Elizabeth Wilson) of the book published as an adjunct to the programmes. She was Consultant to the British Council fashion exhibition 'All Dressed Up: British Fashion in the Eighties', touring Eastern Europe from 1989 to 1991. She is principal lecturer in the Department of Design and Art History at Brighton Polytechnic.

Teal Triggs is a lecturer in Historical and Theoretical Studies at Ravensbourne College of Design and Communication. She is also a practising photographer whose current series of work explores women's roles in advertising.

Carol Tulloch studied fashion design at Ravensbourne College of Design and Communication. She has had work published in *City Limits* and *Fashion Weekly* as well as working as a freelance designer. Carol was born in Doncaster, South Yorkshire, of Jamaican parents.

Lee Wright is a lecturer in the History of Design at the University of Ulster at Belfast. She was co-editor of *Components of Dress*, and has contributed articles to a number of books on fashion and design.

Further Reading

Books

Alison Adburgham (1961). *A Punch History of Manners and Modes*, London: Hutchinson.

—— (1981). *Shops and Shopping: 1800–1914*, London: Allen & Unwin.

Isabelle Anscombe (1984). *A Woman's Touch: Women in Design from 1860 to the Present Day*, London: Virago.

Juliet Ash and Lee Wright, editors (1987). *Components of Dress*, London: Routledge.

Judy Attfield and Pat Kirkham, editors (1989). *A View from the Interior*, London: The Women's Press.

Lois Banner (1983). *American Beauty*, New York: Alfred Knopf.

Roland Barthes (1985). *The Fashion System*, London: Jonathan Cape.

Cecil Beaton (1954). *The Glass of Fashion*, London: Weidenfeld & Nicolson.

Quentin Bell (1968). *On Human Finery*, London: The Hogarth Press.

Wendy Chapkis and Cynthia Enloe (1983). *Of Common Cloth: Women in the Global Textile Industry*, Amsterdam: Transnational Institute.

J. Cordwell and P. Schwarz (1979). *Fabrics of Culture: The Anthropology of Clothing and Adornment*, The Hague: Mouton Press.

Cecil Willet Cunnington (1941). *Why Women Wear Clothes*, London: Faber & Faber.

Caroline Evans and Minna Thornton (1989). *Women and Fashion: A New Look*, London: Quartet books.

Elizabeth Ewing (1974). *History of Twentieth-Century Fashion*, London: Batsford.

—— (1978). *Dress and Undress: A History of Women's Underwear*, London: Batsford.

Jane Gaines and Charlotte Hertzog, editors (1987). *Fabrications: Costume and the Female Body*, New York and London: Routledge.

Madeleine Ginsburg (1982). *Victorian Dress*, London: Batsford.

Dick Hebdige (1979). *Subculture: The Meaning of Style*, London: Methuen.

Anne Hollander (1975). *Seeing Through Clothes*, New York: Viking/Penguin.

Claudia Brush Kidwell and Valerie Steele, editors (1989). *Men and Women: Dressing the Part*, Washington: Smithsonian Institution Press.

René Konig (1973). *The Restless Image*, London: Allen & Unwin.

James Laver (1969a). *A Concise History of Costume*, London: Thames & Hudson.

—— (1969b). *Modesty in Dress. An Inquiry into the Fundamentals of Fashion*, London: Heinemann.

Sarah Levitt (1986). *Victorians Unbuttoned*, London: Allen & Unwin.

Angela McRobbie (1989). *Zoot Suits and Secondhand Dresses*, London: Macmillan.

Stella Mary Newton (1974). *Health Art and Reason: Dress Reformers of the Nineteenth Century*, London: John Murray.

Paul Nystrom (1929). *The Economics of Fashion*, New York: Ronalds Press.

Roszika Parker (1984). *The Subversive Stitch*, London: The Women's Press.

Annie Phizacklea (1990), *Unpacking the Fashion Industry: Gender, Racism and Class in Production*, London: Routledge.

Ted Polhemus (1978). *Social Aspects of the Human Body*, Harmondsworth: Penguin.

Aileen Ribeiro (1984). *Dress in Eighteenth-Century Europe 1715–1789*, London: Batsford.

—— (1986). *Dress and Morality*, London: Batsford.

—— (1988). *Fashion in the French Revolution*, London: Batsford.

Edith Saunders (1954). *The Age of Worth*, London: Longman.

Valerie Steele (1985). *Fashion*

FURTHER READING

and Eroticism, Oxford: Oxford University Press.
—— (1988). *Paris Fashion: A Cultural History*, Oxford: Oxford University Press.
—— (1991). *Women of Fashion*, New York: Rizzoli Books International.
Lou Taylor (1983). *Mourning Dress: A Costume and Social History*, London: Allen & Unwin.
Jane Tozer and Sarah Levitt (1983). *Fabric of Society: A Century of People and their Clothes: 1770–1870*, Carno, Powys, Wales: Laura Ashley.

Christina Walkley (1981). *The Ghost in the Looking Glass*, London: Peter Owen.
Nora Waugh (1973). *The Cut of Women's Clothes*, London: Faber & Faber.
Gordon Wills and David Midgley, editors (1973). *Fashion Marketing*, London: Allen & Unwin.
Elizabeth Wilson (1985). *Adorned in Dreams: Fashion and Modernity*, London: Virago.
—— and Lou Taylor (1989). *Through the Looking Glass*, London: BBC Books.

Videos

For programmes on the BBC contact the BBC shop, for programmes on Channel Four contact Channel Four, for programmes on ITV contact the television company concerned.

CHANNEL FOUR

What Can I do with a Male Nude? (a film by Ron Peck), 25 October 1985.
Irish Angle (a series on Irish Design – tailoring), 1 December 1985.
Asian Arts (a film on fashion designer Aisha Patel's work), 18 June 1986.
A People's War (a film on the 'Austerity' period), 24 November 1986.
The Media Show (The 'New Man'), 13 May 1987.
Dreams and Recollections (The Glasgow School and James Rennie Mackintosh), 28 December 1987.
Irish Reel (Irish Youth in the 1980s), 21 October 1988.
Fair Play (Women's Sportswear), 19 March 1989.

BBC

Now the War is Over ('Make do and Mend'), 4 October 1985.
The Clothes Show (Photographers and Models), 15 February 1986).

The New New Look (Saturday Review), 14 March 1987.
The Clothes Show (Manufacturing Fashion), 18 March 1989.
The Clothes Show (Sportswear), 16 April 1989.
Network East (British Asian Fashion), 3 June 1989.
Through the Looking Glass (a series on the History of Fashion), 20 November 1989 (and five following weeks).
Soul II Soul (Late Show Special), 4 July 1990.
Portrait of a Marriage (fictionalised film of the relationship between Vita Sackville-West and Violet Trefusis), October 1990.

ITV

The South Bank Show (Vivienne Westwood), 8 April 1990.

OTHER VIDEOS

The Soul II Soul Video
The Green Consumer Video, World Wild Life Fund.
Fashion Means Business – Teaching and Learning Design: IVCA Award Winner, 1988, (includes a section on Darlajane Gilroy's business – see Carol Tulloch's article).

Index